GOOSEBUMPS

THE MAKING OF CULT KIDS' TV

GOOSEBUMPS
THE MAKING OF CULT KIDS' TV

LUNA GUTHRIE

BearManor Media
2025

**Goosebumps
The Making of Cult Kids' TV**

Copyright © 2025 Luna Guthrie

All rights reserved.

No portion of this publication may be reproduced, stored, and/or copied electronically (except for academic use as a source), nor transmitted in any form or by any means without the prior written permission of the publisher and/or author.

This book is for educational and entertainment purposes only, and is not to be used to train or develop AI.

Published in the United States of America by:

BearManor Media

1317 Edgewater Dr. #110
Orlando, FL 32804

bearmanormedia.com

Printed in the United States.

Typesetting and layout by PKJ Passion Global
Cover design by Nimesh Niyomal.

ISBN–979-8-88771-857-6

Contents

Thanks and Dedications vii
Introduction 1
"I've Got the Rights to the Hottest
    Kids' Book on the Market" 7
"A Sweetheart Crew" 14
"You Do Need a Personality for a Kids' Show" 27
"Figure Out How to Make It Cinematic" 51
"A Rite of Passage for Toronto" 65
"All Kinds of MacGyver Solutions" 81
"That Will Scare the Little Buggers!" 93
"You Can Learn an Awful Lot in The Deep End" 102
"The World's Biggest Train Set!" 125
"One of the Key Under-Acknowledged
    Magical Elements of That Show" 143
Let's Get This Show on the Road 151
Opening Band for The X-Files 175
"Let's Just Make It Fun,
    Like an Amusement Park Ride!" 182
The Era of Kid-Vid 204
The Beginning of the End 212
"What Have We Got to Lose?" 236
"Splendors Situated Beyond the Tomb" 245
Afterword 260

Thanks and Dedications

This book has allowed me to cross paths with some fascinating, insightful, hilarious and warm-hearted people, all of whom just happened to have something to do with my favorite childhood show. It was touching how many of them thanked me for giving them an outlet for reminiscence, and a reason to look back on what was almost invariably such a special time in their lives. For a humble fan, this book has been an incredibly rewarding experience. I've got to know the people who brought to life a show that was so special to me, and had the opportunity to thank them for their work in creating it. My most sincere gratitude to the following:

Bill Turnbull was a joy to chat with, and gave fascinating insights into the world of child acting.

Brian R. R. Hebb is a great guy, full of passion for life and his work. We bonded over our respective British upbringings.

Jim McGrath was most helpful in offering the technical details of his craft and the wider world of film scoring, as well as fond memories.

Afrah Gouda is an incredibly accomplished and delightful woman who was more than happy to reminisce about her time on the set.

Bryan Renfro very kindly shared some photos for this project, and some of the many stories of his fascinating life and career.

Craig Pryce is such a fun, friendly guy who shared some great tales from his early foray into television.

David Winning's insight into the practicalities of set life were brilliant, and he was a pleasure to get to know.

Jonathan Whittaker was most obliging in not only telling me all about his shenanigans at Horrorland, but in taking the time to chat to my daughter, for whom his episode is a favorite.

Neal Shusterman leapt at the chance to talk to me about *Goosebumps*, and it was great to hear his process and thoughts on the craft, writer to writer. He also indulged my questions about his earlier work on the life of my favorite rock star.

Melody Johnson, for whom *Goosebumps* is not the only iconic horror on her resumé, was full of appreciation for her colleagues and amusing anecdotes, as well as an infectious bubbly energy.

Peter Keleghan may not remember every detail about his time on the show, but he was still happy to tell me everything he could, and offer his more personal insights.

Scott Pietrangelo has been a joy to get to know. He is full of great memories of the show and it was lovely to reunite him with the words he wrote as a young teen.

Tod Fennell was happy to offer me all the resources he could, and shared some great memories, not just from *Goosebumps* but also from his time on *The Worst Witch*, another childhood classic for a British '90s kid.

Bob Sprogis, as everybody promised, is a sweet, insightful and very talented guy. We discussed the common labor of editing, whether in video or literary form.

Stefan Scaini is one of the rare figures who keeps everything connected to his work. Scripts, storyboards, call sheets—he keeps it all, much to the chagrin of his wife! He offered invaluable insights.

Randy Bradshaw, just as teddy-bearish as Steve Levitan promised, offered a great look into the psychology of directing, and much encouragement. He believed in this project, and was kind enough to contribute photos and memorabilia.

Don McCutcheon took a real interest in my work and why exactly this was the project I had settled on. I appreciated the reciprocal nature of our discussions, and his providing some fabulous pictures.

I had a whale of a time chatting to Judah Katz, who is an insanely fun guy (no pun intended). Thanks to him for his time, humor, and for the boost my ego needed by granting his first ever *Goosebumps*-related interview to me, because he believed I could make this book happen and do it justice.

Ron Stefaniuk is a busy guy, but he still found the time to share his memories, passion and expertise with me.

Matthew DeWilde is an absolute doll, with loads of great insight, and many amazing photos. Many thanks to him for sharing them for this book.

Jack Lenz, an absolute gem who always made me feel like a fellow artist.

Beki Lantos was one of my first interviewees, and trusted me with some deeply personal experiences. I took her confidence incredibly seriously, and hope that I have managed to tell her part of the story properly, with sensitivity and kindness. Thanks also for the wonderful photos she shared.

It was a delight to meet Corey Sevier and hear about his multiple experiences on the show and how instrumental they were to where they are now. Such a friendly and knowledgeable person.

Ian Brock is jam-packed with enthusiasm, stories and behind the scenes tidbits that were crucial to putting all this together.

Sir Ronald Oliver, the man, the myth, the legend. Exactly as hilarious and warm as everybody told me he was. I knew out of everybody, it would be him to recognize the three Porno Chic posters on my living room wall. A man of taste!

Mpho Koaho is striking in his wisdom, his humility and his philosophical approach to life. He sees beneath the surface of things, and seems to live immersed in the beauty of it all. He is generous with his time, and his spirit, and was more than happy to meet my daughter and discuss with her everything from *Saw* to *Goosebumps*, to being a kid. He's a one-of-a-kind dude.

Amos Crawley's lifelong immersion in the arts has given him some really fascinating perspectives on life, childhood and adulthood, what constitutes work and art. We chatted at length about the horror genre, about what it is really like for children in the entertainment industry, and where the art world is headed. Another kind, friendly and thoroughly interesting guy who is so easy to talk to.

Michael Caloz and Alex Fallis, who politely declined to be interviewed for this book, but did so with such grace and kindness that they deserve a shoutout.

Many thanks to Darryl Triebner and Debby Corneal at Camp Samac for going above and beyond to aid my research. Also, to Brendan Whelton at Bay Street Video and Howie Levman of the legendary Queen Video in Toronto, and Lori Kirk at Centreville, all of whom were very obliging in helping me piece the puzzle together.

Kingsley Abbott, without whose wisdom and guidance this book would have been the death of me. Every time I felt like giving up, he managed to make the way forward look so clear, and gave me the energy I needed to carry on.

My friends and colleagues Emma Kiely, Anna Miller and Emily Bernard, who cheered me on from the sidelines, and understood exactly how excruciating a long-term writing project could be. They were always interested in hearing how it was going, and quick to offer support and guidance.

The incredibly talented Nimesh Niyomal, whose creative and sometimes bonkers designs have always been a source of great joy, and now serve as the face of my labor here.

My dear friend and fellow artist Jo Turland, one of the most wonderful, sensitive and caring friends imaginable.

To my equally dear friend Rowan French, for hearing my frustrations and lending his critical eye as a proofreader when I needed one.

Dr. Ian Newey, a beacon of wisdom and humor without whom my life would be adrift.

R.L. Stine, for acknowledging and encouraging this project, for introducing five-year-old Luna to horror, and making a lifelong degenerate out of her on account of it!

This book would never have been possible without its major tentpole, Steve Levitan. He was the first person I approached, and he got back to me within an hour, excited to tell the story of how the show came to be. His comprehensive understanding of *Goosebumps* formed the skeleton of this book, as well as many of the ligaments, and he entrusted his wealth of memory and experience to me. He has been an absolute joy: generous, patient, accommodating, and just an all-round awesome bloke. Steve, thank you for helping me take this important step in my life and career, and for fulfilling the dream of this *Goosebumps* fan. Thank you for being the one to set the ball rolling on the show that influenced my life.

To my wonderful partner Geoff and my daughter Willow, my *Goosebumps* girl. They have always believed in me, and encouraged me to make this dream a reality, even when it meant prioritizing it above all else.

My mum Shelley, brothers Ali, Sam and Joe and sister Relly, who has always shared my love of *Goosebumps*. Thank you for your encouragement and celebration of my achievements.

And finally, to the biggest cheerleader of them all, my Pop, Mark Alexander. Without his belief and support by any means necessary, I would never have had the confidence to even dream of this project, let alone get out there and make it happen. I escaped to his apartment to write when I felt like I was being pulled in a million different directions, and he always knew I could do it. This book is the achievement I always knew I had in me, but for so long lacked the faith in myself to see through. I know you're proud.

Introduction

X-treme Childhoods

The 1990s was *the* time to be a child. All the environmental stars had aligned to produce a near-perfect era for a new generation to grow up in: the threat of nuclear annihilation had largely subsided, economies were robust in ways they hadn't been in decades, and the entertainment industry was evolving. *The Simpsons* had come along at the turn of the decade and transformed the ways that families consumed media, by leaning away from the happy-go-lucky perfection that defined 1980s TV and embracing the humble, the everyday, even the dysfunctional. In the US, Clinton's presidency broke a long spell of Republican rule, while the New Labour movement of the UK gave way to the Cool Britannia era, which embraced the working classes and celebrated the underlings. Society was becoming less defined by what was considered proper, breaking out into unexplored territory, and ambitious grass-roots movements in the art world were reflecting this mood swing.

This is characterized by the entertainment industry of the 1990s. Cinema saw a boom in large-scale action and spectacle, a self-aware revival of the horror genre courtesy of *Scream*, and CGI was making its mark with massive hits like *Terminator 2: Judgement Day* and *Toy Story*. Meanwhile, TV sitcoms and series were moving away from the family-oriented in favor of young adult shows like *Friends* and *The Fresh Prince of Bel-Air*, and the weird like *Twin Peaks* and *The X-Files*. Video games were presenting more complex and immersive worlds, extreme sports like skateboarding, BMXing and roller-blading were massive, and the World Wrestling Federation combined the two trends for extreme sport and extreme entertainment. If there's one word to sum up the era, it's x-treme.

Of course, all this awesomeness was catering to children as much as to teenagers and adults, and kids were getting their own brands of extreme entertainment. Channels specifically catering to kids were emerging, with Nickelodeon embodying the loud, wacky tone of the time with original cartoons and bucketloads of slime, and Fox delivering on the action-packed offerings of Saban and Warner Bros. spin-offs. A look at the Nickelodeon time capsule buried in 1992 gives a keen insight into the flavor of this era: MC Hammer and Michael Jackson CDs, GameBoys, Barbie dolls, skateboards, VHS copies of *Back to the Future* and merchandise T-shirts.

Movies and TV were taking on a more rough-around-the-edges shape, tapping directly into the excitement of their target audience, and selling them merchandise at Toys"R"Us. *Mighty Morphin' Power Rangers* took a low-budget kids' show, captured the childish imagination, and by the end of the '90s had raked in an incredible $6 billion in toy and merchandise sales, never mind the fear that the show was inciting violence and a craze for karate kicks and "hai-YAs". The Tickle Me Elmo craze of 1996 left toy shop employees with broken limbs and parents with criminal records. There was no doubt that kids wanted cool, they wanted edgy, and they wanted to spend every penny in their piggy banks on taking their favorite shows further than the television screen. Children's entertainment was causing mania in the '90s, and it seemed producers were only ever one good idea away from making a serious impact on this pop culture landscape.

Producer Steve Levitan characterizes the 1990s as "the peak of children's television. One: you could do scripted television. Two: there were dedicated kids' channels which were the only places kids could go to get content." An industry geared specifically towards young viewers had emerged, in which kids got more than a couple of hours every Saturday morning or after school. They had their very own channels that would reliably turn out content that they enjoyed, without the six o'clock curfew bringing the fun crashing down with news or soap operas. "There was a lot of scary stuff, but fun scary stuff," says children's author and screenwriter Neal Shusterman, "and I think *Goosebumps* got that started. There was a lot more then than there is now for that age group, and there were many more markets to sell those things than there are now."

"It pushed boundaries. It was less safe," says director Craig Pryce. "But that was the fun of it! The storytelling was, for want of a better word, less corporate, and there was more freedom. Cos now when you direct, it's sometimes more the showrunners, 'This is how you do it', and things like that. I would say there was more freedom for the directors, and for the writers, actually. They were trusted and they were hired for their talent. You would scare the kids. Now there's so much concern, with censorship and things, 'You can't do that, you can't do this'. There's a lot more voices now. It was a really creative time and a fun time to entertain kids." From a young viewer's perspective, actor Amos Crawley agrees: "The nineties was a bit of a wild wild West. We were kind of the last generation to go unchaperoned through much of the day. We were the last generation to not have cell phones, so kids' entertainment was a bit more vast in that sense."

Director Randy Bradshaw remembers the late '80s and '90s as "a simpler, more gentle time" in entertainment. "The stories these days are, I think, a bit more dark. I think some of these stories are asking kids to maybe delve into more difficult, emotional terrain. There just isn't as much fun out there anymore, or that fun comes with a terrible price. *Goosebumps* was a tremendous amount of fun, but there was never a deep, cynical, dark place. It was an exercise in developing the imagination of children. The children's entertainment landscape was, you know, apart from being specifically about entertaining and making compelling and fun programming, was also teaching them about something in a gentle way, where nobody was going to suffer. The entertainment landscape was not about dealing with those difficult things for the greater part. I guess the short answer is that I think television then for kids was simply about letting kids be kids."

For those dreaming up and making the entertainment, it was a time of creative freedom, with barely a hint of micromanagement in sight. "It was the inmates running the asylum," jokes director Ron Oliver. "They really left us alone, and there was respect. I'll tell you the difference, there was a respect for the kids' imaginations during that era that disappeared almost overnight in the 2000s. At that time we understood and respected the fact that kids deserve really high quality entertainment." Indeed, just as the '50s had given way to this strange new breed they called the teenager, the '90s prided itself on understanding the youth, and making sure they got what they wanted, and it was with this in mind that a new youth culture emerged.

The children's horror market was booming in the '90s, thanks in no small part to a Canadian anthology TV series, *Are You Afraid of the Dark?* Based and filmed in Montreal, it was the brainchild of Ned Kandel and D.J. MacHale, and told a different story every episode, held together with the framing device of The Midnight Society, a group of adolescents who regularly gathered around a bonfire to tell each other scary stories. It was a big hit on its home channel YTV and across the border at Nickelodeon, and arguably ushered in the kids' TV horror craze of the era. Kids were a big market, and they were being listened to.

This market didn't stop at toys and television. In the summer of 1992, a children's book titled *Welcome to Dead House* was published by Scholastic, quickly followed up by *Stay Out of the Basement*. They belonged to a new anthology series called *Goosebumps*, written by Ohio native R.L. Stine. Having made a living as a children's author for over twenty years, Stine was well-versed in penning scary stories for young readers, but his wife/editor spotted a gap in the market, and urged him to try out horror for seven- to ten-year-olds. Reluctantly, Stine obliged, and a craze was born. In a way that only kids can pull off, word of mouth made it known that these creepy books were *the* thing, and before too long, the series was selling a million copies a month. The author's ability to keep producing new material at such a high rate meant the series could keep up with demand; it was more like a magazine than a book, in that readers could rely on a new title on an almost monthly basis. Kids were fickle, but there was always a new *Goosebumps*. So the rabid enthusiasm of young readers paired with Stine's incredible fecundity made *Goosebumps* a runaway success. It seemed inevitable that the worlds of literature and television would eventually collide.

R.L. Stine pictured with some of the show's monstrous creations.
Photo courtesy of Matthew DeWilde

"I've Got the Rights to the Hottest Kids' Book on the Market"

The Creation of a Monster Hit

Steve Levitan holds up a framed black-and-white photo of himself at ten years old, proudly showing off his family's first television set. "I got all dressed up and insisted that they take a photo of me standing next to the TV set. As far back as then, I wanted to make movies or TV shows," he says. Survivors of the Holocaust, Steve Levitan's parents couldn't afford to throw him a big Bar Mitzvah party, but had a whip-round of friends and family to fund the occasion, promising him any leftover dollars as a present. He is certain that the party would have swallowed up all the funds his folks raised, but still they stumped up $150 as a gift for their son. With $50 he subscribed to *Weekly Variety*—a subscription he maintains to this day—and with the remaining $100, a Kodak Super 8mm Instamatic Movie Camera. He began making movies from that day.

At eighteen, "I was ready to hitchhike to Los Angeles and sweep the floors until they gave me a camera, but my mother persuaded me to go to university and get a degree that I could at least fall back on," he explains. It just so happened that Levitan's local university had recently opened Canada's first film school, and after three years of study, "I decided to hitchhike to Los Angeles and sweep the floors until they gave me a camera!" His ever-sensible mother convinced him to defer his L.A. dreams one more time and enrol in law school. "As a youth, I was arrogant enough to think that I could make great movies! I just couldn't figure out how anyone could be crazy enough to give you a million, two million, let alone ten million dollars to basically transform your idea into an hour and a half or two hours of time-waste. I thought that law school might help me to understand that, and it did not!" he laughs.

In the '60s, says Levitan, the movie industry was just beginning to take off in Canada, with few players other than the national broadcaster and national film board, and all the action was happening in the USA. But by the 1970s, when he graduated law school, the industry was emerging north of the border, and so he decided to declare himself an entertainment lawyer, a move he figured would be a neat segue into the industry he had longed to break into since childhood. "It was an easy move because there were no entertainment lawyers the way there were in Los Angeles, and there was no one saying I didn't know what I was doing, and that way I got into contact with all the early players in the industry," he says. After a good decade of finding his feet, Levitan was hired by a client to run their company Sunrise Films, where he had his first run-in with Scholastic on a show called *My Secret Identity*, introducing him to co-founder and president of Scholastic Productions Inc., Marty Keltz, a contact who would prove to be instrumental in later years. Once Levitan's contract with Sunrise Films expired, he felt the time was right to go into business for himself, and he launched Protocol Entertainment in 1993.

When asked what exactly creating a production company entails, Levitan laughs. "Everything and nothing! It really depends what kind of business you want to be in," he says. Family members on his wife's side were well-versed in the entertainment industry, working in West End theater in London and owning drive-in theaters in Ottawa, and gave Steve some valuable advice on getting started: "The trick is to choose between being small or large, and if you choose large, you have to keep growing and growing and growing and never stop, and if you choose small, you have to keep shrinking and shrinking and shrinking until you're working out of your shirt pocket. In those days, that seemed like a metaphor, but now we have this," Levitan says, holding up his cell phone. He chose to keep things small, intending his company to comprise just him, his assistant, and his contact list. With enough money in the bank to pay expenses and support his family for about a year, Levitan took the plunge, hoping that by the end of the year, things would be going well enough for Protocol to fully launch. Sharing these plans with a friend while at the gym, a business partnership was born, one that would last for about a decade, until illness necessitated his partner stepping down, and Levitan bought back full ownership of Protocol Entertainment.

He is tickled pink when asked to explain exactly what a producer does. "That's a great question, because most people don't ask me that question! Most people say, 'Wow, it's so great to be a producer, you're so lucky!' There's so many different kinds of producers. There's producers that get credit as executive producers, because they were an agent that represented a star and when they couldn't get the salary they wanted, then you've gotta give me and my agent a credit. But they actually have relatively nothing to do with the show," he explains. "To me, the way I operate as a producer is to identify at the earliest possible stage a property or an idea or concept or IP that feels like it would be a popular piece of audio-visual entertainment. And you need tons of those, because one in twenty gain any traction. And it's not because your guess is wrong, but because the market isn't ready or the talent isn't there."

The goal was to never be in a position where they were chasing deals just to pay bills, a common pressure for production companies, particularly when it comes to picking up the tab of evolving technologies. Levitan's goal was to be small enough that he could retain a certain selectiveness, not necessarily over which projects he worked on, but which people he worked with. "I only wanted to be involved with people I liked and respected and could foresee enjoying being joined at the hip with them, for a year if it's a movie, or for three or four years if it's a show like *Goosebumps* was. It's like getting married, and then you have a child."

Protocol was in its infancy, starting from scratch with nothing but a list of contacts, and Steve Levitan was rearing to go, on the lookout for the first big project that would get the company going and make an impact. His first move was to make the rounds of his contact book, making stops in New York, Los Angeles and London, and asking to be introduced to anybody worth knowing. He hobnobbed with entertainment figures, expanding his network and getting to know everybody, while trying to gauge where their interest lay, and what sorts of projects would generate enthusiasm from networks and studios. It was during this crucial time that Marty Keltz popped up, and mentioned a series of children's books that were "flying off the shelves". He took Levitan to meet Deborah Forte, an executive at Scholastic who was overseeing *Goosebumps* affairs. She handed Levitan three books—*Welcome to Dead House, Stay Out of the Basement* and *Monster Blood*—just before he boarded a plane back home to Toronto, and the fledgling producer tore through the titles one after another at 35,000 feet. By the time he landed back on Canadian soil, Levitan was smitten with the world of *Goosebumps*, and was certain that he had found his big project.

So eager was Levitan to secure the television rights to the *Goosebumps* books that he scribbled out a handwritten agreement while still on the plane, which he presented to Keltz over the phone as soon as he could get to one. In spite of a lot of competition, and a pre-existing agreement with Fox for the film rights, a deal was worked out. What won him the rights was his insistence that *Goosebumps* be a live-action series, while every other competitor was aiming for an animated show. Levitan made this call based on his unfamiliarity with animation, and insistence that a live-action show should uphold the scare factor of Stine's books: "It's one thing to have a cartoon kid standing beside a cartoon monster and acting scared, it's another thing for a real kid on a real stage standing beside a real monster and acting scared," he says.

The first step was finding the IP, and then presenting it to broadcasters to gauge audience interest. Although he's seen plenty of the inside of Production Hell, Steve says that as long as decisions are being made one way or the other, it's not quite as hellish as it sounds. The real labor comes with working out financing deals. Nowadays, with streamers dominating the market, a lot of properties are kept in-house, with giants like Netflix funding entire projects in exchange for exclusive rights to the work. The '90s was a different beast, and there was much more collaboration going on. License fees were smaller, and broadcasters would usually offer a percentage of the budget, leading to the likes of Canada's subsidies and tax credits filling in the gaps. Finding the appropriate combination of financing to support production in the right way was a considerable task, one that Levitan says had more to do with citizenship and who paid taxes and where, than anything creative. Then a distribution company may come into play, complicating things further. "It's an extremely complicated and time-consuming job for a producer," says Levitan, "one that happens simultaneously with assembling the creative team. There's a ton going on. You're either in an office, or you're on a plane, or in somebody else's office. Lots of phone calls." This is where Levitan's background in entertainment law, as well as his status as creative producer, rather than just a financial one, came in handy. Protocol had only been in business just over a year when *Goosebumps* went into production with three people on board, but Levitan's unique combination of creativity, legal expertise and knowledge of the industry would prove vital to the success that was to come.

With television rights secured, Levitan's next job was to find a network that would host the show. This proved to be more of a challenge than he had anticipated, given how hot the property he now had was. He called up all of the home broadcasters that handled children's programming—CBC, CTV, YTV, Family Channel—to make them an offer that they surely couldn't refuse. "In those days, *Goosebumps* was like *Harry Potter*, only bigger, because every month there was a new book released and they were selling millions of copies," Steve Levitan recalls. "I said, 'I've got the rights to the hottest kids' book on the market'. All of them refused, they said, 'Not interested, never heard of it, don't want it'". For whatever reason, all of Canada's big networks passed on the opportunity, so Levitan began looking further afield and pitching to major networks over the border.

Fox Kids Network was a giant of children's programming, and had a reputation for airing many of the most popular shows of the time, notably *Mighty Morphin' Power Rangers*. Fox was enthused about the project, recognizing it as the perfect addition to its x-treme lineup of badass entertainment for badass kids, and in early 1995, agreed to bankroll the show significantly enough that for now, Levitan could relax about not having a Canadian broadcaster on board. This was a rarity the producer was very fortunate to encounter, with the majority of Canadian productions simply not having the money to discount their own homegrown audience. With Fox money in its pockets, the show was greenlit in April of 1995, and *Goosebumps* officially went into production that summer.

The plan had been to begin shooting once school let out in 1995 to accommodate the child actors, with a production schedule commencing around the end of June, and wrapping up toward the end of October, because Canadian weather wasn't conducive to shooting out and about as the show would often require. This gave Levitan just a couple of months to get everything in order, and it was a daunting task that his youthful ambition allowed him to rise to. "If somebody pitched that to me today, I'd say, 'It can't be made,'" he says. "On *Goosebumps* we were lucky, because Fox Kids came in with a substantial enough license fee as a percentage of the budget that I felt comfortable going into production with just that, even though we had a big gap still to fill. Even though all the Canadian broadcasters who were appropriate for that show initially rejected it, which is still unbelievably difficult for me to understand."

Midway through shooting of its first season, the show received an unexpected perk brought about by the very audience it was being made for. Steve Levitan got a call one day from a Canadian commissioner he had previously pitched the show to, asking to be reminded of that project he had brought to them. It turned out that the commissioner had just spent the weekend with her nephews, who were going crazy for the *Goosebumps* books, and their enthusiasm for the series prompted her to reconsider the show. An offer was made, empowering Levitan to go back to the other broadcasters who had declined a deal and try again. "I said, 'I have an offer for this now, and you might want to do some research and determine how successful these books are.' And we actually ended up with a bidding war, which turned out to be much more lucrative for me than it would have been if somebody had had the wisdom or did the research and actually cared to look into what *Goosebumps* was. They could have got it for probably half of what they ended up spending! But that's the Canadian marketplace," he explains. "It is reactive, not proactive, and I've had plenty of situations like that on other shows. Canada is a small country in a very, very large place."

The bidding frenzy concluded, and YTV became the home of *Goosebumps* in Canada. As the country's first dedicated children's network, it was the perfect place for *Goosebumps* to flourish on its home turf, which makes it all the more puzzling that they passed on the show the first time around. Levitan says that once the show got its bearings, there was very little interference from broadcasters with regard to the style and scariness of the show. It was a big success, and they were largely left to their own devices, so now it was on them to get out there and make a show with the same cultural impact as Stine's books. Financing was in place, and it was time to hire the creative team who would bring Levitan's ambitious project to life.

"A Sweetheart Crew"

Assembling the Team

As the green light flashed on *Goosebumps*, a huge operation got underway to build an infrastructure that could support the television adaptation of the biggest children's books of the era. It was a period of fine tuning the creative vision, lots of reading, meetings and conversations with the right people. It was before the internet had become a central fixture in the industry, and so ideas were exchanged either over the phone, through the mail or via fax. "Time consuming and awkward" is how Levitan remembers the process. Luckily, they had some pretty serious money at their disposal, which would help them secure the best people Canada had to offer. "As far as I know, it was the highest-budgeted kids' TV show at the time, which probably makes it one of the highest-budgeted ever, because those were the peak years of kids' television," Steve Levitan explains. "I can't tell you the exact number because the financing agreements all require confidentiality, but the comparative would be—and this is extremely unusual for kids' television—if you think about it per minute, our scripts were about twenty-four minutes of running time and a movie is, let's say a hundred, we were about the same cost per minute as a Hollywood studio movie would be. That doesn't mean millions of dollars an episode, but it is an extraordinary number. It's certainly the most expensive kids' show in the history of Canada, which is actually saying a lot, because most kids' shows are not actually shot in America, or weren't in those days. It was quite high."

In addition to a sizable investment from Fox, there were perks to being a Canadian production company. "There were tax credits in the '80s which really kick-started the whole industry in Toronto," explains production designer Ian Brock. "They allowed you to write off a hundred-percent write-off on your taxes for investments in films. So, all these rich guys—mostly dentists and lawyers—they started putting in all this money." It was in this environment that many of those on the crew got their start in the film industry, and now Canada was the place to be for more financially-rewarding film production. It wasn't just the money, though. Toronto as a city became a very accommodating place, which was happy to make arrangements for productions. Need to plant palm trees on the waterfront to make it look tropical? Go for it. Wanna drive a car off a cliff? Be our guest! 1990s Toronto really was the best place for film and television production, and through the many challenges *Goosebumps* presented, the city was there to help.

Production may have been buoyed by a considerable cash float, but they were going to earn every cent of it the hard way. There were three years of incredibly long and demanding working hours ahead of them, but the entire team jumped at it with gusto, and maintained a stamina akin to that of professional dancers, by never letting it look like hard work. It was no small task, and one of the first steps was establishing a headquarters from which everything could operate. Toronto had a considerable amount of architecture leftover from the Victorian industrial era that sat more or less derelict, and among these buildings was the former Molson's Brewery on Fleet Street. It was vast, spacious and in a central location—it was perfect. Producer Patrick Doyle was the one to find the place, and when he showed it to Steve Levitan, he was sold. On the waterfront and right next to the expressway, it was accessible, sizable and malleable. It was, however, in a state of disrepair, but this meant that production could get it on the cheap. Due to be torn down entirely, *Goosebumps* saved it from extinction. "It was just an ideal place," says Levitan.

"It's like this giant building. It was derelict, which is great because we go shoot on it, and all the kettles have been removed, and it's full of dead pigeons, and it was just gross," recalls Ian Brock.

This ramshackle old bird graveyard came with a number of perks though, not least of which being the hollow floors where brewing tanks used to go. "We had these empty floors where we could store all the scenery, so we never threw a thing out. So we just kept recycling and recycling as we went through season after season," Brock explains. "We could build up from below. So, we could do stunts, like throw kids in and throw them out. You could build a pond or whatever in the studio."

The building spanned several stories, which would later prove useful once Protocol's catalog expanded and the company was straddling a number of projects simultaneously. One floor of the old brewery would end up being home to *Goosebumps*, another was for *Animorphs*, and crew were free to wander from one to the other as required. "I would move my office from one level to another level, depending on what production," director Ron Oliver recalls, "so I'd go and do two episodes of one show, and I'd move upstairs and do two episodes of another show." The grounds of the Molson's building were expansive, and the exteriors of the building were stylistically well-suited to a horror show. So much so that the site would later be used for some exterior shots in episodes like "Say Cheese and Die," and "Chillogy." The only real issue was that parking was cramped, which proved to be an issue when Levitan's young nephew was hired as a driver, and kept crashing the van into other vehicles, but in every other way, the old Molson's building was perfect. *Goosebumps* had its home base, and now it was time to find the team to work in it.

Steve Levitan had his work cut out for him when it came to assembling the team that would bring *Goosebumps* to life, but a key figure was gifted to production in the form of executive producer Bill Siegler. He was onboard the *Goosebumps* train as a Scholastic representative, acting as the middle man between the publishing house that unleashed the books on the world, and the television adaptation that was taking shape. A resourceful and well-connected man with a background in theater direction, who Levitan frequently describes as "the heart of the show," he opened many doors and helped in the quest to find the right people to do the right jobs. "He wore the Scholastic/R.L. Stine hat", says Steve Levitan.

As Levitan remembers it, Siegler was friendly with the creative team behind *Friends*, who recommended he get in touch with Dan Angel and Billy Brown, a writing and producing team already making a good impression on the industry. The duo met with Siegler and the Scholastic gang, and then with Steve and the Protocol crew, all of whom were immediately certain that they were the perfect people to make *Goosebumps* happen. "It took a while of planning, it took a while of finding the right team of writers. Dan and Billy were absolutely the perfect people to write this show, but it took a while to search them out," says Steve Levitan. The two were positioned as the executive story editors, and with their help and contacts, the show was quickly beginning to take shape.

Alongside Bill Siegler was Lena Cordina, another of those in the higher echelon of the production team, whose job it was to bridge the gap between corporate and creative and make sure everything ran smoothly. With a property as big as *Goosebumps*, and a network as big as Fox, this was one hell of an assignment. "The production manager is so important because so many other things are going on in the episode, unlike cookie-cutter shows like *Friends*, for example, always the same three sets, always the same six actors," Levitan explains. "Lena Cordina and [production coordinator] Bernie Burford made everything work, and that was just a huge job. Huge. Their office was beside Bill Siegler's office and the three of them were like a unit that just made everything work. Their professionalism, their ability to foresee things, they'd make sure stuff was there before we needed it. They were just so important to the creative process, and a production coordinator is not normally seen as a creative person, but they are." Another key name on this rung of the ladder is Patrick Doyle. The producer was a happy-go-lucky sort of fellow, bursting with energy and ideas. He would fill in for minor roles, offer his house out for filming odds and ends, and always had a solution for any problem. He was greatly missed when he died unexpectedly between seasons, to the extent that he would continue to be credited for producing the show, even after his death.

Determined to make this as Canadian a production as possible, Levitan put together a list of Canadian directors who he considered a good fit for the show, and carried out further brainstorming with Siegler, Brown and Angel to pull together a solid team of creatives who could make the show happen. Between them, they pooled their contacts and began reaching out to writers, directors, production designers and cinematographers that they felt would be valuable assets to *Goosebumps*, and bring the magic to life. In practical terms, this also meant an effects shop, a post-effects wizard, and, importantly, an animal wrangler.

It turned out that magic was a good starting point when assembling the team. Director Ron Oliver describes the world of R.L. Stine as one of "fantasy, illusion and the darker side of fun. Magic and directing or filmmaking are so similar, because you're creating the illusion of something, with various tricks and subterfuges. And I love that, there's nothing I love more than fooling an audience," he says. Oliver cites *The Twilight Zone* as having given him his first glimpse into the magic of directing. "A lot of people forget how low-budget that show really was, and they would have really smart directors on that show who would solve problems." From Rod Serling's signature show, he recalls a shot of clapping hands which, when compressed, gave the impression of a huge crowd when in reality it was six or eight people. "I remember seeing that as a kid and thinking it was genius," says Oliver. Before venturing into directing, he began in the performative world of stage magic, following in the footsteps of other greats of the creative arts like Orson Welles and Johnny Carson, and feels that, paired with his love of the old horror classics, this background set him up well to direct horror. He cut his teeth on the camp icons *Hello Mary Lou: Prom Night II* and *Prom Night III: The Last Kiss*, before venturing into the world of children's horror.

Coincidentally, he was running in the same circles as special effects artist Ron Stefaniuk. "When I was sixteen or seventeen, other people would go work at Burger King for eight hours, and we'd go do a magic show for, you know, forty-five minutes and make enough money for the whole week," Stefaniuk regales. For him too, magic was an important initiation into the world of film. It represented the key to the unreal, to that enviable position in which you could make something impossible happen, and cast waves of amazement through an audience. So it seemed fitting that just a few years into their respective careers, the two Rons would unite for the common cause of entertaining young audiences on the small screen.

Ron Stefaniuk had nestled his way into the industry in an unconventional way. Having got started in stage magic, the theater buff frequented summer stock and amateur dramatic productions, and would wait at the stage door to meet the people who worked on the shows he watched, to sing their praises and share ideas he had for maximizing onstage effects and stunts. "The first puppets people build at a puppet company are hand puppets—the very first puppet I made was twenty-six feet long, seventeen feet high!" he says. When he heard that a local theater company was looking to put a diplodocus on stage, he took the weekend to draw up designs. "Two guys would wear it, it would be on backpacks, and the weight would be transferred to our hips. The tail would balance the head, and the head would lift and the tail would lift, and we could move it," he explains. "So, I drew it all up, and walked into the meeting and said, 'You should build this'. And he said, 'OK, you're hired.'"

Stefaniuk threw himself in at the deep end, an attitude to his work that would define him, and leave a lasting impression. He credits his comprehensive skill set to finding him the most interesting work. Having spent the last few years learning on the job to build not only puppets and masks but also sets and props, he had more to offer than the average puppet shop or special effects artist. Ron Stefaniuk was a young and highly ambitious creator who was just getting started when *Goosebumps* came his way. Not only was his portfolio impressive, but it was comprehensive. This show would require special effects makeup and full body costumes for actors, as well as animatronics and puppets, and Stefaniuk and his crew could do it all. Given how heavily Stine's world relied on its monsters, it was essential that whoever took on the task of translating his fictional creations to the screen could do so faithfully. Having a one-stop shop for all practical effects, helmed by a man for whom no job was too big, was exactly what the show required, and the Stefaniuk crew were eagerly recruited. "I don't think even *Are You Afraid of The Dark?* did this, because of the nature of their show," says Steve Levitan, "but we needed to have an attached animatronics team and we needed a post-effects team, although the decision was that we would do as few post-effects as we possibly could."

Having pledged to create as much on-screen, practically, as possible, Stefaniuk's work was crucial, as was that of the stunt team. Although not exactly a rival to *Terminator 2: Judgment Day* in the action department, *Goosebumps* still required its fair share of stunt work, and with so many young actors on board, safety had to be given even heavier consideration. Anton "Tye" Tyukodi was brought on as stunt coordinator, and he was everything a '90s action man should have been: helicopter pilot, paramedic, stunt performer. He could do it all, and most importantly, make people feel safe and respected while doing so. "He was so good with the kids," Ian Brock recalls. "He was just like, 'It's okay, I'm just going to hang you up by your ankles!'" Tyukodi was a very close friend of fellow stunt performer Bryan Renfro, who continues to sing his praises to this day. He made sure everything, from falling off a bike to driving vehicles, went safely, and was fun for all involved.

Between every other family having a dog with a hardcore name like Vandal, and the many snakes, spiders and other creepy crawlies that would come into play, it was vital that an animal expert was on board. The show would use a number of animal wranglers over the course of its run, but the one everybody mentions is a fellow affectionately called Jim Bugs. Jim Lovisek, to use his real name, was not only an expert animal wrangler but an avid geology enthusiast who owned huge rock collections. Sadly, there were some instances of small creatures not making it through production. The few occasions that called for piles of worms, such as "Go Eat Worms" and "Stay Out of the Basement," meant that worms would overheat from being packed together, and some would die. Those that lived would be given to the crew to take home and put in their gardens.

Production required a solid and experienced director of photography to establish an atmospheric style that would sell the terror of the show. Canadian Brian R. R. Hebb grew up in England and began his career by taking souvenir photographs for tourists on the seaside promenade of Blackpool, later training in still photography, but always dreamed of making it into the movies, with pictures like *Lawrence of Arabia*, *Doctor Zhivago* and *Blow-Up* inspiring him to hone his craft. After moving back to his native Canada, he joined the CBC and travelled the world as a documentarian, before making the move into film and television. He was already friendly with Steve Levitan, who put his name forward for consideration as director of photography on *Goosebumps*. His extensive work on shows like *Alfred Hitchcock Presents* meant he was not only versatile, but well-versed in creating tension on screen, and used to anthological projects. It didn't hurt that he was just a swell guy, too. "He was also a sweetheart. A lot of these people were just puppy dogs," Levitan says fondly.

The 'every week a mini movie' approach of the show worked well for Brian Hebb, who felt he had never really developed a signature style because every project he worked on was so different and required an entirely unique approach. "I would try many different styles even though many people would tell me later that they could spot my distinctive quality," he says. "Sometimes my approach to a particular genre was instinctive after I had done my initial research. I would read the books, the scripts, and approve some locations. I would screen some feature films of a similar style and try to find a different way with the look." This was exactly what *Goosebumps* needed. As a show that could be in a medieval English castle one week and a Louisiana bayou the next, there was no one-size-fits-all approach, and it was important to establish different atmospheres with each episode while maintaining a distinctly *Goosebumps* look to it all. Hebb was their guy. The show was shot on Super 16mm film, the inherent graininess of which Ian Brock describes as "extremely forgiving." Although CGI was a thing, it was still in its early days, and was in danger of looking "hokey" on screen, so it was quickly decided that the 16mm format was the way to go. Some crew members recall switching over to digital for Season Four, but for the most part, the show was shot the old-fashioned way. Beyond the film stock itself, they wanted to achieve a visually cinematic quality with their camera setup. "We shot single-camera," says director Craig Pryce. "We still had a second camera, but we shot it like a film, whereas ever since *Hannah Montana*, most kids' shows are three cameras in a studio, with very loud acting and sitcom-style performances. I think they were more realistic then. It was a really creative time where you could shoot things with style and unique camera angles."

There was still some element of trial and error with the production crew, and not everybody who was brought on at the beginning would stay the entire run of the show. Initially, Armando Sgrignuoli was positioned as the show's production designer, and captained the art department for the majority of the first season. However, towards the end of the Season One, he would be replaced by Ian Brock. Steve Levitan puts it down to creative differences. Sgrignuoli was "an artiste" and incredibly emotionally invested in his work, enjoying talking through the minutiae of his creations and explaining his process. This passionate approach wasn't really conducive to the rigorous schedule of the show. "Too much emotional investment in something on a TV schedule," Levitan explains. "We just have to keep going. We can't just discuss how wonderful this is. Internally, we have to move on. And so, when it came time for the next season, Ian, who was younger, you know, closer in mentality to Dan and Billy, he was kind of the same generation, same kind of mindset, just was a better fit."

Ian Brock had studied art history at university, but finding it too theoretical, started taking film classes so that he could enjoy the more hands-on aspects of the craft. He started working in the industry straight out of university, landing gigs on commercials and in theater productions before getting his introduction to movie sets on a sci-fi picture titled *Firebird 2015 A.D.* Rock music videos were really taking off around this time and Toronto was something of a hub for them, so he expanded into the music video world, where he got used to short turnaround times and having to be resourceful on minimal budgets and schedules. He also studied with the Design School of the Canadian Broadcasting Company, and started making his own slasher movies. This hodgepodge of creative experience and knowledge made him a welcome addition to the *Goosebumps* gang. It was an added bonus that he lived a seven-minute bike ride away from the studios. He was brought in at the tail end of Season One, replacing Armando Sgrignuoli as production designer/ art director (terms which are, according to Brock, interchangeable: "There was a whole transition period in the '90s where we went from being art directors to production designers.") "They just wanted a change, and I don't know if they didn't like Armando. I think they just wanted someone different from the second season. They were going to try someone else," Brock explains.

He recalls a cushty arrangement he was offered when he became part of the *Goosebumps* team. "I was on a retainer the whole time I was there. So they buy me back, which is pretty great, and I kept it on the DL at the time, but literally, they say, 'We finish in November and we'll come back in March. OK, we'll just pay you for the winter half your salary for four months, so go off and do whatever else you want, and then, as long as you showed up on March 1, then you were theirs." Given the seasonal nature of the job, it suited the production designer just fine, and he felt very fortunate to have been offered such terms. It's not clear just how widespread such an arrangement was throughout the rest of the crew, but even if some were not on a retainer, it looks like they were always happy to return for a new season. The issue of burnout, however, was never far away.

Brian R. R. Hebb would not remain with the show for its entirety. By Season Three, he was burnt out creatively, and was going through a divorce, prompting him to take a well-earned hiatus and hand the reins over to cinematographer Barry Bergthorson, who would see out the remainder of the show as director of photography. Despite these occasional reshufflings, the production crew remained a close-knit and well-oiled operation that worked hard and played hard, and there were never any hard feelings when somebody decided to bow out. Director Randy Bradshaw remembers Barry Bergthorson as a very experienced cinematographer who was great to be around. "Wonderful man! Made me laugh. He was the guy that carried a lot of the weight of making sure the unit was kept going. No matter how crazy the thing was you were asking him to do in how little a period of time, you know, he'd never lose it." Bergthorson was in good company, as a resourceful, hard-working guy who was up for a challenge and would always give it his best. He was also instrumental in keeping everything moving, prepping second unit while first was still working. As an all-rounder and good friend, he was the perfect person to continue what Brian R. R. Hebb had started.

Then, of course, they needed someone to slice and dice whatever days on the set turned out, and through a good old-fashioned printed advertisement, Levitan would be introduced to one of the show's most valuable players. Bob Sprogis started out with hopes of being a DJ with the midnight-6 slot, but ended up at the RTA School of Media where he trained in editing, and got started on industrial and educational films before going freelance. Sometime in 1995, he saw an advert with the Directors Guild of Canada looking for people to work on *Goosebumps*, and composed a hand-written letter applying for the job, which he dropped off in person to the Molson building. It took a while, but he was called in, and later told that his incredible calligraphy had set him apart from other applicants. He secured the job and, unbeknownst to him at the time, it would be the start of a three-year-long gig and an even longer working and personal relationship with Steve Levitan and Protocol. He says that the rule of thumb he adheres to in making it in entertainment is similar to that espoused by Anthony Hopkins: "You learn your lines, show up on time, and don't be a dick." Thanks to Steve Levitan's keen eye for good personalities, everybody on the show was on board with this doctrine.

Although plenty of thought and careful planning went into putting together the *Goosebumps* team, it ran on equal parts instinct, and Levitan set the show up for success just with the people he hired. The major throughline of *Goosebumps* production is that everybody just had a great time. They made friends, had each other's backs, shared the passion and work ethic, and were always willing to think big, think creatively and maintain the central ethos of making a show that kids would love to watch. "The producers put a great crew together," says Randy Bradshaw. "I think the industry term for situations like that is you have a 'sweetheart crew.' Just everybody, you're friends with, you respect each other." He says that this is of particular value in the television format, where the demands of the work make a solid team a real commodity. "Episodic television is a machine, right? It keeps moving regardless."

For Steve Levitan, it all came back to respecting his crew as people, and most importantly, as creative professionals. "When you work on a television show, there's no separation between creative and just labor. Even the guys who moves apple boxes around, they have to have a creative sensibility to know exactly when and where and how to fit in, to support the creative process of the people who do what are considered to be the traditional titles of creative positions on a crew. So, I consider everybody to be a creative contributor on that show, even the drivers."

"You Do Need a Personality for a Kids' Show"

Directing Goosebumps

Directing is far from a catch-all job. The distinction between directing for film and television is substantial, and even greater still is the distinction between directing your average episodic TV series and an anthology. Between its young audience, its massive success as a book series, and the anthological format of the show, *Goosebumps* was a fairly unique task to the directors who helped bring it to life. Although as varied as the weekly stories in terms of personalities, the directors who worked on the show were united by four common principles which Steve Levitan laid out at the beginning of his search for the right team.

"First and foremost, we needed directors who understood how to work with kids," Levitan explains. "All the rest of it is fairly routine filmmaking, but getting a performance from kids that kid viewers could relate to…" He needed directors who understood the difference between real kids, and what adults imagined kids were like, and could relate to kids on a personal level. Secondly, any director to come on board had to be up for a challenge that required more than just standing behind the camera. Prep was an intensive week for everybody, with everything from writing and locations to monster-making and prop work having to be completed within about five days, so directors needed to be willing to take on all aspects of production. "You needed directors who could handle that kind of prep before shooting an episode, and that's very different prep than you would have on a regular episodic series, because the directors would have to weigh in on set design, costume design, location scouting. It's a lot more work than just coming in to do another episode of *Law and Order*, where it's pretty much all in the studio.

So, you needed directors who were up for that kind of challenge, actually enjoyed that kind of challenge." Steve Levitan attributes the adaptability of the *Goosebumps* directors to their respective filmic backgrounds, which he feels nurtured creativity more than standard episodic television did. If they were making a mini movie each week, the show needed directors who could make each episode feel like a movie.

The third requirement leaned in a more creative direction: "The ability to build suspense in an old-fashioned way, kind of how Hitchcock would, you know? That's a phrase that would always come up. We want to do this the way Hitchcock would build suspense instead of the way, let's say Roger Corman, would build suspense. So that's more doing things in-camera, doing them with shadows, doing things with close-ups rather than with fright cuts or jump cuts, or, you know, graphic shock imagery. So, an appreciation of that kind of filmmaking." And finally, and perhaps most importantly, every good *Goosebumps* director needed a sense of humor. "These are all tongue-in-cheek scripts, and the best of them had a great comedic twist at the end, which let the kids off gently. We needed them to be able to shift, and do a final scene that was sometimes comedic, ironic, and also terrifying at the same time, like in "The Haunted Mask."" An additional piece of guidance: "We would tell all the directors, 'Don't waste time doing multiple takes, because with kid actors, they're more likely to give you a good take if you can let them say it the way they would normally talk,'" says Levitan.

It was with these four specifications that Protocol went looking for its directors, and it was an exercise in proving the power of networking. The Toronto entertainment circle was already a small, close-knit one where people would cross paths all the time, and as it happened, many of those who would go on to work on *Goosebumps* had worked on projects together in the past, and would continue to do so afterwards. The feelers were put out for directors known to the producers, and for some, it was just too exciting an opportunity to pass up. "There were a couple of other things I was involved in at the time, but *Goosebumps* was just so much fun that I always try and make it work to do it," says Randy Bradshaw. An early team of regulars and semi-regulars was compiled, consisting of William Fruet, Ron Oliver, John Bell and Timothy Bond, with David Warry-Smith and David Winning putting in one-and-done appearances in the first season. Later seasons would see René Bonnière, Steve DiMarco, Randy Bradshaw and Don McCutcheon come into rotation, with Craig Pryce, Stefan Scaini and cinematographer Brian R. R. Hebb helming one episode each. Editor Bob Sprogis was due to direct an episode at one point, but it never came to fruition. John Bell and Timothy Bond emerged as frontrunners early on, with Bell directing the first episode to be shot, and Bond helming the first episode to air, and the first hour-long special. However, it wouldn't take long for William Fruet to become the dominant director of the show, ultimately directing twenty-seven of the seventy-four episodes. Although there was a certain amount of trying people out and seeing who fit, it was mostly a matter of scheduling that allocated who worked where. All of the directors who worked on the show were busy guys, and it was usually a case of seeing who was available when. "They became our staple list of directors and when they were available, we would book them," says Steve Levitan.

Although in an ideal world, it would be preferable to allocate certain episodes to particular directors based on its suitability to their style or strengths, it wasn't usually that sort of deal. Directors also did not get a say on which episodes they felt would be fun to work on. "In television, you don't give the director the choice of what episode they're getting," Levitan chuckles. "That would be suicide, and scarier than anything we ever did in the show!" As much selectivity as could be exercised was, and there were scenarios where one wonders what an episode would have looked like in the hands of another director (kooky Ron Oliver serving Horrorland, anyone?), but the old industry cliché of scheduling conflicts meant that the perfect lineup wasn't always doable. For the most part, things worked well, and directors were happy with the episodes they were given.

Director John Bell had a considerable responsibility on his shoulders. Millions of dollars had been invested in bringing the world of R.L. Stine to life for the small screen, and everyone was acutely aware of the expectations being aimed at them. If they screwed this up and failed to translate the magic from the page to the TV set, it would be a hot property down the drain. They simply had to get off to a strong start, one that would set the bar and hopefully cast the show off in the right direction. John Bell had a substantial television portfolio to his name, having started out in Canadian sketch comedy and various Eugene Levy projects. His forte was firmly in the comedy world, which makes his detour into children's horror an interesting, but not unwarranted one.

"John was that kind of guy, great with kids. Also, he had kids of his own that would come to set occasionally," Steve Levitan recalls. "Great energy, very creative. Everybody loved working with John. He was extremely reliable." Between his jovial nature, extensive television experience and understanding of young viewers, Bell was positioned as the very first director of *Goosebumps*. The first episode filmed was "The Girl Who Cried Monster," and it was one that immediately ran into some teething issues, which made the producers all the more glad that they had brought in someone as dependable and capable as Bell. His resilience and resourcefulness made sure the bumpy first week on the set was recovered from quickly, arguably setting a positive precedent for future episodes that any issue could be overcome. As director on the first episode, with a newly-recruited crew, it was up to Bell to bring every department into the fold, making sure they felt comfortable and confident with what they were doing. It is no mean feat to direct the first episode of a brand-new TV show, let alone an anthology show that would almost never feature the same characters, locations or plotlines. This was a territory in which everything could, and would, happen, and without John Bell's steady hand, who knows where the show as a whole could have ended up.

"For the first few episodes in the first season, you're extra careful because you want to get renewed," Levitan explains, "and you don't really know what the machine that you're building is capable of producing yet." Bell would be the one to find out, and so successful was he at doing so, that he was soon brought back to direct a number of later episodes. Actor Afrah Gouda would work with him on the episode "Return of the Mummy," and she describes John Bell as "a visionary", who was kind, patient and accommodating. "He has the image in his head, and that's what he wants. He was a great guy to work with. I was really lucky to work with everybody, even the producers. All of them were wonderful people," she says.

Although it was Bell who would kick off the show on the practical side of things, to the viewers at home, the debut was in the hands of Timothy Bond. "The Haunted Mask" functioned as the show's grand debut for Halloween 1995, and whatever went on behind the scenes, the impact of this hour-long special was the be-all-and-end-all for *Goosebumps*. Bond had extensive directing credits mostly encompassing episodic television, but occasionally dipping into feature territory. He had notably worked on multiple episodes of both *Alfred Hitchcock Presents* and *Friday the 13th: The Series*, as well as a number of other sci-fi and horror-adjacent titles, and had even worked previously with one of his young cast members, Amos Crawley. Evidently, his background made him the perfect match for *Goosebumps*, for although he would not go on to direct as frequently as Fruet or Oliver, his episodes packed a hell of a punch.

Timothy Bond and Kathryn Long on the set of "The Haunted Mask." Photo courtesy of Matthew DeWilde.

"The Haunted Mask" was as impactful a debut as any show could hope for. Thematically rich, brilliantly acted and remarkably scary for such a young audience, it was the ultimate sizzle reel that showed just what this show, and the creative minds behind it, were capable of. It is hardly surprising that Levitan remembers Bond as someone who loved to go to the extreme. "He liked to go scarier all the time. He liked the darker, more shocking interpretations of the script," which is ironic given that he is simultaneously described as "a big, roly-poly, jolly old guy." Crawley deftly summarizes Bond's strengths as a director: "He was good with kids. He was good with making you laugh and keeping it easy and he was a real pro in that he knew how to run a set. He made his rules very clear early on, and his expectations very clear." If John Bell set the practical bar, Timothy Bond's combination of structure and personality set the tonal one. He wasn't scared to tell people exactly what he needed, and was known to get a bit exasperated at times, but he was a hit with the cast and crew, particularly with the assistant directors, who were always glad to have a boss with a clear vision.

By far the most prolific of the *Goosebumps* directors was William "Bill" Fruet. He spent the majority of the 1970s and '80s directing Canadian horror movies of various flavors, before transitioning into television work which, like Tim Bond, included *Alfred Hitchcock Presents* and *Friday the 13th: The Series*, which put him in the perfect position to take on a majority share of a horror anthology show. Despite being brought back so frequently, Fruet's reputation doesn't exactly seem to fit the mold, with Steve Levitan describing him as "the grumpiest director" of the bunch. "Bill Fruet started the day mad, no matter what was happening, he was very intense and very focused." Somewhat more charitably, "The Haunted Mask II" actor Amos Crawley remembers Fruet as "a little more old school, a little more aggressive with us. Not in any, like, bad way, necessarily, but gruff. I got the feeling he didn't get along with kids so well." Despite being remembered on the surface as one of the more tightly-laced directors on the show, actors and crew agree that he was a good guy, a talented director, and one who encouraged creativity, particularly in his young performers. Actor Beki Lantos remembers feeling nurtured and supported by Fruet on the set of "Stay Out of the Basement." "The director, William, was so lovely and kind to me. He truly made me feel like a professional and like I mattered," she fondly recalls. Despite his no-nonsense attitude, he worked well with his team and got the best out of his actors, and nobody has even hinted at disliking him. His by-the-book approach got stuff done, and in a predictable, reliable fashion that such a fast-paced show needed. "He would always resist [improv], because the script was the script, he would insist on shooting it the way it was written," says Levitan. "Always extremely reliable, would never go over time, never go over budget. The crew loved working with him because you knew where you were gonna be, because the script and the shooting schedule, the call sheet for that day was going to be followed to the letter."

Bill Fruet with Lucy Peacock, Judah Katz, Blake McGrath and Beki Lantos on the set of "Stay Out of the Basement." Photo courtesy of Beki Lantos.

"Looking back, I think my favourite director was Bill Fruet. He seemed to be the one with the good ideas," says cinematographer Brian R. R. Hebb. "He was quite creative. He always gave me a workout." Actor Tod Fennell agrees, characterizing Fruet as "focused. He was good. He wouldn't be afraid to do many, many takes and get exactly what he was looking for." Actor Judah Katz says Fruet was a great director to work with, someone who trusted the talent and instincts of his cast, aligning with Katz's attitude of, "If my instincts are wrong, then you chose the wrong actor." Knowing Katz could take care of himself, he focused mainly on his two young stars. "Bill was very easy for me to work with. Very creative. He knew what he needed and wanted, and he would just explain to me what the shot is, and then I did it my way. I don't remember there ever being a problem. I think his main concern was the kids."

Fruet's legacy is an interesting one. Looking back on his directing team, Fruet stood out to Levitan: "They're just happy to do it. Except for Bill Fruet, who was always miserable!" he laughs. While actors and crew agree that he was dedicated and quite precise, he is remembered very fondly for fostering a creative and supportive environment, and for his ability to bring gravity to a children's show.

Although Steve Levitan says that directors were never given a choice of which episodes they would direct, the producers would do their best to allocate them based on their individual styles and strengths, as much as their availability. To this end, "you would give [Bill Fruet] the ones that were more serious, a little bit more on the scary horror side. You would give Ron [Oliver] the ones that were more lighthearted and more campy."

Mention the name Ron Oliver to anybody who has worked with him and watch their face light up. His reputation as a hilarious, jovial and thoroughly unique character very much precedes him, and of all the people to direct *Goosebumps*, he seems to embody all of the qualities that made it so special, both on the screens and behind the scenes. Brian R. R. Hebb describes him as "a real character!" Production designer Ian Brock had already worked with Oliver prior to *Goosebumps*, and thinks it may have been the director who brought him onto the show. "He was amazing," says Brock, "he's a crazy guy!" Actor Corey Sevier calls him "the most fun director, maybe, that I've ever worked with." Although Amos Crawley never got to work on one of his episodes of *Goosebumps*, the two had formerly collaborated on the *Are You Afraid of the Dark?* episode, "The Tale of the Ghastly Grinner." Crawley fondly remembers how Oliver had blasted a 9 Inch Nails album while shooting, specifically because the young actor loved the band so much. "He was fantastic. He was just a lovely, lovely, dude. Talk about making a mark on people's childhoods!" Beki Lantos, who worked with Oliver on both *Goosebumps* and *Are You Afraid of the Dark?* remembers him as "a flamboyant and outspoken man. I loved working with him."

Ron Oliver was on the furthest opposing end of the spectrum to Bill Fruet. A flamboyant and fun-loving guy who was openly gay even from the early days of his career, he had done everything from stage magic to interstitial TV jockeying. He was made for the world of show business, and loved every minute of it. The ultimate movie buff with a particular weakness for horror, he often took inspiration from movies he loved, and found ways to pay homage to them in his work. "Night of the Living Dummy 2" had elements of *Halloween*, and other haunted doll movies, while "Perfect School" pulled from *Twin Peaks* and *Mission: Impossible* to set its young star Shawn Roberts up as the next action hero. He also enjoyed placing his own little Easter eggs into his episodes, including hanging a portrait of his friend, horror novelist Michael Rowe, on the wall and putting one of his favorite magazines in the hands of a young character. Whatever episode he got his hands on, you could bet it was brimming with reference, homage and a lot of heart.

So good a fit for the show was Oliver that Steve Levitan would do his best to work the show around the director's schedule: "We would find out what his availabilities were early in the season, and book him, and then try and steer the right scripts to those slots as opposed to waiting until we had a script, and then saying, you know, which director will be hired." Oliver was known for always wearing a dress shirt and tie on set (even if paired with shorts), and bringing along a bright yellow Jeep boombox and stack of CDs everywhere he went. "It would go from The Beach Boys to punk rock," Steve Levitan fondly recalls, "dancing around, trying to get the crew to dance. It was just heaven!" But, he emphasizes, there had to be a measure of balance, which Oliver was always able to bring, making his sets more of a work-hard-play-hard environment. He nurtured friendships with everybody he worked with, and to this day seems like a walking who's who, with industry friends up to his eyeballs. Steve Levitan remembers the two Rons—Oliver and Stefaniuk—being a particularly dynamic duo: "He'd have a riot working with Ron Stefaniuk, coming up with these monsters. The two of them together were a trip!" It's not a wonder that the two Rons would get on like a house on fire. Through my conversations with them, it is obvious that they are big kids at heart, and they get a real kick out of carrying out their work as if their younger self were watching the finished product. They make shows like what they enjoyed as kids.

But Oliver's direction never veered into pure comedy, and he explains his ideas behind each episode with surprising nuance. For example, when it came to presenting the dynamics of the family unit which was often integral to *Goosebumps*, Oliver explains some basic but effective framing techniques, starting with framing the family together, then breaking them into separate shots as they begin to fracture. Ron Oliver doesn't remember doing this consciously, putting it down to a standard approach to filmmaking that becomes inherent after a while. "I run a lot on instinct," he says.

On top of the classic horror elements, he liked working with stories that he felt had a deeper meaning he could resonate with. "Perfect School" bears resemblance to another Oliver-directed episode, "Welcome to Camp Nightmare," in that it features a band of young boys conspiring against an institution they feel they can't trust. When asked about this, Ron Oliver says this is the kind of story he loves to tell. "Kids are essentially powerless at that age, and they get shipped off to these various places. I'm sure there was a subtextual element of gay conversion camps, and that boot camp phenomenon. As opposed to fixing the parents, we decide we'll go fix the kids, and I really have an issue with that kind of thing. I definitely have an affinity for those stories," he explains.

When asked exactly why he thinks he became one of the major directors on the show, Ron Oliver puts it down mostly to his comprehensive skill set. He wrote as much as he directed, and by the time Season Four came around, he was producing too. "I guess the short answer is, I kept delivering shows that were popular and that people liked, and I wear a tie on set! So I think once they got into bed with the devil they were like, 'Well, we'll just stay with him!'"

Steve Levitan agrees that Oliver's practical skills on set were a definite factor. "He was incredibly fast, great with kids, getting performances out of them and always ready to solve any problem, which was why we had him on so frequently. Fantastic sense of humor, great spirit, terrific energy and very inventive about how to get ambitious scripts done within the budget, and the timeframe that we had, which was always a challenge." More than that, his rapport with young actors was really the key to making a great episode, and Oliver had an eye for spotting talent and nurturing it. Levitan credits Oliver with discovering Ryan Gosling, having put his name forward for auditions early on in the show.

Director Randy Bradshaw was also a real hit with his child actors, with a chill demeanor, a fun approach to filmmaking and a hefty stock of dad jokes at his disposal. So prominent was his cheesy sense of humor that it ended up getting a shoutout on the final day of shooting "The Blob That Ate Everyone," when both he and actor Scott Pietrangelo brought their copies of the book to set, and passed them around for the cast and crew to sign. Pietrangelo cheekily signed the director's copy with the message, 'Randy, Quit it with the corny jokes!!!!', to which the director responded with his own message, 'Now you don't have to put up with my corny jokes anymore!' Pietrangelo still treasures this little memento of his time on the set of *Goosebumps*, and has a good laugh telling the story. Bradshaw also has his signed book—one for each of the episodes he directed—and shares them with me.

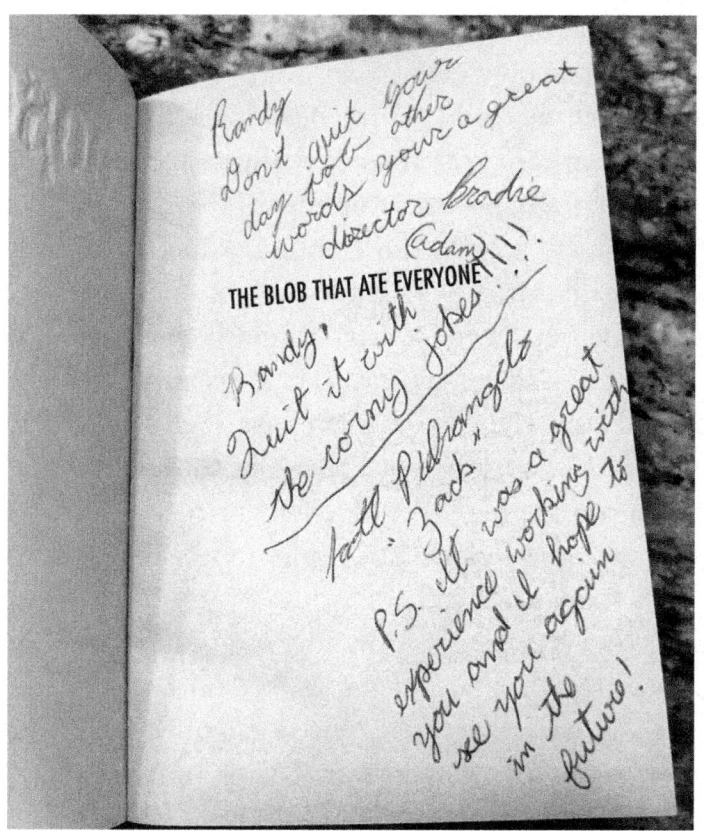

Randy Bradshaw's copy of *The Blob That Ate Everyone*, signed by the cast and crew. Photo courtesy of Randy Bradshaw.

Pietrangelo is delighted to see the message his adolescent self wrote to the director again after more than two decades, and assures me his handwriting is nowhere near that neat anymore!

Randy Bradshaw was what he considered old school, in that he preferred being next to the camera, right in the thick of the action, while directing, as opposed to hiding out in video village. However, this wasn't always possible, such as on a cramped set during the shooting of "An Old Story," when Steve Levitan found him directing from a sofa in the next room. "I thought he was sleeping!" Levitan chuckles, "So he was that kind of guy, and everybody just had fun and relaxed around him. Randy Bradshaw was kind of like a teddy bear. He was a sweet, huge, big, hairy guy who the kids would just almost like, cuddle up with."

Bradshaw felt he could get the best out of actors by communicating with them directly, either verbally or otherwise. He always lived by the advice of an old actor friend, who said that on Woody Allen's sets, direction came down to four simple instructions: quieter, louder, faster, slower. "What a director does is to really try to understand the person in front of them," he explains. "You know, you can go up to an actor and say, 'That was really good, but I need another one.' And then they might say, 'Well, OK, what do you want?' I said, 'Just do it better,' and walked away, and that'll do it. And then, of course, there's the psychology, right? And sometimes it really worked well with kids. Positive reinforcement was always the number one thing to do."

Randy Bradshaw studied photography at art school, but the endless hours spent alone in the darkroom left him longing for more collaborative projects. He moved to a polytechnic college and enrolled in a two-year film class, majoring in television direction, and got work straight out of school, mainly in the educational film arena. It was when he was accepted to the BBC Director Training Program that his career went off in the direction of entertainment, under the tutelage of Leonard Chase. Like Bob Sprogis, he heard of *Goosebumps* through the Directors Guild of Canada newsletters, and sure enough, his reputation was such that his agent called one day expressing an interest in his work from the Protocol gang. Coming on board in Season Two, he had the assurance that this was a big, successful show, a number one hit for the Fox network, which helped to sell him on it. He chatted to another director on the show, and took a script away to mull over. At first, he wasn't sure that he would be a good fit for the show. "I didn't come to *Goosebumps* with that kind of historical professional background. I was a drama guy. Some action and adult stories. So, the whole process was a bit of a learning process for me, of course," he explains.

Despite directors being at the symbolic helm of the ship, Bradshaw found that even the captains were safe in the hands of the *Goosebumps* crew, and would get all the support, guidance and encouragement they needed. "The first day of any series where a director walks on the floor, and they're all new people, they're kind of standing back and saying, 'OK, what's this guy gonna do?' And you think, *how can I make my mark? How can I add to this?*" He knew he had a big property in his hands, and that this was a make-or-break sort of deal. "I don't want to be the guy that makes a bad *Goosebumps* episode! I found on *Goosebumps* that everybody was very accommodating and supportive."

While even the most experienced directors would sometimes require an ease-in to the thick of *Goosebumps*, there were some who were just starting out when they got the gig on the show. "It was one of those right-place-right-time moments," says Craig Pryce, who had been set on attending business school until he saw a brochure for York University's film school at the career counselor's office. His first movie, *Revenge of the Radioactive Reporter*, was made fresh out of film school, with the backing of Andre Bigio, a mentor and investor who taught Pryce the ropes and offered much wisdom. "If it wasn't for Andre, I wouldn't have got my first film made," he says. Starting in horror features, he quickly became well-versed in the uncertainty and considerable time frames of making movies, so looked for an alternative. "I eyed episodic TV as a way to work and pay the bills and still pursue my passions," he explains. "*Goosebumps* came along and it was a great opportunity!" He'd previously worked on *Are You Afraid of the Dark?* and was thrilled for the chance to do more television work in the genre he'd got his start in with the episode "Calling All Creeps."

One of the regular directors on the show had a scheduling conflict come up, so Pryce pitched himself on having done both film and television and having a strong genre background. He knew of the books and the show's success and high production values, so was eager for the chance to work on it, in spite of how intimidating such a large-scale operation was to him. The show took a chance on the young director, and he got straight to work, asking producers to recommend favorite episodes of the show for him to familiarize himself with. Watching most of the first season, he particularly loved "The Haunted Mask," and any time Slappy made an appearance, and was eager to try his hand at contributing to the show.

Being such a young director, only in his twenties at the time, he felt that he could really connect with both the child actors on his set and the viewers watching at home. "I was trying not to get that kid-style acting, for want of a better word," he explains of his approach. "I was trying to ground it more. Child audiences are more intelligent than people think and you think you're making something for a fourteen-year-old and you're actually making it for an eight-year-old. I tried to, with the tone of their performances, make it more grounded and real. There's some nice twists and turns, so I really wanted to build up to those moments. We've got a great hook here, so let's make sure we capture that."

To this end, he was going for more of an eerie feel than a horror feel, and wanted to focus more on atmosphere than on explicit scares. "I was trying to use a more psychological approach, where it's not what you see but what you don't see. Because it's a kids' show, you can't have gore and stuff, so I was trying to bring the tone and have it feel more like a psychological story than a horror story. I'm big on motivated camera moves, so I think being genre, you can use more angles, and try to make as much movement as possible with the actors and the cameras." This kind of creativity was welcome on the set, and he found that despite being "very new and green," he was given the perfect amount of freedom to make the calls he felt were right, and really lead the project.

He would only make a single episode of *Goosebumps*, something he puts down to not being part of the regular rotation of directors, and still being fairly new in the industry. But his one-and-done status was never a bone of contention. To the contrary, Pryce was thrilled to have had the opportunity to work on such a big show, and feels that it only ever served him well in his later career. "It was awesome to have that opportunity," he says. "I had fun and I was very focused on the kids, and that was my main thing. With the crew, they were great, they were professional, they were union. So, I knew after I said, 'These are the shots', when we came back, they would be ready."

Unfortunately, it wasn't such a fond farewell for another one-time director. David Winning's short spell in Season One with "It Came from Beneath the Sink" was a great shooting experience, with a somewhat undesirable aftermath. Just as Steve Levitan had feared, post-production effects were not achieving the same level of quality that in-camera effects were, and a shot in the finale of Winning's episode required the evil sponge to expand and contract, changing sizes on camera. Despite playing around with different techniques on set, they couldn't get it quite right, and so it was decided that the sequence would be passed on to the post-effects team. On a mostly problem-free show, this incident was apparently about as hair-raising as it got, and Winning was not asked back for later episodes.

When asked whether the expanding sponge debacle may have had anything to do with this, he says, "I never got blacklisted, it's just that when you look at the seasons over the years you think well, I never got a phone call. Must be something I did." While it's possible that the sponge problem had a hand in his being a one-and-done, more charitably, it is probably more a case of other directors simply being a better fit for the show, more available, or both. Winning himself characterizes the eventual format of a select few dominant directors as something typical of the television industry. "They shake down the people that they like, or that gel with them. Like *X-Files*, for example, by the end of the *X-Files*' run, it was really just two directors that were rotating because they got to know the series really well. I'm fine with that, you know. It doesn't always work out," he says with an air of *c'est la vie*. He may have never gone back to *Goosebumps*, but he values his time on the show all the same, and remembers it very fondly.

Steve Levitan remembers it more as being an issue of suitability than any sponge catastrophe. Describing him as a "great feature film director" and more of an auteur, Levitan recalls David Winning being a slower, more methodical director—perfect qualities for art cinema, but not so well-matched for an anthology kids' show on a tight schedule. "I feel if you're too slow, everything gets thrown off, performances get thrown off, effects get thrown off, the editing gets thrown off. And I felt him to be a bit too thoughtful, which feature film directors would tend to do. Not that he was bad. It was just a different vibe on the set. I think his heart was really in kind of independent feature films for adults, not so much kids."

Don McCutcheon, on the other hand, was very well-versed in the television world. He always had his sights set on directing, but paid his dues by starting at the bottom as a production assistant and working his way up, getting his big break directing the show *The Campbells*, which four of his *Goosebumps* contemporaries would also work on. After a good decade of building up a reputation and portfolio, "*Goosebumps* just kind of landed in my lap. I guess my agent had pursued it, and they brought me on board." He was well aware of the hype around *Goosebumps* and other kids' horror media, with his own children being big fans. Not only this, but he had those same reliable qualities that Bill Fruet did, ones that put the producers at ease, knowing that whatever they gave him, it would be turned in on time, within budget and to a decent standard.

"Don McCutcheon was terrific," Steve Levitan enthuses. "Some of these directors, you don't hire them for their creativity so much as you do for their ability to just get it done right. You know, you read a script when it comes out of the writing room, and you go, 'Oh, well, this one's gonna be tough. Who do we give this to?' And if Don McCutcheon was the one that was booked, there's a sigh of relief. You need directors like that in your roster. If I can use a baseball analogy, he's always gonna get on base. You're not gonna necessarily count on him to come up with the clutch home run, but you can guarantee on him to not strike up. He'll get on base and give everybody else a chance. So, he's that guy."

While it constituted just a small portion of his substantial TV career, *Goosebumps* was a special time for McCutcheon, one that turned out one of the top five proudest moments in his career in the form of "Awesome Ants." "It was kind of a unique little period of my career to have been involved," he says.

It was an equally unique ride for Stefan Scaini, a busy director who'd built a reputation for working well with both children and animals, so he was determined to one day get to work on *Goosebumps*. "I always said I'd love to do *Goosebumps*. It's a great show. 'If you can find a slot for me, please give me an opportunity.'" It so happened that Scaini had previously worked with the show's first assistant director Andrea "Raff" Raffaghello, who called him when a particularly animal-heavy episode came up. Scaini leapt at the opportunity.

The director only worked on a single episode, "Teacher's Pet," and he showed signs of being somewhat ahead of his time. One of the qualities he particularly liked about *Goosebumps* was how user-friendly it was, appealing to boys and girls alike. It transcended the gender divides that were so prevalent in children's entertainment of the time, and he was eager to work on stories that broke down such barriers. "I said, 'Guys, come on, let's open this up. Everybody can enjoy these things.' When Raff wrote it I said, 'Can you make the lead the girl?' Nowadays you don't have to say that, but back then it was a thing. It was the female performers that were driving the story, so it became like a girl adventure. We always pushed for that."

While doing what he could to make all viewers and characters feel welcome in the world he directed, he was also conscious of finding the right level of scare for the young audience. "Let's have fun, let's play scared. We still need to play that," Scaini explains, "and we do have a young audience, so we don't want to make it too creepy. We don't want to traumatize these kids. So, it's finding a performance tone that is kind of, it isn't *Scooby-Doo*, but it isn't *The Shining*, either." Scaini was focused just as squarely on his young performers as his young audience, and being experienced in directing child actors, worked closely on the logistics to make sure it was as smooth an experience for them as possible. "Every director handles child performers differently," he explains. "I had the approach of having to be very efficient when they're there and also making it a calm, safe environment for them… You're looking at about eight hours, six, eight or ten, depending on their age. So, what we did was spend a lot of time on the schedule, and we'd sometimes use a stand-in to do the over-the-shoulder so that one kid could do school while you're shooting the scene. There is a real process on your board to schedule everything. When you're dealing with kids, we call it a pumpkin."

René Bonnière briefly entered the rotation in Season Two. Working in film since the 1950s, he made the shift toward episodic television in the '90s, and would carry on well into the mid-2000s. Easily one of the most experienced directors to ever grace the set, he brought with him a wide and varied wealth of expertise, and although Steve Levitan doesn't feel like his two episodes, "Be Careful What You Wish For" and "You Can't Scare Me," really "came alive" the way others did, he undeniably got great performances out of his young casts. As the only French Canadian to direct, he brought a different cultural flavor to proceedings, and as such, the producers felt that the more down-to-earth stories were the best fit for him.

Meanwhile, David Warry-Smith made a brief appearance in Season One with "My Hairiest Adventure," a shooting experience he has almost no recollection of. At the time, he was just breaking into directing, having spent years honing his craft in various assistant director roles. *Goosebumps* is only his second credit as a director, and while his time on the show was brief, it introduced the Warry-Smith lineage to the show, continuing later through his son Dan, who would star in "Attack of the Mutant" and "Click." Despite not remembering much of his time on the show, Warry-Smith maintains that it was an enjoyable experience, and one he was very glad to add to his resumé.

Steve DiMarco, despite his limited run on the show, was an unforgettable addition to the crew. Incredibly outlandish by '90s standards, the kids he directed thought he was the coolest, and most of the adults did too. "He dressed very outrageously, like, you know, black leather lederhosen with fishnet stockings. His head was half-shaved, and he had the Rolling Stones kiss right here on his forehead," Ian Brock says, describing how DiMarco cultivated his alternative persona. "When he started in the film business, he looked like Poindexter or something, he looked like something from *Harry Potter*, and then he adopted this persona." The heavily pierced and tattooed rocker was an adept director, who would arrive on set in leather miniskirts with huge grungy boots. "I was afraid of Steve DiMarco!" Steve Levitan laughs, "He was off the charts a little bit but he was great. He did a good job."

Although his appearance made a hell of a statement, his work did too. "He was really fun to work with. He was a really good director," says Brock. He was also known for his efficiency. "When you get into that jam, and you say, 'OK, we've got four episodes left, and instead of shooting them in five days, we need to shoot them in two days,' he's the guy you would hire. He would figure it out." Steve Levitan remembers. "There's nobody who would shoot faster than Steve DiMarco. He would just get it done in lightning speed." The go-to guy for troubled or pressured shoots, he could get an episode shot in less time than was standard, all the while retaining a calm demeanor and a fun atmosphere on set. Sadly, his time on the show would be short-lived thanks to a bit of internal power play on Scholastic's part, and this big friendly giant would be shown the door in a move reminiscent of the tactic attributed to Orson Welles in *Friends*.

Despite this rare example of behind-the-scenes tension, there was never a time that a director didn't gel with the show or the people who made it. "There weren't any directors we didn't like," Steve Levitan says. "We would interview them really intensively before hiring them. You know, we broke all of the rules of the kind of conventional wisdom of movies—don't work with kids or animals or monsters. And we did every one of those, almost in every episode. So you had to have the right kind of director."

He fondly recalls how the roster of directors he got on board were an integral part of the spirit of the show. "You know, it was such a fun show to do because of all these characters, and I've done lots of episodic television. Not all of them have this kind of attitude, but *Goosebumps* was such a wildly ambitious show in the first place. The kinds of people it would attract would be the ones who are in it for the creativity and the challenge, not because, 'It's a job, and I need to work, and I'll take that one.' So, it was fun. I can't think of any directors we had for just one episode that we wouldn't hire again. I would work with any of these guys again. You do need a personality for a kids' show. You need a director that doesn't have to be jolly, but you need a person that has a strong personality, because kids, especially twelve-year-old kids, will totally take advantage of every opportunity they can to have fun!"

Although the director gets the final say on set, and usually most of the glory in the credits, he is nothing without his assistant director (A.D.), as Ron Oliver is eager to express. "They help you with the management of all of the moving parts, and I've been so lucky to have had so many great A.D.s, like so many wonderful ones." He explains that on a TV series, assistant directors are typically on a rotation, staying with the show and knowing it intimately, which puts them in a strong position to acquaint the director with the feel, tone and mechanics of the show. "Their job is to make sure you are comfortable in that world, and they bring your quote-unquote 'vision' to life. So much of episodic television as a director, you're essentially a traffic cop, and you come in and you stand here, because the actors know the characters, the cinematographer knows the look of the show, and so much of that world is already set in stone. But a show like *Goosebumps*, as a director you were really fortunate because you could create your own world each time. So having a great A.D. is like having gold!" Steve Levitan agrees: "The A.D.s are worth mentioning, too, people like John Pace and Raff. The A.D.s were amazing because they would wrangle these directors into shape, because they would get carried away with the atmosphere and start having too much fun. They would keep them on the straight-and-narrow."

The set was a busy place to be, and even if they were technically at the helm of an episode, it was impossible for a director to keep track of everything. It also fell to the A.D.s to conduct the weekly production meetings, and manage everything that was going on. Levitan describes them as "key planners." Randy Bradshaw is equally appreciative of his assistant directors: "You probably have a couple dozen different things going on on the set at the same time, so you quickly determine the things that you don't need to worry about, and then deal with the things that you might have to worry about, or just think a little bit more." He says that first A.D.s were generally the ones to deal directly with extras, and keep all the small parts moving, and that without their integral input, the set would be a much more chaotic place. "The director has his or her own vision, and the AD..s have coordinated that vision," explains Steve Levitan. "They have their own strategy for how they're going to get through the thirty-five pages of the script in five days."

Despite bringing their individual personalities and quirks to the set, every director who worked on the show had the same essential qualities that made them so perfect for it. All of them are described by their colleagues as patient, hard-working, friendly and most importantly, great with kids. There was never any tyranny, any foot-stomping or screaming matches. None of the ego, tension or brutality that makes up some of Hollywood's most infamous stories. The set of *Goosebumps* was a great place to be, where fun was had, creativity was encouraged, and everybody tried their damnedest to make a show that kids would love.

"Figure Out How to Make It Cinematic"

Writing Goosebumps

Are You Afraid of the Dark? stood as the dominant kids' horror show by the time *Goosebumps* came around, and had amassed a significant following, thanks to its diverse cast, themes and approaches to storytelling. When it came to bringing *Goosebumps* to the screen, there was, rightly or wrongly, the looming presence of *Are You Afraid of the Dark?* and it was much closer to home than other contemporaries. The concept of an anthological horror series for kids was one thing, but then there were the people who worked on it. Given the familial vibe of the Canadian television scene of the time, there would end up being significant crossover between *Goosebumps* and *Are You Afraid of the Dark?*, with a considerable number of people both in front of the camera and behind it working on both shows at some point. Ron Oliver, David Winning and Craig Pryce all directed episodes of *Are You Afraid of the Dark?* and actors including, but certainly not limited to, Kathryn Long, Amos Crawley, Dylan Provencher, Daniel DeSanto, Tod Fennell and Aron Tager appeared in episodes. The scale of the crossover between the two shows is vast, but Steve Levitan says that the success of *Are You Afraid of the Dark?* had no bearing on *Goosebumps*. "We didn't pay any attention to that show on the creative side at all. The audience is big enough to have two shows. It wasn't a competition or an issue or a threat or anything."

Amos Crawley was one of the many actors to have worked on both shows, getting started on *Are You Afraid of the Dark?* before crossing over to *Goosebumps*. As a kid of the era, he could examine the two shows from both a personal and professional perspective. From a work standpoint, he saw it as more of a communal effort to entertain kids than a face-off between opposing shows. "The great *Are You Afraid of the Dark/ Goosebumps* rivalry, that's not really a rivalry, because it was all the same people on all those shows!" he insists. Artistically speaking, he felt the framing device of The Midnight Society in *Are You Afraid of the Dark?* afforded the show more of a weekly-viewing feeling. "Even though it is an anthology series, it feels a bit more cohesive, in a way. As a viewer, you know, I think you have relationships with those characters that have a longer arc than maybe the relationships you have when it's a different story every week." When it comes to the million-dollar question of which show was scarier, Crawley's vote is for *Goosebumps*. "I feel like *Goosebumps* was a little scarier. They pushed the envelope a little bit more." Actor Scott Pietrangelo also worked on both shows, and sees it differently: "I think there's a bit of campiness and silliness to *Goosebumps* that isn't in *Are You Afraid of the Dark?*, there's a darker edge to *Are You Afraid of the Dark?* Even the opening title sequence is spooky." He felt that there was more of a fun vibe to working on the show too, getting to play at being scared around things that could clearly not happen in real life. Effects artist Matthew DeWilde agrees that *Are You Afraid of the Dark?* was the scarier show, comparing his creations for *Goosebumps* to The Muppets. "The stuff on the book covers looked more frightening than what we were making," he says.

Although Levitan paid little heed to the presence of a rival show, it was certainly on the radar over at Scholastic. Ron Oliver recalls an early meeting he had with Deborah Forte at the Four Seasons, which involved a very good martini with a blue cheese-stuffed olive, in which the producer laid out what she was looking for in an episode of *Goosebumps*. "She said, 'Look, here's what we want. We want it to be scarier than *Are You Afraid of the Dark?*' And I thought, *well, I bet that's not what you really want. What you really want is something slightly different*, and *Goosebumps* had much more money than *Are You Afraid of the Dark?*" Oliver was snatched straight from the hands of *Are You Afraid of the Dark?* to work on *Goosebumps*, and got into the habit of commuting back and forth between Montreal and Toronto in order to work the two shows simultaneously. He saw the projects as pretty distinct from one another, mostly down to tone. He thought *Are You Afraid of the Dark?* often had "downer endings. They had endings that you would go, 'Whoa! That's pretty dark,' whereas *Goosebumps*, I think, had a slightly lighter tone to it, and because it was broadcast TV, they're kind of big on having, I don't want to say happy endings so much, but more of a resolution. So, the kids aren't going to lie there in bed, terrified."

Randy Bradshaw agrees that the tone of *Goosebumps* was lighter and more digestible for young viewers. "The beautiful thing about *Goosebumps* was it was scary stories but in an age of innocence," he opines. "There was a sweetness to the characters. I think R.L. Stine did a wonderful job with that." Bradshaw considered courage to be the cornerstone of the show, with Stine's stories bestowing kids with a certain resilience that they could carry into their adult lives. He saw the adventures as "giving them kind of a preview of a grown-up experience."

Steve Levitan recalls young viewers saying that they liked *Goosebumps* better, but that *Are You Afraid of the Dark?* was scarier. Meanwhile, he considered his project to be more ambitious, requiring more elaborate production values to do Stine's vision justice. Although almost everybody brings up *Are You Afraid of the Dark?* affectionately enough, director David Winning, who worked on both series, characterizes Scholastic and the wider *Goosebumps* crew as being "anti" the show. "They didn't like *Afraid of the Dark*, because it was scary, but they always ended happy," he says. "Big difference was *Goosebumps* always wanted to have that nightmare, sort of *Night Gallery* last-stab scare at the end of the shows, which probably made it more scary and terrifying for kids." Evidently, those who viewed and worked on the two shows each saw them in a slightly different way, but the bottom line was that *Are You Afraid of the Dark?* and *Goosebumps* each brought something different to the table, so there was no reason that the two couldn't co-exist harmoniously.

Along with the general attitudes ranging from indifference to a certainty of the town being big enough for the two of them, there were other fundamental differences that distinguished the existing show and the upcoming one. As an original concept with no literary basis to fall back on, *Are You Afraid of the Dark?* stood on its own two feet, which Steve Levitan says presented different creative limits and benefits to *Goosebumps*. Although there were certain expectations to meet when it came to adapting a wildly-popular literary series, the concept also came with a built-in fan base that would be easier to convince to tune in, if they played their cards right. On the other hand, *Are You Afraid of the Dark?* effectively existed in an artistic vacuum, with its entire world contained within the show itself, putting different kinds of pressure on the cast and crew.

When it came down to writing *Goosebumps*, there was a certain amount of distinction being sought that would enable the show to stand as a very separate entity to *Are You Afraid of the Dark?*, but with R.L. Stine and his wife Jane having creative control over first drafts of every script, there was never really much danger of the show wandering onto its competitor's turf. It started with Dan Angel and Billy Brown, who were the creative heads of the writing department, and would usually control the direction stories took. "Dan and Billy totally got the books, they got the show, and they were never off the mark. They were just a delight to work with," says Levitan. "The two of them are very different from each other, but they were great." Steve Levitan and his crew recommended writers to work on certain episodes, basing their assignments on written samples and conversations they had with writers. Soon a small pool of regular writers emerged, just as it had with the directors, with the likes of Rick Drew and Charles Lazer often taking the helm whenever Angel and Brown did not. Some worked on just one or two episodes, and director Ron Oliver worked on a few himself, usually also directing the episodes he wrote.

Neal Shusterman had been writing across a number of markets by the time *Goosebumps* arrived at his door. Primarily an author of young adult fiction, he had also worked in film and TV writing, which proved to be a very different experience to writing books. "Books are a finished product, whereas a script is a blueprint for a movie or TV show that might not get made. It's difficult when you see your babies languishing in development hell," he explains. He was working on a television anthology adaptation of one of his own short story collections when an offer came his way from Scholastic. "As is always the case, what you're trying to do always opens doors that you weren't expecting to open. I never set up that series, but they asked me if I wanted to write for *Goosebumps*," he says.

Shusterman ended up penning four episodes of *Goosebumps*: "The Werewolf of Fever Swamp," "Awesome Ants," "Night of the Living Dummy III" and "The Ghost Next Door." Always keen to keep on top of his market, he was already familiar with *Goosebumps* when the Scholastic offer came his way, and felt the series would suit him well as a writer. "It was a good fit, very much the type of stuff that I was writing, especially when it came to short fiction, supernatural, *Twilight Zone*-type of stuff, which is very much what *Goosebumps* was." As a fiction writer, this new job presented him with some interesting challenges, particularly when it came to transferring the written word to the very visual medium of television. "What I was able to have fun with was fleshing out the characters a little bit, really getting into the characters' heads," he says. "I knew from my own experience adapting my own books to scripts that many times when you're doing an adaptation, you have to fracture what was there and figure out how to make it cinematic."

Indeed, this is what Steve Levitan says largely governed the decisions of which books to adapt to the screen. "The process was 'Which of these can we physically produce?' Some of them were so difficult on a five-day shoot that they would have been prohibitively expensive or too complicated," he says. It was fairly smooth sailing in the early days, because there was a decent number of books to consider for adaptation, and it was only growing on a monthly basis, thanks to Stine's constant output. By the third year of production, Brown and Angel were feeling the pressure, and feared they were running out of material that could translate to the screen. It was with this in mind that the show started to get a little creative, and deviate from the source material somewhat.

"Once or twice, even though we weren't technically allowed to do it, we went back and got permission from R.L. Stine and we invented some stories," says Steve Levitan. In a strange turning of the tables, this reversed the creative process and allowed Stine the opportunity to write and publish the ideas that the writers on the show were coming up with. Levitan emphasizes that this was because production was getting difficult, and they felt a very sincere obligation to *Goosebumps* fans to keep the quality high. "They were chosen based on 'What can we actually shoot in a way that's faithful to the book,' because we did not want ever to have a kid read the book and say, 'Can't wait to see that on TV,' and then walk away saying, 'That was lame.'"

There were times that the output of the show and the book series would collide, and an episode would go into production before the book was released. Director Craig Pryce recalls this being the case with "Calling All Creeps." "When I got the script, it wasn't published yet, the book. So, it was really exciting. I'm always looking at how I can take this script and bring elements that are going to elevate it, and jump right off the page," he explains. "One of the things it had going for it was a psychological element, a lot of mystery and intrigue. I spent a lot of time on locations, designing it, breaking it down technically, so then I can focus on the creative. So, when I got to set, I could focus on the kids. I would block very quickly, so I had more time to rehearse with them and more time to shoot, because I want to make sure I'm getting the coverage and the style that I want to tell the story." Pryce feels that the show and the book series ended up complementing each other, with one giving the other a boost of attention and popularity. "I'm pretty sure they wanted the books out to generate interest in the show. I do remember walking into the bookstore and seeing a big display for *Calling All Creeps* and it was super cool, and I believe that was just before the show came on." Indeed, once the show was in production, new books would have stickers on their covers urging readers to tune in to the show, and later, a run of TV special reprints would use stills from their corresponding episodes on the covers. The two were working together to promote the wider world of *Goosebumps*.

Outside of such circumstances, there was a typical running order to the process of adaptation. Breaking down the writing process for *Goosebumps*, Neal Shusterman says it went like this: with an episode in mind, story editors Dan Angel and Billy Brown would approach a writer, who would then give their thoughts on what could be done with it. If this approach was to Angel and Brown's liking, the writer would be officially brought on to bring the book to life. Step one was to read the book and produce a treatment for an episode, which would then be submitted to Angel and Brown, and looked over by them, Scholastic and the Stines. A variety of notes would come back. "Taking all those notes, and putting them together and figuring out how to make it work was always an interesting creative challenge," Shusterman explains, "and when you work with parameters like that, it opens up your own creativity. You say, 'OK, I know this is working for them, but this isn't working for the Stines. How can I work this so it will work for everybody?' It was a really interesting process to do that." From there, an average of three drafts would be produced—a draft, a rewrite and a revision—all with plenty of feedback from others. "By the time it got to the end of those drafts, the timeframe was very, very tight and I had to do a very quick turnaround of those drafts."

Steve Levitan summarizes the schedule to which writers were working: "We aimed to publish a script every Friday, and every Monday we start shooting. The script we publish today would go into prep for that particular episode, the unique features of that particular episode, that prep begins on Monday. If the Episode 3 script is published on Friday, then on Monday, two things happen with two different teams: on Monday there's the production team which has begun shooting on Episode 2, because that prepped all this week. And then Episode 3 goes to the prep team, so that they can be ready to shoot Episode 3 a week from Monday. You're prepping one show while you're shooting the show before it." Got all that? This is a key example of the rolling nature of production on *Goosebumps*, and how it was never a straight-forward process of managing one task at a time. There was a consistent overlap, with an episode effectively being passed along a conveyor belt from one department to the next, and when one was passed along, another was received in its place.

"On Fridays, before shooting begins on a Monday, you usually have a big production meeting," Levitan explains, "where all of the heads of all of the units sit around the table and review where they're at, make sure everything they need is the right thing, is creatively appropriate, doesn't have any delays or issues and is ready, so that when the first shot is called for at 7am on Monday, we can just go ahead and work." Final drafts of scripts were generally delivered on a Wednesday and published on a Friday, but on some occasions, would run over schedule, having a knock-on effect on the remainder of the week. The writing team were solidly reliable, as was everybody else on the show, and if something ran over, they were willing to work faster and harder with what time they had left to make sure everything came together in the end.

For Ron Oliver, the enviable opportunity to direct his own writing cropped up with *Goosebumps*, and as a director, he brought a more practical eye to his scripts. "I find it much easier to direct my own stuff on set," he explains, "because when I'm writing something I tend to visualize it. I tend to picture in my mind exactly how I'm going to do it, and then when I go on set, it's just a case of following the instructions I laid out in the script." Even when not directing his own material, Oliver makes a habit of conducting a "director's polish" on any script he is given, which he says mostly involves the logistics of translating action from the page to the screen. "The challenge with many writers is that they seem to have spent their entire lives growing up in their parents' basement," Oliver chuckles, "and they have no idea how physics works! Or how human emotion works." His preferred method was to give any script handed to him a once-over, to iron out any kinks and figure out the mechanics of setting up shots, camera movements and so on, so as to maximize filming time on set.

He may not have written for the show in any official capacity, but Craig Pryce recalls how the role of director would often spill over into at least some writing. He looked over his script and went back to the writers to discuss his thoughts. "I would bring script notes and say, 'This is your baby, take it or leave it.' I would also bring production notes. So I have this whole process for prep. I prep very hard. On the first day of prep, you get a script, and on TV that script might even change, so you have to be flexible. If it means me doing fourteen-hour days because my shot list came through halfway through my already short schedule, I actually put more into prepping hours than shooting hours." For directors, the script was just as much about logistics as it was about dialogue, and there was a lot to consider when a script ended up in their hands.

The process of adaptation from page to screen can be a tricky one, with fans of the books often taking a puristic stance on preserving everything as it was written. For myriad reasons, screen adaptations often make changes to the source material. Asked about the ways in which some episodes stray from their literary counterparts, Neal Shusterman says it was often due to the collaboration between writers and story editors. "I would say the deviation was mostly my doing. Sometimes I would deviate too much and they would pull me back, but they liked the changes that I made." There was also the ever-present issue of the practicality of pulling off the stories on screen. "*Goosebumps* books are very cinematic already, they are very visual, but there is always that process of having to transfer it from something that's an internal experience—reading a book is an internal experience—to now it's a visual experience coming at you from the outside," says Shusterman. He felt very little compromise was necessary in terms of the quality of the writing, but practical and budgetary constraints necessitated some creativity on the part of the writing team. Whether it was a case of too many locations, too many expensive effects sequences or not having the time to film so many different scenes, there were elements of transferring a children's book to television that required some corners to be cut. Shusterman saw all this as an exciting creative exercise that sharpened him as a writer. "Knowing that there were real-world considerations on what could be done, it informs how you write it," he explains.

Importantly, writers had to consider the wishes of the man at the center of it all. Their having the rights to the books came with a number of caveats, the main one being that R.L. Stine retained the right to creative control over first drafts of all scripts. This put a lot of power in his hands, and the hands of Jane Stine, who is known to be fiercely protective of her husband's work and legacy. The sudden and immense success of a writer is liable to go to their head at some point, but R.L. Stine proved to be down-to-earth, friendly and trusting in the show's independent success. "[Stine] technically had right of approval over first draft scripts, and we often got comments from him," Levitan says, "Stine was never a problem, there was never an obstacle with Stine. He was always helpful, and whenever we did get notes from him on a script, they were always really good notes. And he was unbelievably fantastic when he came to set to do intros for the one-hour videos. The first time he was just thrilled to be there and see his books transformed with a small army around them. I think he was there when we had Adam West. I have nothing but positive things to say about R.L. Stine, which is not common. I think even if you get a candid interview with people from *Harry Potter*, I don't think they'd always tell you that J.K. Rowling was a dream to work with! But he was."

There can often be a tangled mass of work and writers behind any completed script, and allocating credit for the final product is such a complex business that there is a whole department whose job it is to figure it out. "It goes to the Writers' Guild for arbitration," Ron Oliver explains, "so they can determine who gets the actual screen credit, because down the road, when the thing reruns for a billion years, there are royalties and so on to be paid." Sometimes a writer feels their contribution to the final product is so insignificant that they opt out of any credit they might be entitled to, as a matter of professional integrity, or simply for not wanting to be bothered with all the hassle over such a small piece of work. Oliver is sometimes credited as a writer on some episodes that he doesn't really consider to be his work, simply due to having thrown a few ideas into the hat, or helped neaten things up. It was always a heavily collaborative effort, regardless of whose name showed up on screen.

Early on in the business side of setting up the show, Steve Levitan had secured a deal with 20th Century Fox Home Entertainment to release one-hour specials on VHS. With the majority of the show being made up of standalone twenty-three-minute episodes, this deal necessitated some expansion, and for certain episodes to be selected for a lengthier runtime. It was decided that this would be a great way to introduce the show to the world, with the first episode, "The Haunted Mask," kicking off the hour-long special format. This wasn't to be the standard, and special consideration was given to which books would receive the coveted multiple-parter treatment.

As the show progressed and ate through its source material, the writers found it more difficult to adapt the books into single episodes while still doing them justice. With quality and audience satisfaction always taking priority in the creative process, the final season would end up entirely comprising two-parters. "After a while, it was difficult to find books that were shootable properly as a one-off," Levitan explains, "and some books were really terrific books that we didn't want to reject just because they were one-offs, and the networks were accommodating enough to let us do that. Networks don't like that because in the days of scheduled television, which we're kind of returning to, oddly enough, the networks want as much freedom as possible to schedule any episode at any time."

The pull that *Goosebumps* had with its network was considerable. Fox was habitually accommodating of whatever the show required, be it more time or more creative freedom. This is not to say, however, that the crew had a blank check to do with what they pleased. "I would never say that we spared no expense, because it was a constant effort," Levitan says. "Lena Cordina, who was production manager, was making a constant effort to maximize every penny and put as much on the screen as possible. We were always frustrated because we were always having to say 'No, we can't do that, it's too much time or it's too much money.'" But what *Goosebumps* did have was the support and belief of the network. Traditionally, a serialized television format is a turnoff because it requires chronological airplay, which is not so simple when it comes to reruns. In the '90s, scheduling was a manual exercise rather than a computerized one, and so the freedom to pick any episode from a show and line it up was preferable. However, Levitan and the team were firmly behind the idea of some episodes being multiple-parters in order to tell the stories properly, and soon, the network came around to the idea too. "Eventually they agreed with us," Steve Levitan says. "It also helps from a customer loyalty point of view to have kids tune in for one episode and then feel like they absolutely have to be there for the next one."

Depending on who you ask, things got either more enjoyable, or more demanding when it came to the episodes which would become hour-long specials. For Shusterman, the multiple-parters were a great opportunity to do what he did best: getting inside the characters' heads and allowing them more room for growth. Steve Levitan says that the adaptation process was already a challenging one, but extra runtime was easier to handle from a writing perspective. "None of the books were easy to adapt to the screen, not one of them. Some of them were very, very difficult, and from a writing point of view it would have been easier to make them a one-hour story with a break, or even a ninety-minute story with a break, than to condense everything into one episode," he says. They also had to consider the workload of multiple-parters on the young actors they hired, who could easily find themselves burnt out by the process. "Not all kids can handle that kind of pressure at that age," says Levitan. "It's a lot of work."

"I like doing two-parters in any series," says director Don McCutcheon. "You've got more story to work with. And that to me is a blessing in any element, because you know, particularly with something like *Goosebumps* or any of the half-hour teen series, by the time you edit for commercials, I think you're only down to something like twenty-two or twenty-three minutes. So that's a short period of time to tell the story, you know? But now, in a two-parter, you've got over forty minutes to tell the story, for the writer and the director. You're with the actors for a longer period, too. It's just sometimes the single episodes are quick, you know, you're in, and the story's quick and all that, whereas the two-parter allows you to kind of play things out a bit more, and just enjoy the luxury of a little more screen time to tell a story."

Although directors and writers often enjoyed the increased creative freedom that came with an extended runtime, multiple-parters were not necessarily given twice or three times as much preparation time as a standalone episode, due to having the same basic elements that needed to be brought together, such as characters, monsters and locations. "On a two-week schedule we would prep for seven or eight days as opposed to ten," says Levitan, "and we didn't do it to save money, we did it to make better shows. Every script is different and you prep it how you want to." Having produced both big-budget shows and shoestring ones, Steve Levitan always found the same issue persisted, regardless: "At either end of the scale, it's always the same. You never have enough time, you never have enough money, you never have enough of the resources you want. You always want more. It's just the nature of the process."

When asked to name the favorites of the episodes he directed, it is notable that the two-parters are the ones Ron Oliver mentions. "Because you could get into the story and you could give the lead character a decent arc, you could really flesh it out," he says. He felt that single-episode work required the storytelling to be whittled down to "get to where you had to go," but the extra runtime gave a shoot a more "lush" quality, with more opportunity to maximize a story's potential. Notably, the multiple-parters were often the most acclaimed, both with fans and with critics, and even attracted awards attention. Although these nominations came at the tail-end of a series that had been immensely popular with its audience, there was something legitimizing about this critical success that went to prove that kids' shows—horror shows, at that—could still have an air of sophistication to them. All you needed were the right minds to spin straw into gold.

"A Rite of Passage for Toronto"

Casting Goosebumps

Goosebumps presented a fairly unique challenge when it came to casting. The standard TV series would entail one bumper casting session at the beginning of production to assemble the key cast members, and then a smaller-scale operation for the duration of the show's run to fill secondary roles that might come along at a later date. However, the anthological nature of *Goosebumps* meant that everyone was running on all cylinders for the majority of the show's run, constantly having to start from scratch for each new story, making for an unrelenting few years for the casting agents. Thankfully, there were plenty of young actors to consider. According to actor Bill Turnbull, the entertainment industry in Toronto back in the late '80s and early '90s was relatively easy to break into for young performers. "If you're a kid and you're willing to learn your lines and stand in place for hours and hours, you can get an agent. If you're willing to go to auditions, you'll get an agent," he explains.

Steve Levitan estimates that they saw every child actor in Canada throughout the run of the show. "We were always casting! Non-stop casting," he says, "and we were always looking for twelve-year-olds and we were always looking for eight-year-olds. Susan Forrest, who ran the casting, was wonderful, and would just bring any kids that she could into the casting sessions." One advantage the show offered was a certain formula, a family unit that remained fairly unwavering regardless of the story. Levitan refers to a formula, "the famous ten rules of *Goosebumps*," which was so central to the franchise that it was written into the contracts. Although Levitan is not at liberty to divulge these ten rules, it is evident that one of them is the character setup, with the lead being around twelve years old, and usually having a younger sibling. Then there is at least one parent who hangs around on the periphery of the story, trying their best but usually failing miserably to be there for their kid in a time of supernatural crisis. This setup left the casting agents with a conveyor belt scenario, in which they were always looking for twelve-year-olds, eight-year-olds, and adults of the right age to be their parents, and sometimes grandparents.

There was always a certain something that the casting gang were looking for in *Goosebumps* kids, an element that may have been more unique to the Canadian entertainment industry when compared to its cut-throat cousin across the border. Where L.A. stage parents had a reputation for grooming children into stardom from a very young age, the Toronto scene was nowhere near as cynical, and the show was looking for kids who could act, but do it in a natural and less polished manner. "It became clear, actually in our first episode, that you had to decide in casting whether a twelve-year-old was good at the reading because she'd been staying up all night with her mom rehearsing, or whether she was good," says Steve Levitan. "They're very different things. Eventually Bill [Siegler] had a really fine sixth sense about which kids had talent and which didn't."

Stefan Scaini was always looking to break down barriers with his work, and when it came to casting, he liked to reflect the diversity of Canada itself in his choices. "Our casting directors were great about that, to have that diversity," he recalls. "You know, Toronto is a very multicultural city. It's funny, in Canada, our own Prime Minister said, 'There's no such thing as the all-Canadian boy or the all-Canadian girl, because we are such a collection of cultures and religions and everything. And that's our beauty." With *Goosebumps* being a staunchly Canadian production through and through, Scaini's sentiment was widespread, and everybody was eager to make the show as representative of Canadian society as possible, while still maintaining that generic American charm that would keep U.S. audiences appeased.

Susan Forrest would be a central figure in maintaining this ethos. She had established herself as a casting agent in the early '90s, alongside her sister Sharon, under the company Forrest & Forrest Casting, and was quickly gaining a reputation for being a reliable and thoroughly loveable figure in her field. She had worked in both film and television, and by 1995, had worked on casting several long-running TV shows, including *Forever Knight* and *The Adventures of Dudley the Dragon*, but *Goosebumps* would prove to be a uniquely challenging task. Additional casting agents were involved to cast the net wider, with Anne Tait and Elizabeth Ritchie also getting involved. It would prove to be a multi-layered affair, with production seeking not just Torontonians, but actors from all over Canada. Although Toronto served as the industry hub for the country, just as Los Angeles does for the U.S. and London does for the U.K., Montreal also had quite the entertainment circuit, and it wasn't unusual for actors to commute to Toronto just for a job. Actor Tod Fennell drove in from Montreal to audition for *Goosebumps*, adding up to a good twelve hours of solid driving in a day for the pleasure of auditioning. "It makes for ten hours of driving for ten minutes in the room," he says. Thankfully, once the job was secured, he was put up in Toronto for a week or two and didn't have to worry about the day-long car rides to which he was quickly becoming accustomed.

Casting sessions took place at Goosebumps HQ in the Molson building, with Steve Levitan, co-executive producer Bill Siegler, the casting agent and the episode's director present. "Another nice thing about this show," says Ron Oliver, "is that they had the director in the casting room, so you weren't handed actors. You actually got to cast the actors, which was cool." For Don McCutcheon, it was a pleasure to work with young actors, and to have a say in casting them. "They're usually quite enthusiastic and willing to give a lot, and it's usually very enjoyable," he says. In the early days, Deborah Forte would put in appearances at the final callbacks and exercise Scholastic's input in proceedings. "Deborah came in to make the final choices of the two or three in each of the key roles," recalls Levitan.

Most remember casting as a relatively straight-forward but enjoyable process. "In those days you would go to a building somewhere, unlike today!" says Amos Crawley, musing on just how much twenty-first century technology has changed the way pre-production works. Ron Oliver also laments the changes that have occurred in the casting game over the years: "I despise the way the casting industry has gone, because you can't be in the room with somebody and feel the energy of that person. Now it's all done through Zoom and self-tapes. It's been detrimental to our industry." Some of the actors who continued in the industry into adulthood notice the same change: "I just audition from hotel rooms!" says Melody Johnson. *Goosebumps*, however, was the best of the era and the industry, allowing directors a day or two to meet people in person, talk to them and get an idea of what they could bring to the role. Oliver says there is now some movement back towards how it was done in the good old days, and he hopes this sentiment continues and rebuilds the bridges between crew and actor when it comes to casting.

The more casual nature of making a Canadian TV show in the 1990s is striking in its apparent lack of pitch-perfection and intense preparation, at least for the actors. "There'd be a table with a bunch of sets of sides, which is like the scene that you're gonna audition with. And you pick it up, and you'd go out in the hallway, and you'd read it over two or three times, and then you'd come in and audition," Amos Crawley says of the casting process. In his early days in the business, fellow young actor Mpho Koaho liked to model himself on Marlon Brando, and just go with the flow, letting his talent speak for itself. "I wasn't as steady as I am now!" he says. "There's a lot on the line for auditions, but I didn't feel like it was that arduous when I was young. I don't think I felt the pressure, if there was any." He was mainly motivated by his previous rejections at *Goosebumps* auditions, determined to impress the casting agents and secure a role on one of his favorite shows. Now, almost three decades into his acting career, Koaho's approach to his work has become much more reminiscent of Olivier than Brando, with extensive care and craft given to every opportunity that comes his way, and he admittedly misses the ability to be so laid back. "I think one of the reasons I still connect so much with *Goosebumps* is the reverence that I see from children, the innocence that I don't think any of us adults should lose," he observes.

Beki Lantos approached *Goosebumps* with a similar verve. She says she didn't really prepare for a role in terms of rehearsal or research, but she always tried to immerse herself in her characters, as much as her young years would allow. "I was only 13, but I still took things really seriously. I'm not a method actor or anything, but I've always felt it really important to be truthful to the story and the character. I'd just use my wonderful and vivid imagination and do it." She wasn't new to the acting thing, but she recognized that this particular show was perhaps more culturally significant than other jobs she'd had. "At the time the job stood out because I remember it being and feeling like a big deal," she says. "This was a syndicated cable show! It had a big budget compared to anything I'd done before. And it was a lead role! I'd practically have to carry the show, or at least, that's what I believed back then. I didn't have the maturity or understanding of how many people it takes to put a project like that together. I truly felt like this was my chance to shine and show people what I could do. It was very positive for me in that way and still is."

Beki Lantos and Judah Katz go over their sides.
Photo courtesy of Beki Lantos.

It was not unusual for actors to audition more than once for the show, and eventually bag a role that producers felt was the best fit for them. "You want to see who's out there," says Steve Levitan. "So, you want to see as many twelve-year-olds and eight-year-olds, because we needed both in every episode, as you can, and then make note of them, if not for the first two or three episodes you're shooting, but for later episodes." The rolling nature of the show presented opportunities for actors that they may not have foreseen. With an endless chain of episodes in the pipeline, it was common for actors to be assigned to episodes or roles other than the ones they initially auditioned for. "Sometimes we would choose kids for the upcoming shows, sometimes we would know we're going to do this title, and that kid would be perfect for that episode down the road," says Levitan. Scott Pietrangelo was originally being considered for a role in "Calling All Creeps," and attended two auditions for it before things were switched up, and he was sent to audition for "The Blob That

Ate Everyone," ultimately winning the lead role of Zack. He was in the midst of a flourishing acting career that saw him going back and forth between Toronto and his native Southwest Ontario when he got an audition for *Goosebumps*. By now, the show had already established itself, and found a fan in the young actor. "I was already a fan of the books, and of the show," he says. "I went nuts when I found out I got the part. As a fan already, it's so cool to know you're going to be part of it." He recalls being given the part in mid-January, and thinks a couple of months went by before he rocked up on set. He was given a color-coded official script, and having never felt confident in his line-learning capabilities, was glad for the time he got to prepare for the role.

Similarly, Amos Crawley had initially auditioned for the role of Steve in "The Haunted Mask," as had many of the other young actors trying out for the episode, and casting agents made their choice for Chuck based off of those tryouts. "I have more of a sidekick vibe than an instigator vibe!" he says. As a big fan of both *Goosebumps* and *Are You Afraid of the Dark?*, Mpho Koaho was beyond disappointed when five auditions for the latter led to nothing. When auditions for *Goosebumps* started coming in, he continued to face further disappointment. But after a number of tries, he finally won a role in the show that he loved so dearly, playing Ben in "Awesome Ants," and was overjoyed at the idea of finally getting to act on a show that he watched religiously himself. Koaho was a self-described nerd for whom the traditional school system just didn't feel like a good fit. "My brain just circulated around baseball and cartoons!" he says. He harbored lifelong dreams of becoming an actor, and despite having family friends in the industry, it was the encouragement and mentorship of an after-school acting teacher that got him started. Having been introduced to an agent by his teacher, Koaho began auditioning for roles at the age of fourteen, and got his start in the industry being hand-picked by Maya Angelou for the role of Thomas Sinclair in her movie *Down in the Delta*.

Angelou's firm but fair guidance on the set had a profound effect on the young actor, and instilled in him a courtesy and humility that he applies to his work and life to this day. By the time he finally got the job on *Goosebumps*, he felt well-prepared, and like this opportunity was long overdue. He was not going to disappoint.

There were occasions when actors returned to the show, either reprising a previous role, or more usually, playing a different one altogether. Editor Bob Sprogis recalls young viewers being particularly eagle-eyed in such cases, and going to lengths to call production out on it. "That was one of the challenges, because we were doing an anthology," he says, "so every episode had to have different kids. And if you didn't have different kids, you get letters: 'She was this character! She can't be that character.'" When it came to the few episodes that were an explicit continuation of a previous one, such as "The Haunted Mask II" and "Say Cheese and Die.. Again!," actors were invited back without having to audition, although in the case of the latter, none of the original actors would return. These instances would come as a pleasant surprise to those involved. Given that stories selected for television adaptation were chosen based on practicality, and certainly not in keeping with the order of publication, there was never any guarantee that a story would get its sequel, even if one was already written for it. Amos Crawley says he was hyped to receive a call one day, informing him that "The Haunted Mask II" was going into production, and they wanted him to come back and reunite with the gang a year later. Of course, there were instances in which actors were unable to reprise their former roles. Young Ryan Gosling's appearance in "Say Cheese and Die" was only his second television role, after an episode of *Are You Afraid of the Dark?*, but by the time the sequel episode was ready to go, he had become a busy actor working on a range of projects, including a movie called *Frankenstein and Me*, which brought him together with fellow *Goosebumps* kids Beki Lantos and Ricky Mabe. This led to Gosling's role being taken over by Patrick Thomas.

When it came time for his second go-round the *Goosebumps* carousel, Corey Sevier was busy working on an adaptation of Louisa May Alcott's *Little Men*, and got a call on the set to say that he had another audition for the show. He went straight from the set and arrived at his audition in period costume, having gone over the lines in the car while on his way to Toronto, and met Ron Oliver, who told him to put the sides down and just talk with him. After a few minutes of chatting, Oliver asked Sevier to hold his hand out. "He pretends to take my pulse and goes, 'You got the role.'" Familiar with Sevier's work and simply covering formalities, Oliver knew he'd found his male lead for "Cry of the Cat," and gave the actor the role on the spot without ever hearing him read. "This is the only time in my whole career this has ever happened!" Sevier says. "It's a real confidence boost as a young actor that he believed in me."

It seems that casting would go a little differently each time, depending on which director was present. Some actors recall being tried out opposite different co-stars and doing chemistry reads, while others only met their colleagues later on. There was an emphasis on seeing what the young actors could handle in terms of the material. "When I got the audition for "A Night in Terror Tower" I was over the moon!" Sevier says of his first appearance on the show. "We went through several auditions. They really wanted to, I think, test the kids to see if they could handle it." Actor Judah Katz agrees that the horror of the show meant the kids had to be able to handle the tone, and that the audition process was as much about measuring suitability to the genre as it was their acting ability. "It's hard when you're a kid to play scared. I'm sure when they're casting, they have to see a lot of kids until they're able to find kids that are able to go there," he says.

Sevier recalls auditions being fairly extensive, involving numerous callbacks and combinations of actors, but making for a very exciting experience for a young professional. "You do the initial audition with the casting director, and then, you know, a few days later you got a call back, so you get all excited and nervous about that. And then the next time I was in there, I believe I was with William [Fruet] and the producers. It was several callbacks. I have this vague memory of doing mixing and matching, which is something they do often with chemistry reads and things like that. So I think my final audition I did read with Katie [Short], which was also my first experience as a very young actor, like, not only is this my audition, but you're auditioning with someone else. Just an amazing experience."

Fully leaning into the role she was auditioning for—that of clumsy Samantha Byrd in "Be Careful What You Wish For"—Melody Johnson decided to make a grand entrance into the audition room by falling through the door. This endeared her to director René Bonnière. "He said he was sold!" Johnson says. Meanwhile, Afrah Gouda made an impression on director John Bell with her business-formal attire and native Egyptian accent, which made her the perfect fit for the role of Nila, the journalist/undead Egyptian princess in "Return of the Mummy." She also got to do a chemistry read at her audition with her co-star Elias Zarou. "They let us read together," she says, "we read a couple of times. Really great guy, very helpful." Gouda was more than happy to accept the role, and never felt like leaning into the classic archetypes of ancient Egypt was silly or caricaturish. "I have an accent and I have the look," she explains, "so why not use it? I didn't really mind it at all. If you have the look and you have the talent and you are able to do it, why not?" It wasn't until she got the part and read the entire script that she realized the role was really that of an ancient Egyptian princess, and that she'd get to wear something far more remarkable than a formal suit.

Bill Turnbull started out as a print model at a very early age and eventually asked his mother to get him an agent so he could start doing TV and commercial work. He was accustomed to the audition process by the time he was sent out to try for *Goosebumps*, having previously auditioned for *Are You Afraid of the Dark?* among many other productions. He went through at least one, possibly two callbacks, and secured the role of Sam Sadler in the episode "Ghost Beach," which was his second credited television role. He was thirteen, and just about to start high school in the fall. Up to this point he had attended private schools, so wasn't subject to the usual strictly-enforced set schooling his fellow young actors were. "I didn't have a teacher being like, 'Here, while you're away, do this and this and this'. So I just brought books, while they were actually doing math and work!" he recalls.

It was a pretty crazy way of life. While many of the young actors tell of childhood experiences typical of that traditional Canadian humility, with normal friends and schools, and parents who didn't make a big deal of the whole thing, there was no denying that it was an unusual and fast-paced way for a kid to grow up. "It's an adult world," says Melody Johnson. "You grow up very quickly." Having basically acted his entire life and grown up in a family of entertainers, Amos Crawley concurs: "When I was young, there was just an expectation that you were to behave the way that any adult would. Which I think is an unfair expectation." He is glad that his generation of industry professionals who grew up on sets the way he did, are now enforcing better, safer and healthier conditions for child actors. He recommends the writings of former child actor-turned-screenwriter and director Sarah Polley, to gain an insight into what it's like to grow up working in the entertainment industry.

For kids just getting their start in entertainment, this was all incredibly new and exciting. For the more experienced actors, it was just a lifestyle they had long since become accustomed to. Peter Keleghan had recently moved back to Toronto after living in L.A. for a number of years and working on American projects like *General Hospital*, *Cheers* and *Seinfeld*. An expired work visa prevented him from doing another episode of *Seinfeld*, and he had become disillusioned with the turbulent L.A. scene, particularly as the father of two young children. As a busy actor being asked to recall events almost thirty years past, he struggles to remember auditioning for *Goosebumps*. "I probably have done six hundred and ninety-two auditions since then!" he jokes. He was one of the few who had managed to totally bypass the whole *Goosebumps* phenomenon, so when the audition came his way, he had no idea what sort of legacy he was stepping into. "I didn't know anything about the books and knew nothing about the popularity of the whole thing," he says. When he was cast as Mr. Burton in "Revenge of the Lawn Gnomes," he was most excited about being reunited with an old friend and colleague, David Hemblen.

Like Keleghan, Judah Katz had also moved back to Toronto from L.A. to ensure his kids had a more stable upbringing, and met casting director Anne Tait, who was already a fan of his work and wanted him to read for *Goosebumps*. At only 35, he was amused by the prospect of playing a man old enough to have two adolescent kids and a doctorate, but was eager to be a part of it, enticed by the prospect of getting to play two characters in one as Dr. Brewer in "Stay Out of the Basement." He had heard of the books, and understood exactly what a big deal this was. "It was a phenomenon!" he says. A trained method actor, it was the perfect thing to have fun with and show his range. It may have been for kids' TV, but he took the job seriously. "If we're going to do this scene, I've got to make it intense. If I sense I'm scaring these kids, then I'm feeling that I'm scaring the kids at home. And as soon as I would turn on 'plant dad', I had those kids' attention," he explains. "The script was good enough for me to find all kinds of fun levels and play around with it. I just kept in mind that I was playing for kids. I was aware of the audience. As an actor, you have to be aware of the genre and the audience." He felt that there was something different about *Goosebumps*, compared to other children's fare of the era, that attracted him to the role. "A lot of kids' shows, especially back then, were really cheesy. Bad acting, bad scripts. Everything was done cartoony. They were all so broad and so big and terrible like really talking down to kids. This wasn't so. This was right up my alley. They wanted genuine characters."

Meanwhile, Jonathan Whittaker made quite the impression when he turned up to his audition for "One Day at Horrorland" on his lunch hour from another show, still in full costume and covered in blood spatter. But for a working actor, it was all par for the course, and to this day he continues to operate on a "spaghetti" policy, in which he throws everything at the wall and sees what sticks. It just so happens that this particular strand of spaghetti was looking for a dad who would find himself at a horror-themed amusement park, so the extra touch of the blood-stained shirt may have helped it stick.

For stuntman Bryan Renfro, the casting session was particularly memorable thanks to the input of his dog, who had come along with him. His furry friend evidently got sick of waiting in a separate room while Renfro met with producers, and got into a little mischief, pushing the door shut as he had been trained to do. Only problem was, the door locked shut, and nobody on site had the key. It took a good half-hour for someone to show up with a key, and by the time they had, the dog had made quite the impression, and bagged himself some stunt work on the show. His owner also got the job.

Casting the show was perhaps more like a traditional job interview than one might imagine, in that there was emphasis on getting the right personalities as well as the right skills from whoever they hired. If the set were to continue being the fun and friendly place it was among the crew, they needed to make sure the qualities they embodied extended to the cast as well. "I think the kids we worked with on *Goosebumps* were, for the most part, very intelligent young people," says Randy Bradshaw. "Bright. They saw everything, they heard everything, and they were incredibly aware." As far as he was concerned, they responded well to direction, and enjoyed being on an even keel with the adults on set, which was something the directors always strived for, as did the wider cast. "What always helped in all of those shows was the adults. I don't think all adult actors like working with kid actors, for a million reasons, right? Most of the actors [we had], I think really, really enjoyed working with kids." Bradshaw says the adult actors deserve a lot of credit for their work on the show, because their experience and professionalism meant they were happy to do whatever needed to be done to work around the kids' schedules, and to encourage their young co-stars in their own careers. "The kids may have been in one or two shows, working with actors who had decades working," Bradshaw says, "and so you just want the actors that were willing to share their knowledge."

For young actors, working alongside far more experienced adults can be an intimidating experience. The added complication of making a horror show, full of spooky scenarios and Ron Stefaniuk's at-times gruesome creations, was that the kids had to be at ease on set, and surrounded by a supportive and fun-loving cast and crew. "You had to surround them with adult actors who played monsters or aliens or stuff, who were able to be scary on screen and supportive to a twelve-year-old actor, which is a very difficult thing for a character actor," Levitan explains. "You can stay in character and be scary, but then the kid is going to freeze up on the set. So, they had to be very well-directed and very flexible actors, so that also made casting very difficult." Once a child had been cast, it was ultimately down to the director to nurture them and create a laid-back set where creativity and fun were top priorities, and to make sure that whoever they cast alongside them were willing to support them and ensure things never got too overwhelming.

Sometimes, the casting process threw out unexpected or interesting scenarios. Perhaps one of the most striking casting choices of *Goosebumps* came with the episode "Strained Peas," in which Tyrone Savage played the son of his real-life parents, Booth Savage and Janet-Laine Green. Director Don McCutcheon says there was no favoritism involved in this choice: "There was no preference or anything given to him," he says. "He was just the best for the role at the time, and it happened to be the real-life son of Booth and Janet-Laine. So even though as young as he was, it's amazing sometimes how professional and polished these young kids can be at a very young age. They're almost well beyond their years in maturity as an actor." McCutcheon feels that having a real family cast enhanced the chemistry between them, but is quick to emphasize that this doesn't detract from their work: "They're still actors at that moment, you know, and they still have to become the character. I think it was probably a unique experience for them, too. I think Booth and Janet had probably worked together a few times. But to actually have their son, I think, was kind of a special thing," the director says.

On the odd occasion, the show had to look for even younger actors, and it wasn't just a case of asking the crew if any of them had babies, or friends who did. The casting of babies was handled just like all other casting, through agents. According to Randy Bradshaw, the babies even got paid the same rate as the rest of the cast, and extra care was taken to make sure they weren't upset, overworked or overstimulated. "When there's a baby like that, everybody was a bit nervous," he recalls. Don McCutcheon says that when working with babies, you just have to do what you can: "Babies are a whole different element. There's nothing you can really do. I think we probably had twins. The reason for that is, if one's sleeping, one's awake, and you just put them back in, in and out. Don't try to overdo it with them."

For a remarkable number of young Canadian actors of the time, *Goosebumps* is an early feature on their resumé. Often, *Are You Afraid of the Dark?* is on there too. A good number of them crossed over from one show to the other. "I had a lot of friends, as an Ontario actor, that I'm still in touch with today, who got to do an episode or two of *Goosebumps*, and it was like a real rite of passage for Toronto," says Corey Sevier. While there are plenty of *Goosebumps* kids who tinkered with acting in the mid-'90s before vanishing off the face of the Earth as far as IMDb and internet presence is concerned, there are just as many who made steady careers as working actors, and a select few who went on to even greater recognition. Ryan Gosling is undoubtedly the breakout star of *Goosebumps*, working his way up from Canadian TV acting into feature film and finally to the A-List of Hollywood. His turn as Ken in Greta Gerwig's *Barbie* in 2023 was testament to his status, and garnered him his third Oscar nomination. Meanwhile, Hayden Christensen achieved huge fame and success—if not audience appreciation—in the mid-2000s as Anakin Skywalker in George Lucas's somewhat controversial prequel trilogy to *Star Wars*. A.J. Cook and Caterina Scorsone went on to long acting careers, and Zach Lipovsky recently directed the hugely successful and entertaining *Final Destination: Bloodlines*. For many young Canadian performers, *Goosebumps* proved to be a vital and formative first step in their careers. "The nice thing about doing kids' shows, especially if you cast a lot of kids, is that some of them grow up to be real actors," Steve Levitan chuckles.

"All Kinds of MacGyver Solutions"

Locations and Sets

The Molson building was the gift that kept on giving for the *Goosebumps* crew. It was affordable, spacious and provided them with a two-in-one workspace, housing both production offices and studio space. Everybody from producers to composers and editors worked from their own offices in the Molson building, forming a central hub that the entire gang could use. If they ever needed a break, or to confer with their colleagues, they were only ever a few steps away. All the interior sets used for the show were built on site, so with the exception of location shooting, there wasn't often a need to venture far from its grounds.

"That Molson building was kind of like a godsend," Bob Sprogis remembers. The vast layout of the old brewery not only lent the floorspace required for a fully-functioning television studio, but came with its own little quirks that could be used to great effect. The hollow floors in which tanks used to be stored were now empty, and could be repurposed as pits, basements and other underground spaces. "We had one show where it came in handy, because it was a show about mummies, and the kid had to fall from one chamber down into another chamber, so we made a hole in the floor. Boom! Down he went." Sprogis recalls.

Although the old Molson building was in many ways the ideal setting for Goosebumps HQ, it did have a few drawbacks, not the least of which being its location on a busy freeway. Such was the noise from the traffic that a running joke soon emerged of everybody pretending not to hear what each other had said. This made recording sound a bit tricky, and all manner of solutions were tried out to soundproof the building. "Patrick [Doyle] found this crazy sound engineer who came in," Steve Levitan recalls. "He had this theory of these strange cylinders. I don't know what they were made out of. He would just put them in key parts of the building, like up on walls and in corners and stuff. They said, 'That'll fix it.' It seemed like mumbo-jumbo to me, but he put them up, and it worked, and it was amazing." Just another day on the job for the resourceful *Goosebumps* crew.

Ron Stefaniuk vividly recalls the Molson building, and both its pros and cons. "We were shooting a lot of it night-for-night. So yeah, working in the middle of the night, with fourteen- and twelve- year-olds, in an old brewery that's half torn down. It's this giant, empty, cavernous, four-story concrete bunker. There's nothing like running around on concrete floors for years to make you understand the words 'shin splints' by the time you're fifty!"

The old Molson building housed two studios, imaginatively dubbed Studio A and Studio B, but Sunnybrook Park in Toronto became such a key player in *Goosebumps* that it received the honorary title of Studio C. It would become many things over the course of the show: a swamp, a theme park, a campsite, pretty much any rural outdoor space it needed to be. Thrilled to be hosting such a big deal of a project, the local authorities were incredibly accommodating of production. "They let us do anything," says Ian Brock. "They even told us that, 'You can cut branches on trees if you need!'" The crew were even given tutorials on basic tree surgery so that they could transform the space however they needed on their own terms, and were provided with a professional digger who would come and create graves, pits, swamps and any other hole required. "Sometimes we got away with murder there," says Brock, but other episodes were easier to pull off, "like times it turned into a Louisiana bog. We just put some dry moss in the trees, and it looked great!"

The layout of Sunnybrook Park made containing the action relatively easy, with the sets encompassing a roughly 300-foot radius from its base camp for the smaller outdoor shoots. Although they were given a fairly free rein by the authorities, the crew were always mindful of treating the space well and leaving it in as good a condition as they found it. "From a technical standpoint, we tried to keep our equipment and our footprint small," says Stefan Scaini. "First of all, for the conservation of the area. Because, you know, it's a sensitive environment, and we wouldn't want to be stomping on things. So, we asked the park, 'Where are we okay to stomp and where are we not?' And they were very clear, and they said, 'This area is fine, people can camp here. Can you please stay out of there?' So, we're very respectful of the environment, so we're not disturbing it too much."

Sunnybrook Park offered the additional perk of giving the impression of wilderness right in the middle of the city. "You can literally step off the parking lot, and you're in the woods," Scaini explains, "so all the scenes when they're walking through the woods, if the camera were to swing around, there's the trucks, there's catering, there's all the cast sitting with their chairs, you pan over this way, and oh, we're in wilderness." A simple forty-five-minute drive from the Molson building, Sunnybrook became the recurrent guest star of the show, and of all the non-studio locations, was ultimately put to the most constant use throughout the run of the series. Its accessible location just made it all the more perfect. Randy Bradshaw explains that whenever they were shooting outside of the studio, they would do their best to cluster the locations to avoid spending unnecessary time and money on moving from place to place. Walking distance would be preferable, and was often achieved.

The more shooting went on, the more apparent it became that Toronto was the perfect place to be. A city surrounded by almost every natural landscape you could ask for, the crew never had to drive more than an hour or so to get to where they needed to be. Beach scenes were often filmed at Scarborough Bluffs, owing to its beautiful white cliffs and the council's tolerance for vehicles being driven off them. Palm trees would be dug into the sand to offer a more tropical setting where required. Those film tax credits put everybody in an affable mood, and crews could largely do what they wanted as long as they were bringing business to the area. "Back in the '80s and '90s, it was a little more relaxed!" says Ian Brock. Meanwhile, Mount Pleasant Cemetery would pop up when needed, like in the "Haunted Mask" episodes, various university buildings and local schools were happy to accommodate shoots, and a number of historic houses, such as Casa Loma and the Cawthra-Elliot Estate, welcomed the gang and helped ensure that the budget recirculated back into the local economy. The crew's use of old or condemned buildings didn't stop at the Molson Brewery. Hearn Power Generating Station cropped up for the episodes "Attack of the Mutant" and "Welcome to Dead House," a location which Steve Levitan says was "a very scary place, but had lots of character." It perfectly captured that bleak, run-down look that certain episodes needed, and the building still stands, though it has long since been condemned. Toronto's famous CN Tower also got to feature in "Attack of the Mutant," standing clearly behind the Mutant's lair, although the area has been significantly developed in the years since, making the layout almost unrecognizable compared to its screen incarnation.

Pickering, just east of Toronto, was the go-to for the more rural locations on the show that Sunnybrook couldn't handle, with a bounty of farms and fields on offer. Apparently, the area had been earmarked for a new airport back in the '70s, but when local officials and communities protested the plans, the region was simply left as it was, making it a great spot for shooting the more timeless, country life episodes. "Scarecrow Walks at Midnight", for example, involved finding a farm and cornfield, which they ended up locating somewhere around Scarborough, according to Randy Bradshaw's recollections. The landowners were very obliging, and the crew returned the favor, taking good care of the house and crops, and doing their best not to damage anything, despite the huge generators and lights that were hauled into their fields. On this occasion, all the interiors were shot at the farmhouse, getting plenty of bang for Fox's buck.

Although plenty of real outdoor spaces were used for filming, this wasn't always necessary, and with a central principle of recycling and repurposing sets and dressing, they could always bring the jungle to the studio if need be. "We built whole forests inside, because we had so much space," says Ian Brock. "We had a greenhouse area just outside. We kept all the plants there in the summer. We'd go buy like thirty grand worth of tropical plants, and then just recycle them all into all our sets." To this end, the bounty of plants that made up Dr. Brewer's workspace in "Stay Out of the Basement" would end up reprising their roles in later episodes. Nothing ever went to waste on the set of *Goosebumps*.

Then, of course, sometimes, they just needed city streets, and Toronto had plenty of those to offer. The problem was, when production required such spaces, especially during the day, a lot of paperwork and red tape was necessary, not to mention a considerable chunk of an episode's budget, for the trouble of disrupting the everyday working lives of Torontonians. This placed pressure on the cast and crew to get in, do their thing, and get the hell out of everybody's way again, and if any issues cropped up that threatened to prolong the shoot, there was little room for maneuver. Thankfully, between the crew's never-say-die attitude and the ever-rolling schedule, there was very little opportunity to become flummoxed, and they always managed to get what they needed in time, without causing too much chaos for the city.

Particularly in its earlier days, *Goosebumps* had a very suburban vibe, with plenty of episodes requiring little more than a charming, middle-class family house to set the scene. "The great thing about Toronto was the Americana feel," says Ron Oliver, detailing the abundance of American-looking neighborhoods within the radius of the *Goosebumps* sets. Given the series was of American origin, it was important to Steve Levitan and the crew that that American flavor be maintained (except, of course, for those tell-tale Canadian accents), and to this end, the location scouts would drive around the neighborhoods of Toronto, picking out the perfect houses that would make American viewers feel right at home.

A good majority of interior shots set in houses were done in the studio with a setup that had been introduced early on and continued for the show's run. Steve Levitan describes sets that were like Lego constructs or flat-pack furniture, in that they slotted together in a very simple fashion, and could be taken apart, rearranged and redecorated as required. As such, a few basic house interior sets were made right at the beginning of production, and as shooting continued they would be dismantled, given a lick of paint or new layer of wallpaper, or simply turned around, and put back again to create the illusion of an entirely new room or house. It was a simple trick, but it worked wonders, and would be the first big step in establishing the show's eco-conscious production standards.

There were occasions that called for something much more elaborate. Episodes like "The Haunted House Game," "One Day at Horrorland" and "Return of the Mummy" stepped further outside the everyday locations, requiring game show sets, giant board games and ancient pyramids. Of everything actor Afrah Gouda experienced on *Goosebumps*, what stood out to her the most was the quality of the set design. "Mummy" was easily the most ambitious of the entire first season's sets, most of which had been relatively suburban, and the crew got hastily to work recreating the inside of a pyramid. The details of the sets were very immersive: sand on the floors, the shapes and angles of the stone walls, the hieroglyphic carvings. As an Egyptian who had seen all of these things for real, Gouda was probably best qualified to judge them, and she was blown away. "It was just as if you were really walking into the pyramids, and I've been there in the pyramids," she says. "It was really beautiful, to the point that I said, 'Who designed this?' So, I spoke with one of the designers, I said, 'That's just spectacular, like I am really impressed.'" Beyond the sets themselves, Gouda was enamored with her princess costume, particularly the intricately-beaded headpiece and necklace. She was told, although she couldn't say for sure, that these pieces were flown in from L.A. and had been used in the movie *Cleopatra*. She sings the praises of the entire design crew, from sets to hair and makeup, for their imagination and attention to detail. While suburban homes may have been the most common sets they worked with, they most definitely had the skill and imagination to pull off the more unusual ones.

When it came to finding film-ready houses, it was the job of a scouting crew to get out there and canvas places that had the right look for the job. While the sudden appearance of a film crew in the vicinity might be quite the talking point for the average citizen, there were particularly picturesque neighborhoods that got used frequently, to the point that local residents were well-versed in lending their homes and communities to productions. The classic middle-America look with picket fences was often the most in-demand, and for some homeowners, another production company turning up at their door was just business as usual.

The scouts would stop by people's houses and ask them if they'd mind production using their home for a week or so, sometimes for as little as a day. Once a contract had been drawn up, the house's residents were put up in a nearby hotel for the duration of the shoot, and the majority of their furniture was moved out so that the set decorating crew could dress the house to suit the production. There were also insurance and liability considerations, which made the removal of the homeowner's belongings a wise choice. On occasion, if it was deemed appropriate, some of the owner's furniture would remain in place and specified in the contract to cover the entirely possible scenario in which damage would occur. "Film crews generally are really careful of houses, but just having, you know, a hundred and twenty people go through a house for a week, there's a lot of occasional damage that occurs because it's just a lot of traffic," director David Winning explains.

Amos Crawley agrees that, particularly with young actors around, damage is bound to happen, no matter how much care is taken. "You take over the house and it's always sort of a funny thing. You're in somebody else's house, and you're not supposed to touch stuff, but you got a bunch of twelve- and thirteen-year-olds, so of course you end up doing that, anyway!" he says. Although things usually went according to plan when on other people's property, the odd inevitable screw-up did occur. Ian Brock recalls an occasion when one person's house needed their hedgerow trimming in preparation for filming. When the crew arrived on set the next day and found the bushes in the exact same state they left them in, they were perplexed. Turns out that wires had got crossed, and the next house over's hedges had received a manicure instead, much to the delight of the owner.

Sometimes, there was a particular quality required of the house or neighborhood. For "Awesome Ants," Don McCutcheon was determined to find a relatively new-build neighborhood that had a "human ant farm" quality to it. "I don't want any trees. I don't want anything like that," he recalls. "We got all the cars removed from the driveways. I just wanted it so generic and just so, kind of a little bit creepy, in a way. You know, it almost didn't look like humans lived there. And so, I remember being very specific on that. We found that street that worked really well."

On the odd occasion, something a bit more spectacular was on the cards, such as in the case of "The Ghost Next Door," which with its house fire set piece presented some interesting challenges. "It was like, 'What do we do? Do we build this set of the burned-out house?'" Don McCutcheon says. "As I recall, it's a question of *how are we gonna do this? Are we gonna build this or whatever?* And I remember we had to actually go into a home. It was a tough one for the art department, because we ended up using an actual home. We had to sort of give it the impression that there had been a fire. But then, having to be able to turn it back, we had to restore it for the people that lived in the house, so there was no permanent damage done to their home." This is where Ian Brock and his crew's ingenuity would really come in handy, throwing handfuls of cocoa powder and the like to dirty things up in ways that could be easily reversed when the residents came back after their week's paid hotel stay. Of all the homes the show filmed in, there were certainly challenges, but never any lasting damage that anyone can recall.

There doesn't seem to have been much of a pattern dictating when a house's interiors would be used for a shoot and when a Lego set would just be put together at the Molson building. Perhaps budgetary concerns governed such decisions, but over the course of its run, *Goosebumps* would spend as much time in and around people's houses as it would in the studio, sometimes just using a house's exterior and sometimes using the whole space for the entirety of the shoot. For exterior shots of homes and neighborhoods, foliage was a cheap but very useful means of transforming the space. In the case of "It Came from Beneath the Sink," the aftermath of the scene in which the evil energy of the sponge has poisoned the garden, required the set decorators to paint the grass and shrubbery brown overnight, an effort that was somewhat hindered by unexpected rainfall. Meanwhile, autumnal episodes shot in summer were helped enormously by greenery. Effects artist Matthew DeWilde recalls giant bags of dry leaves being brought to the set of "The Haunted Mask" to sell the October vibes in what was really midsummer.

Just like with the greenhouse full of tropical plants, the crew thought up an arrangement that could save time and money on the things they needed most. "We're doing a couple of kids' bedrooms every week, which is a lot of kids' bedrooms to do a set design for!" explains Ian Brock. "So, we made a deal with a furniture store: instead of buying stuff, we'd rent it. And they said, 'As long as you put it back in the box perfectly, we'll let you rent it,' and we paid like 25% of the value for the week. Great! But it's always like this giant lineup of boxes that you couldn't go near, because everything was unpacked, meticulously put on the set and put back in a box and returned to the store, because otherwise you end up with so much stuff!" So, unbeknownst to Toronto locals of the '90s, they may well have in their homes, to this day, a genuine piece of *Goosebumps* set. How about that?

Many of the cast and crew have lamented the loss of certain characteristics of the industry as it was in the mid- to late '90s, but non-industry folk may be surprised at just how bureaucratic things can get behind the scenes of film and television nowadays. Ian Brock recalls buying a poster store for the show: "Like a thousand posters, in all the racks, crazy posters from the '70s and '80s and Jim Morrison pictures, and we just use them all. At the time, the producers think, *well, we're going to get sued for that.*" He recalls one of Scholastic's higher-ups accepting the challenge, and simply saying, "Let them sue us!" According to Brock, modern TV and film is never as straight-forward as buying a poster, sticking it on a wall and filming it. "We have to send pictures of all the sets to lawyers before we shoot them, which is really hard to do," he explains, so tight are the legal restrictions surrounding IP. He says that even fonts have to be cleared by lawyers these days. The '90s truly were a simpler time.

Haggling for cut-price rented furniture and buying old poster shops are just a couple of the many indicators of the central production ethos: resourcefulness. Although they had the best budget of any show of its kind, and the backing of major networks, it was always a matter of making that money stretch as far as it possibly could, to make sure a good show was being put on for the millions of kids that made *Goosebumps* the hit it was. Steve Levitan says that this format was put in place early on by Armando Sgrignuoli, and carried on for the show's run: "The key creative work of the show was done by Armando. The first season set up that formula of how, in an anthology series, we could, with the same resources, make every home look like a different home. Ian's job was really just occasional extra things that came up based on that week's script, and just making sure that the existing machine worked the way it worked. He was brilliantly talented. I'm not saying he wasn't. It was just the heavy lifting was done by Armando, and Ian just made sure that it kept going."

For Ian Brock, production design was a matter of begging, borrowing and stealing. He tells of he and his crew earning nicknames like Ali Baba and His Forty Thieves and The Dumpster Diving Designer, because they were always rummaging around for objects and materials that they might repurpose for the show. "Burlap, chicken wire, glue, all that sort of thing." Hay was an often-used resource for making a space look ratty, autumnal or abandoned, but once the crew felt that it may have become overused, they got the idea from another show that wrapping surfaces in burlap gave off the same vibe. One of the painters had a gig with MAC Cosmetics, and would bring industrial-sized units of iridescent powder to set, which were then mixed in to make custom paints. Food coloring was another common commodity, again ordered in huge quantities for fairly low prices. Brock says that nowadays things can be done quicker and easier with computers—everything from mixing paint to 3D printing small props—but that it was a labor of love for *Goosebumps*, and everybody got involved to make their production lines happen.

Brock says they were working with a fairly minimal design crew of seven or eight people, along with eight full-time carpenters and four painters, and when needed, everyone from set dressers to props guys would get involved to create the illusion. Sometimes interns were brought into the art departments to paint, saw and thread individual hairs into creatures. "It was an all-hands-on-deck kind of thing," Brock explains. "There's always the little projects spun off, ten or fifteen little jobs going off. The problem is with *Goosebumps*, there's like five-day shoot, five-day prep. Very short time for designing and organizing stuff, right? So every morning you're filming, every night you're filming, mostly in the summers, and then in the daytime you're running around building the next episode, working with the directors." Though this may sound like a maddeningly chaotic pace, Brock says that it was actually a pretty sweet deal by industry standards. "But five days for a half-hour [episode runtime] is pretty good, actually, in the scheme of things, because we do a lot of one-hour shows in seven or eight days."

So fast-paced was the show that the usual poring over design sketches went out the window, in favor of rolling up their sleeves and seeing what they could pull off. The occasional use of miniatures, such as in "How to Kill a Monster" and "Chillogy" was about as by-the-book as the show got. "We didn't have time to do a lot of drawings and stuff," says Brock. "We would just literally go downstairs to our 10,000 square foot warehouse of stuff that we could recycle. It's like building blocks. And we were just like, 'OK, what do we do?'" This handy and thoroughly eco-friendly attitude has never evaded Ian Brock, who is currently constructing an entire house out of recycled sets. Steve Levitan fondly recalls the creativity of the art departments. "We tried to use whatever we could. The scripts were so ambitious for a five-day shoot on a kids' show budget that we had to invent all kinds of MacGyver solutions!" Although Ian Brock says the producers were "amazingly generous," *Goosebumps* always maintained a down-to-earth, grass-roots innocence to it. "It was pretty much like a high school show!" he remembers.

"That Will Scare the Little Buggers!"

The Music of Goosebumps

Sound is an integral component of any good piece of horror media, and *Goosebumps* was buoyed by distinctive and highly memorable work in the audio department. From its creative musical stings and sound effects to its iconic theme song, every episode was unique in its approach to heightening the visual drama with spooky sounds, while maintaining a distinctly *Goosebumps* flavor. Jack Lenz started out in L.A. working with rock bands. It was a demanding life—one his wife wasn't crazy about—and so, as many Canadian creatives do, they ended up returning to the safer and easier pace of Toronto life. He had been composing for film and television since the early '80s, writing jingles for news programs and commercials, and even some Olympics shows. With the goal of composing full scores, he founded Lenz Entertainment in 1992, and he really began to make a name for himself, both as a composer and an all-round great guy to work with.

"I got a call from Steve Levitan saying that he was looking for somebody. He knew about my work on a couple of things and he asked me if I'd be interested in writing a theme. And the theme really then turned into, you know, 'Would you be willing to score episodes?'" Jack Lenz explains. He was, at this point, completely unaware of *Goosebumps* and R.L. Stine, but the show presented a fairly rare opportunity in his industry: a long-term gig. Lenz was ridiculously busy, spreading himself over several simultaneous projects, but this offer was too enticing to pass up. "I had two of those going at the same time, which was unheard of, right? But *Goosebumps* was a lot easier because of the producer [Bill Siegler]." Lenz got straight to work, bringing in a musical partner and setting up shop at 20 Duncan Street in Toronto, at the Einstein Brothers' office on the second floor, later moving over to Adelaide Street, affording him a distance from the main creative hub of *Goosebumps* HQ and its infamous lack of soundproofing.

"I learned a lot from Jack," says Lenz's assistant and orchestrator Jim McGrath. "He's a brilliant, very talented guy, and he certainly has a highly developed, sophisticated musical style." A trumpet player by training, specializing in jazz, McGrath found the idea of studio work and film and TV scoring to be a more realistic ambition than pursuing a career as a recording artist. Although he had also never heard of *Goosebumps* before getting involved with the show, he worked at the same production company as Lenz, and had previously assisted him on a number of projects, so followed him over to the show. Lenz knew, after years of working with musicians with a good ear but no formal training, that he needed someone on his professional level to make this all work, and McGrath was perfect. "I had studied classical piano, and I went to university and studied orchestration. So, I had the advantage of being trained, and if you're trained, it's always better," Lenz explains. "Jim McGrath is a highly trained musician. Jim is a very capable musician and composer himself."

Lenz was used to a fast working pace, having spent years composing music during the day and working with bands at night, but there was a lot of pressure to ensure that this major show for a major network would consistently be delivered on time. So, although he and his team had great fun working together, "We never really had any opportunity to collaborate. We just had to deliver a show every week. It's still a service industry. Within literally two weeks [of shooting], we'd be doing post. Yeah, that's how fast it moved, you know."

But Steve Levitan and Bill Siegler ensured that a good balance was struck, and that quality work was turned out by creatives who felt appreciated, despite the time crunch. "Steve was sort of an interesting balance between a money producer and a creative producer. Bill was a creative producer," says Lenz, explaining the different sorts of personalities that are attracted to producer roles. For artists, producers who care about the work more than the money or deadline are always preferable, but there has to be someone managing the project and making sure everything comes together. In this way, Steve Levitan was the perfect combination, and when paired with artistically-minded Bill Siegler, they made for a very agreeable duo.

Lenz ended up composing the entire show, first with Jim McGrath and later with Brad MacDonald, and Jack's working style was indicative of an almost instinctive approach to creating music. He refers to his style as intuitive scoring. "What I've done for my whole life is I play piano to picture. And whatever I played—and it wasn't much different with the theme—you get an idea, you put it down, simple keyboard, or maybe it's electric piano sound, or maybe it's a percussive, you know. It just depends on what sort of strikes you at the time, and then you have to fill that out," Lenz explains.

Unlike most movie scores, they didn't have the luxury of a manned orchestra to perform their music, instead working almost entirely digitally with a piece of equipment they referred to as The Box. "Whatever sounds were available that the programmer would have in the gear that he had. Then I fill it out and orchestrate it, based on the sounds that hopefully, I can find that sort of match the idea. Orchestrators have got a pretty good intuitive sense, and you pretty quickly find the sound that you're hoping will sort of bring this little piano part that you played into life," says Lenz of his creative process.

An average day in the studio involved watching the finished edits of an episode and playing around with different sounds and arrangements to fit what was happening on the screen. "He would basically compose spontaneously to picture all day," says McGrath. Producers would then rock up at the office for so-called spotting sessions and hear what Lenz and McGrath had come up with and offer their feedback, at which point any necessary revisions were made, and all the technical polishing applied.

"I show up at every mix, and sit there, usually with Bill Siegler, not always, but almost always, and with Jack Lenz, and we would just sit in a dark room with a screen and these two sound mixers at a big circuit board, and just have a ball for hours," Steve Levitan recalls of the process. "That would be half a day with no sunlight!" Jack Lenz loved working with Steve Levitan during these sessions. "He had such a great sense of humor. He was easy-going. Really, really a sweetheart." They remain friends to this day. "We chat about the good old days, because, you know, the production climate is very different now than it was. It was a great experience with both Bill Siegler and with Steve Levitan." It was almost always Levitan and Siegler who would sit in on these scoring sessions and cast the deciding vote; once in a while, Deborah Forte would show up to see how things were going.

"It was always an interesting process, but again, time pressure," says Jack Lenz. "At a certain point they stopped spotting and we would just get the episode and write it, and then Bill would show up on Friday and say yay or nay, or change this or do that." The engine was well-oiled enough for the music department to be left to their devices by this point, and the only issue they would come across was what the show's periodic back-and-forths often came down to: "Usually it was all around the issue of how scary it was," Lenz recalls.

"We would always push for it to be scarier," he continues. "If visuals obviously were terrifying, why wouldn't the music sort of support that? But there's often this kind of dialogue about, 'Well, that's too scary'. I said, 'Well, what's too scary?' 'Well, that big orchestra strike just scared the crap out of me', and I said, 'And the visuals don't?!' It was an interesting kind of tension-and-release kind of thing, because sometimes you'd get away with it, other times you wouldn't." It was never quite clear who got to draw the scary line, or where that line was. "Who's the arbiter of scary, right? Most horror movies are based on the concept of surprise. That's just how it works. So, you want the music to support that. I used to remind Bill, 'Well, you didn't have those limitations for the theme.' He would always say, 'We can't scare them too much,' but then, every time we'd finish an episode, he would say, 'That will scare the little buggers!'" Lenz laughs.

The process of recording the music was "quite primitive by today's standards," McGrath explains, "but it seemed to work OK then!" The work was delivered in stereo mix form on DAT tape, along with a list of time code numbers indicating where to start each cue, which engineers at the mix theater would then position alongside the visuals. It was typical of *Goosebumps*' fast-paced and highly creative production process, but it usually came together without issue. Despite the industry's reputation for hectic schedules, and the constant and very fast turnover rate of the show itself, McGrath recalls it being a fun and fairly relaxed process in the sound department, with a reasonable schedule and no particularly gruelling deadlines.

Of course, the theme tune for *Goosebumps* is among the show's most memorable elements, with its eerie piano riff giving way to a full-bodied and menacing piece. When it came to composing the theme, Jack Lenz already had a few basic criteria in mind: it had to be in a minor key, and preferably catchy enough to be memorable. "Then it had to have an epic kind of quality. I really like this idea that even though it was a minor key, I could use the major 6th in the scale." He quickly threw together a piece that sparked his imagination, and he played it to himself over and over again in his office. "I liked it so much that several people, when they were walking by the door, said, 'Will you please stop that?' I remember telling Jim, 'We're gonna close the door now!'"

For McGrath, the theme is the highlight of his work on the show. "I was always quite proud of the theme. I had a fair bit to do with the arranging and production of that." And for those who have ever wondered about the canine choral contribution that plays over a clip of a golden retriever from "My Hairiest Adventure," overlaid with glowing yellow eyes, McGrath reveals he "may have even contributed the dog barks on the melody at one point!" The whole dog thing is something both musicians remain amusedly pleased with. "I thought it was fun if the dog did it," says Lenz. Fans around the world agree to this day.

"We were presented with sort of the sketch of what [the credits] was going to be like, because you generally, even with theme writing, you're scoring to some kind of picture," Lenz explains. "You're seldom writing the theme in isolation from visuals, and because they already had the visuals sort of mapped out, I felt like it could be this kind of very compact, sort of that little descending melody against the minor, and then I could open it up into the diminished when it goes to the four-chord." So accustomed is Jack Lenz to the fast pace of his work that he seems almost nonchalant when he reveals that the theme took no more than two hours to write and record. Voice actor Cal Dodd, who would go on to provide a number of voices for the show, was brought in to deliver the "Viewer beware, you're in for a scare" line of the theme song, giving his best Vincent Price sneer. Lenz was thrilled with how it all came together.

Steve Levitan was under no illusion of how difficult a job he had given Jack Lenz, despite the composer's never-say-no approach. Having shot the opening sequence for the show, it was passed on to Lenz, who had to compose a theme tune that would fit perfectly to the visuals they had already locked in. "He had a specific emotional agenda to achieve [with the theme song] in a specific amount of [run]time, and that's really hard," says Levitan. "I think we gave him like ten minutes or something. I'm sure it's not ten minutes, but it was probably on a Friday, we said, 'Can you do this by Monday?' And Jack never said no to anything."

Lenz's favorite part of the theme remains the ominous bass line, although the most recognizable part, the *dundun-dundun-dun*, is also a source of pride. "It was like the kind of scary music you always wanted to write, but no one would let you. I think I just remember that as being an incredibly fun day," he says. But even the most accomplished composers can feel the pressure of expectation. "I don't know that anybody can do anything creative without having this crazy thing in the back of your mind that says, 'I wonder if people will like this', and it can be a tremendous hindrance."

Dispelling any illusion of a Hollywood-style scene in which producers listen to their shiny new theme song and their eyes light up in immediate recognition of what a hit they have, Jack Lenz says the unveiling of the *Goosebumps* theme was rather unceremonious. "They were in such a hurry, they just said, 'That's great.'" He recalls a story he heard about fellow composer Randy Newman, and the problem with overthinking creative choices: supposedly Newman presented "You've Got a Friend in Me" to Pixar, and the more they listened to it, the more they picked holes in it. He eventually lay down on the floor, eyes closed, and when asked what he was doing, replied, "Lowering my expectations." Such is the preference, Lenz says, to play a composition once and get it signed off on, before higher-ups have too long to think about it and reconsider. "It was such a great process, and partly because we didn't have a lot of time. You're just under that pressure to deliver." According to the composer, another saying the industry lives by is, "There's cheap, good, and fast. You can only have two." Lenz says that despite the impact of music on a final project, studios often underestimate its importance, and can allocate as little as 1% of the budget to composition. Although this wasn't the case with *Goosebumps*, the revolving door of new episodes necessitated fast work that didn't allow anybody too much time to get cold feet, and the music department was required to be just as resourceful as every other.

So, the theme was good to go, and the show was off and rolling. Now came the opportunity for real creativity. It is striking just how differently each episode was treated when it came to orchestration.

While the more suburban episodes don't necessarily stand out so much, those with interesting environments or themes presented fun challenges for the music department. "A Night in Terror Tower," for example, takes a lot of inspiration from its medieval English setting. Court-type brass is used for the more regal scenes in the tower, and modest penny-whistle-style woodwind accompanies the shots of muddied-up peasants in the courtyard outside, while those booming choral arrangements that the show does so well emphasize the menace of the dungeons and appearance of the Lord High Executioner.

On the opposite end of the spectrum, episodes like "How to Kill a Monster," "You Can't Scare Me" and "Scarecrow Walks at Midnight" go for a more American country vibe, with lots of banjos and twanging string work. Jack Lenz's favorite episode score was probably the first he composed, given that it was for "The Girl Who Cried Monster," the first episode filmed. "I think part of the fun of those stories is they were diverse enough that you could stretch out. My favorite one is still the library, because it was just that that guy was so creepy. He even scared me! We used a lot of sort of tuned bells and kind of spider-like, what we thought were sort of spider-like sounds."

Over the course of three years working on the show, Lenz saw how popular the property was, and how well his compositions were going down with fans. To this end, he frequently pitched a soundtrack album release. "I even assembled one, and I had some songs written for it by some artists in Toronto, mostly rap artists," he recalls, the rap preference framing this squarely as a product of the mid-'90s. Siegler and Levitan were fully on-board and pitching the idea, but Scholastic continually shut it down, choosing to stick to what they knew, which was books. So, after years of a *Goosebumps* soundtrack going nowhere, and a twenty-something-year reprieve in between, Lenz was astounded when he was contacted by Enjoy The Ride Records, who wanted to put out a vinyl special edition of the album. Lenz said, "Well, you don't have any trouble with me, but good luck with Scholastic!" Through some intense wheedling, the record company managed to get Scholastic's approval, and the vinyl was pressed. "It was just such a thrill, even twenty-five years later, to see that somebody actually would put out a soundtrack, after all the efforts that everybody made, you know, to try to convince Scholastic that it was a good idea," Lenz says.

Notably, when the *Goosebumps* movie was in production in the mid-2010s, Scholastic denied them the rights to Lenz's music. What changed between then and 2024 is anybody's guess, but Lenz says that the record producer told him, "I don't even want to tell you what it took." Intellectual property rights for film and television scores are almost always split, and so with Lenz retaining just a portion of the IP rights for his work, he was only ever in a position to lend his support to an idea and wish the makers luck with wrangling Scholastic. On this occasion, it actually worked. In early 2024, Lenz's soundtrack for *Goosebumps* was released on vinyl by Enjoy The Ride Records, a New York-based record label specializing in limited edition releases, with a subdivision dedicated to soundtrack albums. It sold out within a few days of its release.

Lenz certainly has enjoyed the ride. "I always used to tell my dad, who was a farmer, that I'd never worked a day in my life," he chuckles. "It probably bothered him because he worked very hard, but I tried to explain that when you love something, it doesn't feel like work. And that's the joy of being able to work in a creative field. Really, you can get just totally lost in the joy of doing, and joy of playing."

"You Can Learn an Awful Lot in The Deep End"

The Effects

When it came to deciding which of Stine's books would get the TV treatment, Steve Levitan says it was all down to what could be pulled off on-screen. Working in a time and with a budget that wasn't conducive to advanced post-production effects, it was all about what could be done in real life, with puppets, masks, costumes, makeup and a lot of magic. With this in mind, production was looking out for an effects workshop that could combine R.L. Stine's imagination with their own, and find ways to bring all of these incredible creations to life in three dimensions.

Ron Stefaniuk came from a theatrical background, working a lot in theater and summer stock, and always finding ways to make the show bigger, brighter and more ambitious. His one true love was puppetry, and he had a knack for devising the most elaborate puppets and operating them himself, which already gave him something of a niche. Early in his career, he and fellow effects artist Colin Penman worked on a couple of monster movies together, and he started to diversify into animatronics and other effects work. "We had only ever done just, you know, quite a small amount of work," he says, "but the first job we got was a full creature suit, animatronic, big giant guy in a suit. That cross-pollination of wanting to be a performer and wanting to be a magician and wanting to be designer allowed me to do the weirdest first four jobs of anybody's career!" He spotted a gap in the market for an effects shop that would do it all: puppets, animatronics, suits, makeup, prosthetics. If he could offer the industry a one-stop shop for all visual effects, there would be no stopping him. It was with this goal in mind that he launched Stefaniuk FX Studio, and gathered a team with a wide variety of skills.

It so happened that this niche would be one of the key factors that secured him the job on *Goosebumps*. Although the studio was in its infancy, it already showed a great sense of ambition, and this was exactly what was needed. "My interview with Bill Siegler, I was just so happy that he would see us, to consider me and my company for the job," Stefaniuk recalls. "We didn't have the biggest portfolio in the world, but the things we had in our portfolio were really, I thought, interesting and fun." Apparently Siegler thought so, too. But more than just an interesting body of work, it was Stefaniuk's attitude to it that really sealed the deal. "My pitch was, 'Do you want to hire somebody that thinks they're doing you a favor by showing up? Or do you want to hire somebody that's gonna kill themselves for you every week?'" he recalls. This promise of energy, humility and creativity ticked all the right boxes for *Goosebumps*, and with that, Stefaniuk FX Studio went into production on their first legacy show.

Going into the job, Stefaniuk was under the impression that it would be a monster-a-week kinda deal, but even with the first episode, it became clear that some, if not most, stories would require more than one big creation out of the team. Sure, the Haunted Mask was the centerpiece, but what about the other masks in the background? Ron was quickly realizing just what a task he'd taken on, so the comprehensive skill set of his crew became a vital pillar of the whole show.

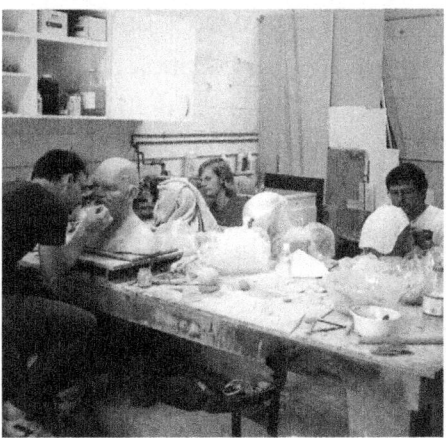

Stefaniuk FX Studio hard at work. Photo courtesy of Matthew DeWilde.

He quickly became known for his ambitious approach to his work, a never-say-no sort of guy. For his colleague Matthew DeWilde, it was a good influence, if a very demanding one. "He was a bit infectious that way," DeWilde recalls. "I mean, he was a really positive man, he was a workaholic, he loved what he did, and he was always trying to come up with some great idea for something." Steve Levitan describes Stefaniuk as somebody for whom no task was too big, no matter how outlandish the suggestion or demanding the schedule. DeWilde agrees, and says that Stefaniuk's ability to manage people and the work going in and out of the shop was a crucial ingredient in ensuring things didn't get too maddening. Ron was constantly busy with something, says DeWilde, conducting meetings, coordinating multiple overlapping tasks, liaising with producers. The work never stopped. *Goosebumps* kicked Stefaniuk FX Studio into overdrive, to such an extent that a secretary was soon brought in to handle all the administrative stuff. "She said she inherited a mess because everything was just so chaotic, and then she had to organize everything!" Matthew DeWilde sympathizes.

As DeWilde remembers it, Ron Stefaniuk's forte was in puppetry, but his trademark quixotism promised everything from masks and prosthetics to makeup. "He wasn't really a skilled prosthetics artist," DeWilde explains. "But he came up with really good creative ideas." Stefaniuk loved and admired the work of Jim Henson, and DeWilde says he would often use the famed puppeteer as a yardstick against which to measure his own work. In his case, WWJD stood for What Would Jim Do? Well, Henson had a large company working together to bring his ideas to life, and that was exactly what Stefaniuk needed. People who could fill in the gaps in his own expertise, and unite to offer the Canadian entertainment industry the most comprehensive effects service out there.

He got straight to work assembling a team who shared his drive, ambition and youthful energy. In the earlier episodes there was a lot of trial and error with different artists, but by the fifth or sixth, a core team soon emerged, consisting of a half-dozen or so, with a revolving door of interns and young artists looking to get their start in the industry by doing the more menial tasks like gluing on Saber's fur. The crew included David Scott, Patrick Gorny, Tony Chappell, Randy Daudlin, Frances James and Graham Chivers. Additional help came in the form of Ron's friend/gofer Brandon, as well as Ron's wife and parents, who would run errands. "His parents were just wonderful people. His wife helped out a lot creatively in the shop at the time," recalls Matthew DeWilde.

David Scott was often the fixer, taking over for others when they had to move on to something else, or just needed a fresh pair of eyes. He toiled over the infamous killer potato from "It Came from Beneath the Sink," and was always on hand to offer a second opinion.

Tony Chappell had a reputation as a prankster, and found that creeping up on people was a great way to break the tension and let loose a little among the nonstop workload. This made him a great fit for Ron Stefaniuk, who describes himself as having a "childish sense of humor." Matthew DeWilde was initially brought on as shop supervisor, but the operation soon became an all-hands-on-deck sort of thing, and his makeup, mold-making, painting, and prosthetics skills were put to good use.

Work commenced almost immediately after Stefaniuk signed on, which DeWilde says is unusual. It was all systems go from the very beginning, and the pace never really let up. Where SFX jobs on movie sets would require weeks or perhaps a couple months of hard work, the rolling nature of the show meant that there was no reprieve. There were times when the team would find each other passed out in the workshop from sheer exhaustion. Stefaniuk was actually living in his studio at the time, which further blurred any line between work and home.

These guys really earned their paychecks. It was not uncommon for them to work through the night in order to get their projects finished in time for the filming week. The show was working to tight schedules, with the SFX crew typically having at best a week or two to design and build all the creations required for a single episode. This labor was always working at an overlap, and the team were prepping up to three episodes simultaneously. When work on one was finally finished, work on another started.

But it did not stop at building the puppets or crafting the masks. The creatures needed to be operated by those who made them, and the makeup and costumes needed to be applied by skilled artists. Nights in the workshop melted into days on the set. The gang would go from finishing Slappy's paint job to lying on the floor of a set, puppeteering him over their heads while simultaneously voicing his lines, the paint on his hair still drying as they did so. It is impossible to overstate the craftsmanship and sheer dedication that Stefaniuk and his team put into making *Goosebumps* what it was. They were being pulled in all different directions. "The people building it are the same people performing it and puppeteering it," Stefaniuk points out. This sometimes extended to suit work as well, such as in the case of "One Day at Horrorland," in which several of the crew played Horrors.

On the set of "Welcome to Camp Nightmare," with Ron Stefaniuk at the controls of Saber. Photo courtesy of Matthew DeWilde.

Ron Stefaniuk has never had a problem finding work or achieving an ambition. He says that when he set his mind to doing something, he just went out and did it, and a combination of his skills and ability to talk people into things has always worked in his favor. He spent his early career throwing himself in at the deep end and learning as he went. In the years since, he has reveled in taking on students and apprentices and giving them a space to learn their craft. "When they come in our shop, they don't spend all their time just sanding something or just mixing fiberglass," he says of his interns. "They find themselves helping to make puppets. They find themselves very quickly in the deep end. But you can learn an awful lot in the deep end."

This mentality seems to have worked out well for Stefaniuk over the years, but he gives much credit to his team not only for making it all happen, but for helping him hone his own skill set. Matthew DeWilde says that he and Ron would often share their knowledge with one another. The ambition crossed with the sense of camaraderie made for a winning formula, and working on *Goosebumps* was the starting point for many talented artists who have since gone on to long and renowned careers in the industry.

There was a fairly neat divide between the effects shop and *Goosebumps* HQ, with most of the correspondence from the production side of things going via Ron. Matthew DeWilde recalls operating from Stefaniuk's workshop on Danforth Ave. and Jones Ave., which worked for him as it was no more than a half hour journey from his home, and given the demanding hours, this softened the blow a little. "I'd be working like a twenty-four-hour day sometimes, and then I would go sleep, and then I would go back to work. So, I was glad it was a short distance for me," he recalls. It was more demanding still on account of the various on-location shoots the crew would be required for. Having to drive an hour out to a graveyard or whatever just chipped away further at their work time.

Despite it all, Matthew DeWilde emphasizes that it was an "exciting" job that he was thrilled to have.

Ambitiousness was always the name of the game for Ron Stefaniuk. Everybody I ask remembers him as full of ideas, energy and resourcefulness. He never said no, and he never failed to deliver, no matter how little time or money he had at his disposal. "I'm always game to follow somebody with a bold idea," Stefaniuk says. "Our company hadn't even existed that long. The opportunity, you know, youthful exuberance, and then the need to do a good job for them, along with their enthusiasm, buoyed spirits quite a lot."

These were all qualities that a show as intensive as *Goosebumps* would require. The very first episode they shot, "The Girl Who Cried Monster," needed a half-face monster mask, which was fitted with animatronics that would allow the stalk-eyes to move. Of course, complex designs mean there's more to go wrong, and the fact that the mask had been crafted to fit the face of a different actor who'd had to drop out for health reasons meant the crew had to scramble to make it fit Eugene Lipinski as best they could. To top it all off, the animatronics eventually broke down, and couldn't be fixed in time to continue the shoot, which necessitated finding a spare moment later, before filming wrapped, to get an insert shot. There was always something in need of tweaking, fixing or patching up. Saber was another of the more ambitious creations, modeled somewhat on the werewolf design from *An American Werewolf in London*. The backend of the creature was pushed along on a wheelbarrow-type contraption while one of the SFX crew physically got inside and operated the front legs manually. Matthew DeWilde recalls a day that Saber got stuck in a cross-eyed position, and fondly remembers the blooper reel for that particular shoot.

What made Stefaniuk's ambitiousness all the more necessary was the budget they were working with. Matthew DeWilde thinks he recalls *Goosebumps* being shopped around to every effects studio in town, and that many rejected the job because they didn't think they could meet the brief with the money they were being offered. Ron Stefaniuk had no such reservations, at least not out loud. Budgeting was a huge concern for Stefaniuk's team, as it was allocated to them on an episodic basis, but some episodes called for much more investment in effects than others did, so Ron would redirect funds towards the episodes that really required it. This sort of careful planning was one of the most important tricks Stefaniuk had up his sleeve in making it all happen. He wasn't just an artist, he was a manager.

Accounts of the budget vary, but everyone agrees that they were being as resourceful as they could to make it stretch further. "Ron used to joke with me like every time it was payday," says Matthew DeWilde. "He'd give me my check, and he'd just go [pained grunt] and it was just a running joke we had all the time. We agreed to a rate when I started the show, and I think he thought it was charging too much money or something, but at the time, it wasn't really that much money. We weren't getting overtime. We were working so many hours on the show to get things completed."

He may have joked about the pain of money running through his hands, but Stefaniuk was proud of how far everybody made it go. "I think everybody tried to do a lot for the budget, like Ian Brock, the production designer, the props person. Everybody was really stretching the restraints of the budget to get a lot out of the project, and I think it shows," he says. "I think if you really knew the numbers, I think people would be surprised that so much was accomplished for the money spent. I thought we accomplished more than the money would allow." In the effects shop, there was a lot to consider when it came to budgeting. Not only was there the manpower to pay for, but the materials, everything from paint to rubber to hair, ate up a considerable chunk of the budget. "There's a lot of foam rubber in a full-size creature!" Ron explains. "The limitations day to day were hard. The time and the money and the budget were very difficult. But I don't think that showed in what we were doing, because while we were doing it, we were having an enormous amount of fun."

For Ron Stefaniuk, the thrifty mindset that *Goosebumps* necessitated became a way of life over the years of his career, and he has repeatedly found that his resourcefulness may have even been his downfall: "Any money saved is money that doesn't go in your pocket. God forbid!" he laments. "That's something I never learned: how to put money in my pocket. If you could save the money, it allowed us to put it somewhere else in the episode, so the episodes got bigger."

Despite *Goosebumps* being the most expensive show of its kind at the time, it was always a case of not enough time, not enough money. Although this never dampened Ron Stefaniuk's spirits, there are those who say that these pressures are very noticeable in the final product. However, this always comes with the caveat of the team clearly having done their very best with what they had. Judah Katz fondly remembers the effects used in "Stay Out of the Basement" as "cheesy… and their budget was nothing! They were relatively young, these guys, like they found people who were hungry or willing to do the job. Really nice guys, but I remember that they were challenged on a few things." In this particular case, the bald cap Katz wore in the final scene was somewhat beyond the expertise of even the multiskilled Stefaniuk team. To this end, Jane Stevenson, a bald cap specialist (yes, that really is a thing) was brought in to fit it to the actor's head, although he recalls that even with such a professional touch, the thing was always a blink away from snapping, and he had to measure his movements very carefully to avoid such a fate.

For the most part, Matthew DeWilde didn't find the work *Goosebumps* required to be particularly challenging. He says that the world of prosthetics hadn't changed much in over half a century at that point, and many of the techniques he used on the show were similar to those used in old Universal monster movies. "Everything was basically made of foam latex. That was kind of the standard, and we could make that do anything. It was tough, it was durable, and it was easy to paint," he explains. "I was using all kinds of different paint systems to get the effects. We needed a lot of fiberglass, a lot of the molds. I was making something called Ultra Kl 30, like a gypsum cement. A lot of the molds are all plaster. We had a basic silicone molding rubber." For masks and teeth, there was a lot of casting and sculpting involved, but for an experienced prosthetics guy like DeWilde, it was all in a day's work.

The show was a fairly latex-heavy one, and Stefaniuk's team would do all the casting in-house before sending pieces off to a local company that specialized in latex. Given the time crunch they were constantly working with, the pieces didn't always come back perfect. "The first two Haunted Mask heads, they came back horrendous!" Matthew DeWilde recalls. "They were horrible castings, and we couldn't use them, so we just thought we'd use them for background. Then they came up with five more that were in really good condition, and those are the ones we used on the show." Latex came with its own set of challenges. All latex pieces needed to be properly washed at the end of each day, ready to be used again the next, necessitating backups. They would go through a considerable amount of wear and tear, so some team members had to be on set to make repairs where needed, as well as to fit and apply the masks and costumes. There were a million little jobs that always needed doing in the studio and on set, and so the crew's adaptability and willingness to lend a hand and take over anything that needed finishing up was crucial.

They were always looking for ways to make things more affordable or less time consuming, Stefaniuk's ambitious nature notwithstanding. "We were actually taking stuff from other productions that [Ron] worked on and trying to make that fit or make that work to save time," says Matthew DeWilde. To this end, many *Goosebumps* creations were repurposed for later episodes. Most notably, Saber from "Welcome to Camp Nightmare" later became Ripper in "One

Day at Horrorland," and his skeleton had already been taken from an existing piece in the workshop. Two of the horror masks were also repurposed for the episode. "A Shocker on Shock Street" effectively became a showcase for the crew's work, with the Haunted Masks, creeps and scarecrows making appearances in a very meta scenario. "We were even repurposing within the bounds of the show itself," Stefaniuk says. This would be another core principle of his work.

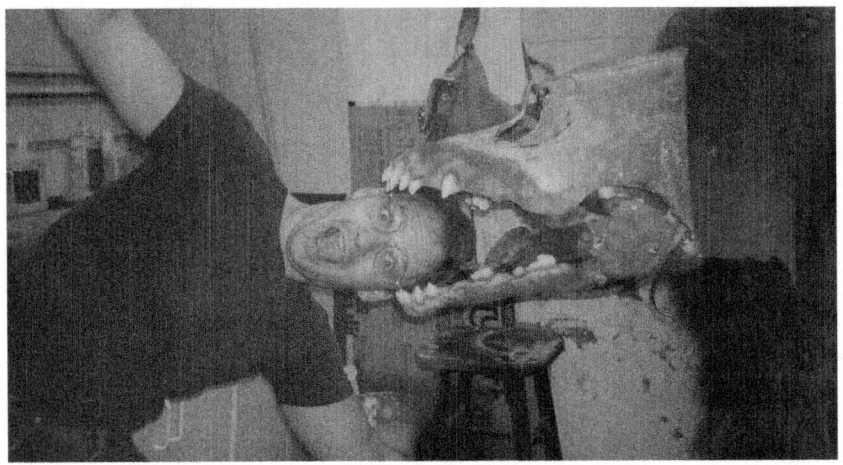

Matthew DeWilde in the early hours of the morning, with his head in Saber's jaws. Photo courtesy of Matthew DeWilde.

"I'm sort of a world class scavenger," he says of himself. "So that exact thing became the template to what my business today is, which is a lot of what I create, I keep, and the ability to take the things that we've built and done and repurpose them. The ability to save money by not fabricating from scratch, that has always been a going concern on how I design. And because the practical realities of the situation of *Goosebumps* just kept reinforcing what I already felt, that all the stuff that we kept and stored in our collection of stuff, we were very good at reinventing, reusing, and then we're not even talking about just puppets, just raw material and objects." Sometimes it was a matter of "cannibalizing" existing pieces. Puppets would be taken apart to reuse the skull, or flayed to reuse the skin. Not only did this approach save money, but it saved time. It wasn't often that something was built completely from scratch.

Stefaniuk says that while his knack for repurposing items almost certainly came into play, it didn't have any direct correlation with which episodes were filmed. "It wasn't a case of, 'You have this puppet, and that could be repurposed into this story.' It was a case of, 'Here's the story, find or make something to fit it,'" he says. He always had to adapt to the show, not the other way around, but adaptability was one of his super powers. Like Ian Brock and his house of sets, Stefaniuk proudly recalls times that he produced almost entire sets out of junk reclaimed from scrap heaps. He is the eco-warrior the industry needs.

The sheer workload and fast pace at Stefaniuk FX Studio is difficult to do justice. They had a little time to get their bearings at the very beginning, but once the crew got into the flow of the show, they were in for four straight years of hard work. Every Thursday would be the day that they worked through the night, starting at 8am and turning up with wet paint at 6am on the Friday. They would then install their creations and spend fourteen hours operating them on set. They'd finally clock out at about 1am on the Saturday morning. To the average person, just staying awake for that long at all is an achievement. "I'm not talking about being awake for forty-one hours," Ron Stefaniuk says, "I'm talking being at peak operational ability, non-stop, for forty-one hours."

Such was the pressure on the SFX team that their work was barely completed by the time it reached the set. "I mean, the Haunted Mask I sculpted, I made that in a day," recounts Matthew DeWilde. "I remember we had the live cast of Kathryn Long's head. You did a live cast on her, and for a young actress she was fabulous. It's not a fun procedure to go through. Yeah, we did it really fast, and we got a pretty decent head cast. I mean, even the plaster was still warm. It hadn't even fully cured." Because of the nature of their work, and the fact that they had to be the ones to apply prosthetics and operate animatronics, the team put in more hours than most on the show. "So, we're very often the first people in the building, other than the grip setting up, and it takes us an hour and a half to get out of the building. The chances are that what we were doing the day before it came to set was staying up all night finishing it," Stefaniuk says. They were usually the first to arrive and the last to leave, and this on-set portion of the job only constituted a fraction of their actual workload. "One of the cruel things of the show is the creature department always got called in for a pre-call to put somebody in creature makeup," Stefaniuk explains, "so we get called two hours earlier to do a makeup." There was no respite for the team, and these long days and working nights soon started to add up.

Of the entire *Goosebumps* crew, the SFX team probably had the highest turnover rate. The hours were absolutely grueling, and for some it was just too much. Before leaving the show entirely, Matthew DeWilde got as far as "The Cuckoo Clock of Doom" and had no choice but to take a week off to recuperate. "I literally stayed in bed for three days, just to get my energy back," he says, "and I was young then, too." Ron was panicked at the prospect of Matthew never coming back, fears that DeWilde quickly assuaged. Of course, a week in *Goosebumps* land was considerable, and by the time he returned, "Welcome to Camp Nightmare" was already in production. "I worked there day and night, practically. I remember my wife at the time, she didn't see me for months. She used to come down on her bicycle and like, bring me dinner and stuff like that," he recalls. It was thanks to Mrs. DeWilde's frequent trips to set that Matthew's extensive photo albums exist, collections he was kind enough to contribute to this book.

The overtime arrangement for the effects crew is described by Stefaniuk as "limited," meaning that all the extra hours and late nights that they put in were because of deadlines and a love of the craft. To add a bit of spice to the hectic schedule, the team enjoyed coming up with unexpected little embellishments to their creations, something that would take everybody by pleasant surprise when they turned up on set with it. "When you get a laugh on set, when you get a reaction from the crew, when something goes really well, those are really fun, exciting moments. You know, the adrenaline carried us a long way," Stefaniuk recalls. In fact, there was always a sense of fun and creativity going on. Just as the set encouraged actors to try stuff out, the vibe extended to the effects team. Ron valued engaging with his team's ideas, and those moments when they hit on something that made him think, "That's gonna make for good television!"

Despite it all, the crew were a solid and very reliable bunch, and they never missed a deadline. In fact, screwups were remarkably few, but there were times when there was a mad panic to get something fixed or repaired, while the set crew agonizingly waited around, not able to do their jobs until SFX had done theirs. Although it was always a collaborative process, especially when they got to set, Stefaniuk was quite particular about drawing a line between his creature workshop and the rest of production design, wanting to keep his passion for creating monsters to himself. "I asked right off the jump, 'Oh, this is fun! Can we design monsters?'" says Ian Brock. "He said, 'No, please don't help me design them, because it's the only thing I get to do. My only job is designing the monsters!'" Brock respected this decision, and although somewhat disappointed not to have a hand in helping Stefaniuk bring his creations to life, was content to handle the rest of the production, which still offered a lot of fun and artistic outlet.

When it came to the design of the creatures and effects, the crew were largely left to their own devices. Although they had R.L. Stine's books for reference, Ron Stefaniuk was not content to just bring his words to life. He wanted to make sure his crew's work felt unique. "Ron just threw the books away. He wanted to make his own original designs for everything, and he wanted what I would come up with," says DeWilde. Brainstorming usually meant five or ten minutes mocking up a quick clay sculpture, getting the thumbs up from Stefaniuk, and going at it. It was a rarity for Ron to not like what his team turned out after his brief specification, and on the odd occasion that it did happen, it was more a case of miscommunication under the stresses of such limited time and resources. One such memorable case was when the crew needed to produce the summoner for "Return of the Mummy," which was meant to be a pocket-sized mummy arm. Wires got crossed, and the team rocked up to set with a full, life-sized arm. But, ever the resourceful bunch, they slapped together an appropriately proportioned replacement in a very short time, and production continued without a hitch.

Ron says that early on in the creative process, they would attend a sort of table read, during which every department would make notes on what the episode would require of them. He would discuss ideas with the director, offering suggestions about what they could achieve. "The decision-making process at the design level was very quick, and eventually, as we went along, everybody was so busy with what we were doing that a lot of times, the design meeting at the end of the week was always very fast. The approval process came more from a sculpture that was three-quarters done," he says. Although this was a high-pressured way of doing things, Stefaniuk actually preferred it. "There was also a certain freedom from not having a lot of time to decide that meant that things moved along very quickly," he says.

He found that sometimes a script would be very specific in its requirements, as was the case for Mr. Mortman's creature design, whereas others were more vague, and open to interpretation. Between the source material that translated to the script, and the director's own vision, it ended up being a "really nice hybrid of ideas," Stefaniuk says, with lots of scope for creativity. "They allowed us to present sometimes very weird ideas. They were really good about encouraging. I think they encouraged all departments, actually, to be very creative about how they went about doing things. I think that encouragement bred enthusiasm, and that enthusiasm shows up on camera."

The enthusiasm was what it was all about. As a kid, Ron Stefaniuk loved the theatricality of visual performance, whether on TV, stage or film, and many of his childhood favorites influenced his own art. He thinks his earliest inspiration was *H.R. Pufnstuf*, the delightfully batty kids' show starring *Oliver!*'s Jack Wild, by Sid and Marty Krofft, who had done *The Banana Splits*. From there it gave way to the Disney epics of the '60s like *20,000 Leagues Under the Sea*, and the rides themselves at Disney parks. Young Ron was fascinated with how it all worked, and how it all entertained. In fact, the imaginative, family-friendly vibe of such influences is still what he prefers: "I'm not actually a huge fan of actual real horror and gore, which is good because *Goosebumps* is not a gory show. But I think our writers definitely had a sense of humor, the sense of humor that's in the books. I thought we were a nice counterpoint to that. The fact is, I think we could find the humor in the puppets. You know the laundry monster? Not my favorite monster, but I thought it was funny, the upside-down underwear being the shape of the eyes and the socks for fingers."

As much as the monstrous side of things, Stefaniuk enjoyed the opportunity to have fun and get silly. Slappy was a real favorite of his, and given that the dummy was effectively an extension of the puppeteer himself, he could really let loose through this snarky little vessel. "I think Slappy is a great puppet," he says. "The ability to be the guy on the day that's making the performance and puppeteering them and keeping them alive, and then figuring how we're gonna rig them and how we're gonna get a guitar over his head, and how we're gonna get him hanging from a building. You know, all these elements." Randy Bradshaw, too, was bowled over by the dummies the crew came up with. "The dummy freaked me out!" he recalls. "It works so well, right? I almost found myself wanting to give it direction!"

Ron's enthusiasm extended to embodying his own creations at times. He enjoyed bringing life to the creature suits he designed, and considered them a highlight of his work on the show. "They're what I really gravitate toward, what I like to build. That hybrid between puppet, rubber and prosthetic." The swamp monster from "How to Kill a Monster" is a firm favorite of his, alongside Saber. Because he knew what it was like to be on the inside, Ron always did his best to ensure the comfort of the actors who would wear his creations. He recalls talking Bryan Renfro through the various features of his werewolf costume, like Q introducing 007 to a new gadget, and did his best to make them as comfortable as was possible, although even their best efforts usually didn't make the costumed performances much more bearable.

The crew often considered their creations a great source of pride, particularly given the blood, sweat and tears that went into making them. Both Ron Stefaniuk and Matthew DeWilde are united in their love for a particular practical effect they pulled off for "The Haunted Mask." In the scene, Carly Beth puts the mask on in front of the mirror just before she heads out for the night, and it seems to sink into her face, emphasizing this as the moment that she and the mask become one. "We put air bladders, really narrow air bladders in the forehead and cheeks and throat," Stefaniuk explains, "and we had those squeeze bottles that suck the air out of it. Real simple, low-tech, but I think to great effect."

"It looked like it became part of her, and that really impressed me," DeWilde enthuses. "Really good, and that was all Ron. That's something he wanted to see happen, live in-camera. I remember at the time, we were in the makeup trailer, and I thought, 'I'm not going to put balloons on her head!' It was totally worth it. So I'm glad he made me do that." Although Stefaniuk was thrilled with the results, he is quick to point out that he can't take all the credit. "The look in her eyes is why that works really well. You can see the horror in her eyes," he says, giving well-deserved attention to Kathryn

Long's performance. Similarly, the pig mask in "Squeal of Fortune" is another favorite, but he insists it's Caterina Scorsone's acting that pulls it all together. "That girl looks so horror-stricken, and was hysterical. Her portrayal of being a hysterical kid that didn't know what had happened to her. It made my skin crawl!" Ron says. Once again, the *Goosebumps* crew show their decency by acknowledging the collaborative nature of their work. "The two actresses in those masks, the expressions they were making came through, and they really sold it," he says proudly.

But it's not just the wearable creations that he still looks back on fondly. "The shrunken head, I think, is a marvel, because it has seven points of motion on it, and the head is smaller than my fist!" he explains. "The brows go, the eyes blink, the eyes look left and right, and the mouth not only opens, but it chews, it goes side to side and opens, all in something that you can hang from your hand like that. And I'm really proud of that. I think for our experience level, that's an accomplishment. And then the simplest, stupidest thing I still think is the best is the evil potato. I probably had that in our monster display for fifteen years, until it rotted away." He delighted in showing off said evil potato and waiting for the dumbfounded response, only to start pushing buttons and pulling levers to show off everything it was capable of. People on the receiving end of this demonstration were often quick to admit that it was pretty cool—for a potato.

As fun and creative as all this was, it was mostly just another day at the office for DeWilde, who didn't consider what he was doing particularly groundbreaking or challenging. "For me it was standard, because I was kind of doing the same work as they do on every other show," he says. "I mean, occasionally it got challenging, like when it came to animatronics or things like that. Most of what I was working with was mainly like the prosthetic end of things. I've been doing prosthetics since I was fifteen or something like. So I kind of understood the process… I never went to school for it. I was just self-taught." Evidently, DeWilde was another graduate of the "throw me in at the deep end" school of thought.

Although it didn't feel like particularly difficult work on a skill level for DeWilde, there were so many factors that could complicate matters or cause a creation to turn out not quite as he had imagined. Despite being arguably the most iconic image of the entire series, he was not pleased with the end result of the Haunted Mask. "I never liked the Haunted Mask," he says, explaining that it was such a collaborative effort that there were elements he ended up hating about it. He wanted to do the teeth as dentures rather than as part of the mask itself, but describes it ending up a slapdash effort achieved with teeth found in a drawer, a pair of pantyhose and a hair dryer. "I wanted it to be more alive in that sense," he says. "But I think that got vetoed. I think it was a time thing, because there was a lot in the episode." At least he was pleased with one of the background heads that he sculpted. He also takes the opportunity to correct a common misconception regarding the color of the mask. "Ron didn't want the mask to be green. Every time I see people that make copies of the Haunted Mask it's always painted green. They were all like a pale flesh tone, with purples and blacks and maroon." So there.

As with any creative project with a deadline, he also feels like some of their creations were on their way to being great, but could really have used more time to live up to their potential. "I think Saber could have been better, but I mean, I wanted to sculpt Saber. I wanted to make a different head, but because of the time frame, it wasn't that good. It tore a lot. I had to do a lot of work on that, and it took me actually longer to fix the thing. I could have made a new one from scratch." Any creative, particularly one whose art constitutes their living, can empathize with this stance. There was sometimes a feeling of too many cooks, and with time and money always perilously scarce, they had to work with what they had. It's no surprise that some works didn't come out exactly how their creators had hoped.

Besides projects not living up to expectations, the crew had more pressing concerns on the job, namely their physical safety. Special effects of this sort—the kind that don't involve stunts or pyrotechnics—may not strike the layman as the most dangerous of fields, but, particularly back in the '90s, there were a number of occupational hazards. "We were using a really toxic polyurethane to fill up the suits. Ron's shop was not a safe place to work, because there was no fume hood," DeWilde explains. He describes Stefaniuk's studio as having a big set of double doors that opened onto a courtyard where they would store things or let them air-dry, and this was the best they had when it came to ventilation. Given that they were working with a number of toxic substances, this was far from an ideal setup. "All the fiberglassing was done inside the shop, so we were trying to sculpt on one end and paint on the other, and then we were making this big, giant, horrendously toxic fiberglass mold on a big creature," he explains. Unfortunately, whether or not anybody realized how dangerous all this exposure was, it was something of an industry standard at the time. "There's friends of mine that started with the same materials back in those days, and they can't work around these materials anymore. They have kidney trouble now or physical problems. They burned through their lungs," DeWilde says.

With all this in mind—the exposure to dangerous substances, the physically and mentally demanding work, the schedule that seemed to forget that sleep was a basic human requirement—it is to be expected that it was a lifestyle that caused burnout, and by the end of Season One, Matthew DeWilde was done. His official reason was that he had already signed onto a film project, but the unrelenting pace of the show was also a factor. "I stayed as long as I possibly could for Ron, because Ron was desperate to keep me there for that time, and then I finally had to leave and had friends replace me," he explains. Around this time, DeWilde established his own company, which as any business owner knows, is one hell of an undertaking.

"I had a lot more fun on the show than I had starting my company!" he says. He feels glad to have been there at the show's peak, citing a slashing of the budget in later seasons that would have made his job all the more difficult.

It seems that starting his own company would benefit DeWilde, as it certainly did for Stefaniuk. Professional creativity can be a funny thing when it comes to deciding exactly who owns the intellectual property rights of a piece of work, and often, it is not the person who designed or created it. Matthew DeWilde explains that in the industry, all the IP rights for original designs are generally retained by the production company. "Ron retained all the intellectual rights to all the creatures in the show, and they're all original designs," he explains, "but he hired me to be the creative artist kind of thing." On account of this pretty sweet deal that Ron Stefaniuk had negotiated for himself, he kept the physical masks and puppets, which he would go on to display in his own little monster museum (some of *Goosebumps'* most iconic faces are behind him as he talks to me). For this reason, DeWilde speculates, Ron was particularly invested in making sure everything stayed in as good a condition as possible. However, they haven't stayed that way. "Latex just goes bad. It goes rotten. But if you painted it properly and stored it properly, they'd last decades, really," DeWilde explains. At one point, Matthew was asked to verify a Haunted Mask (probably the one gifted to Steve Levitan years earlier) and while it was genuine, it was in terrible condition, and had been painted green! DeWilde, for his part, kept nothing from the show. At least deliberately. In a makeup box he had in storage, he recently found a pair of fangs worn by Mrs. Dark in "The Girl Who Cried Monster," something he'd long forgotten having in his possession. A fan ended up buying them off him.

While he retained the IP and physical creations, Ron Stefaniuk is eager to express his appreciation for his entire team, and decry the fact that they were not formally credited for their work, as is the industry standard. He says that in almost every other department in film and television, people are named and credited individually on every production they are a part of, whether they're doing payroll, craft services or driving. "But there's nothing that says that they're obligated to say more than, 'This is the shop that built [the special effects].' I find our department has always gotten the short end of the stick in accreditation."

Although Ron Stefaniuk's impressive portfolio has expanded tremendously over the decades, *Goosebumps* remains his most identifiable work, and he still gets a lot of appreciation for it. Matthew DeWilde has also done incredibly well for himself, branching out into more of the gory stuff that Stefaniuk was never a fan of. DeWilde says he learned a lot from *Goosebumps* and from Ron—and taught him a few things too—and it's stuff he brought with him into his later work. "I remember doing these other shows after *Goosebumps*, thinking like, *I wonder how Ron would approach this?* I could thank my *Goosebumps* training from Ron on that. So that's where that collaborative effort helped me in the future. And I hope Ron learned a lot of my techniques." DeWilde's only regret is that he didn't hang around. "I wish I'd actually done more than just the first season," he says.

He considers himself a lucky guy: "I love it. I mean, I'll never retire. I'm just going to keep working and working. I'm not obsessive about it, but it's almost like I have to build something every day to make me happy. If I'm not on a set, or if I'm not in a shop, I don't know what to do with myself." He even taught his daughter the craft, and although she works in an entirely different industry, she has helped on a lot of his projects over the years. He loves to spread the joy of his profession.

As of 2025, DeWilde and Stefaniuk both work on the hit show *The Boys*, albeit in fairly separate capacities: "He's doing mechanical effects, and I'm doing the prosthetic end of things," says DeWilde. Their hard work, enthusiasm and creativity are fondly remembered by their colleagues on *Goosebumps*. "[Ron]'s always really great to work with," says Randy Bradshaw. "Always full of ideas. Very creative guy. Ron was also a guy who would put in a lot of hours. He was fully engaged in the show." Meanwhile, the other Ron on the scene praises the work of the effects team. "I'm kind of glad that these shows back then were practical effects," says Ron Oliver. "To use CGI for stuff now, the experience is cheapened somewhat. Depressing, frankly. I did not get into the movie business to stand in a warehouse covered in green screen."

On the day of our meeting, Ron Stefaniuk hasn't slept, and the dog keeps scratching at his door. In this time alone, he demonstrates that immense mental clarity he maintains, despite external factors trying to pull it away from him. "We used to work long hours, and that wasn't a problem," he says. "Now, when I work long hours combined with being older, that's a bad combination. Your brain stops working. It didn't used to. We used to just power through." Back in 1995, when everyone was young, lively and their shins and lungs weren't shot to shit from years of hard work, the gang made a promise. "Me and the people we brought with us collectively did what I promised Bill Siegler, which was we would give it all we had," Ron says. Boy, did they deliver.

"The World's Biggest Train Set!"

Life On Set

The running order of the *Goosebumps* set was a twist on your traditional working life. Production ran Monday to Friday, occasionally including weekends and nights, but largely sticking to a standard format to accommodate the young actors. Mornings may have been early, and nights may have been late, but it was only ever an eight-hour day for its young stars. "The clock actually started when they hit the studio," explains director Randy Bradshaw. He recalls the young actors' parents being very involved on set, and keeping a close eye on their children, but the strict labor laws were something the crew was very cognizant of, and did their best to uphold. This was most certainly not the case for everybody else, who would end up working all hours of the day and night to get an episode finished.

The format was that shooting for an episode would begin Monday morning and wrap Friday evening, unless they were working on a two-parter, which tended to secure them a few extra days. Meanwhile, behind the scenes, the crew would be busy preparing next week's episode. On set, Monday meant the start of shooting a new episode, whereas in the offices, it meant the start of prep on the episode that would follow. After the show's first season, the network's renewal notice would arrive in February or March, and production would run from June to October or November, depending on the order size. This gave the crew an average of three months between receiving the season's order and arriving on set, during which time they would get to casting, writing and organizing schedules. If they had an order for twenty-two episodes, it effectively meant twenty-two weeks of production, and they could figure out from there how long a season would take to complete. There was a continual, rolling basis to shooting a season. "It could be very creative and intense," says cinematographer Brian R. R. Hebb. "I would put everything into my work and would go home exhausted. My profession was never just another job. I always put 100% into the art and craft because I enjoyed it so much."

The crew of *Goosebumps* worked hard to not only turn out a great show, but to make the set a friendly, encouraging and enjoyable place to be. "It was just a pleasant, pleasant, pleasant atmosphere to create in," says director Don McCutcheon. "What do they say? Animals and kids!" Despite the old adage of not working with children or animals, which *Goosebumps* did consistently, there was not a trace of the adults looking down upon, or feeling the need to contain or wrangle, their child actors. "I loved getting to hang out with all the crew," says actor Beki Lantos. "It felt like I was with my people, as silly as that sounds, since I was a kid and they were all adults." For a big-time show with a lot of people counting on it, the *Goosebumps* set was blessedly void of those standard industry horror stories of divas, predators and hard-nosed producers. That familial feeling of the *Goosebumps* set was widespread. "I enjoyed the people, the crew, the editors, the cast," says Brian R. R. Hebb. "They all became family for a while. It was all very colourful."

It was also a great opportunity for many of the newbies to get a soft-launch into filmmaking in a safe, encouraging environment. "I loved learning about all of the different roles and responsibilities it took to make a project — the director, the director of photography, the continuity person, make-up, grip, lighting, sound, sets, costumes, crafts people, line producers. There were just so many people and I thought they were all fantastic and fascinating," Lantos recalls. Director Craig Pryce recalls a story from the set of "Calling All Creeps," in which a young actor got a crash course in the basics of production. He was shooting a closeup of one of the kid actors in conversation, and while rolling, heard the voice of a girl saying,

"Excuse me." A young actress was confused as to why she was delivering lines without the camera being on her. "She goes, 'I'm talking but the camera's not on me.' She was so sweet! So, I said, 'Well, just so you know, we're gonna film him, but when he's done, we're gonna put the camera on you and you get to say your lines. So, you both have your lines, but then we cut it together, so we can go back and forth.' And she goes, 'Oh! Oh, OK!'" Pryce chuckles. The adults on set were always happy to explain these things, and the kids felt nurtured by a crew who didn't seem annoyed by their presence or lack of industry experience.

The administrative side of the show largely tended to be a similarly convivial affair. Production manager Ian Brock describes the whole Scholastic-Protocol system as "the best company. They were really generous. It was like a family-run business, in a way." Although executive producer Deborah Forte was mostly an in-name-only sort of entity, there was a feeling of accessibility to the higher-ups, thanks to the likes of Steve Levitan, Bill Siegler and Martha Atwater. Forte would make occasional visits to the set to make sure everything was going smoothly and that the *Goosebumps* brand was being upheld. It was largely down to Siegler and Atwater to act in Scholastic's interest in her absence, a pairing Steve Levitan describes as "family. They were just a dream, and you know, it was kind of like father and daughter. They were very close, and Martha was kind of like his surrogate daughter while he was up here, but they worked together so well."

He says there were two key pairs of people who made *Goosebumps* what it was: Dan Angel and Billy Brown, and Bill Siegler and Martha Atwater. "Martha was really great at production, one of the best I've ever worked with, and Bill was everybody's grandfather. Billy was the dark side of *Goosebumps*, Bill was like the family side, and Dan Angel was the funny side." For his part, Steve Levitan prided himself on being a creative producer. "Producers should be storytellers!" he insists. "A lot of them aren't, they're incredibly boring people who just get the money together. If you're not driven by telling stories, you shouldn't be a producer."

"Bill Siegler was [Deborah's] eyes and ears and brain on the show," says Levitan. Although she wasn't often actually on set, her presence was felt. One story from the crew involves Deborah Forte showing up for a production meeting, having asked a driver what he thought of the show, only for her to relay his criticisms back to the team. This led the crew to assign her a particular driver who was given a script to follow, only saying good things to minimize the kickback they would receive when she did show up. Apparently, that worked.

It was a crazy, fast-paced environment that never allowed a moment's rest for the hard-working crew. "They all sort of blend together like this one crazy pastiche! It was like a haiku!" says Ian Brock. For Siegler, *Goosebumps* was a welcome reprieve in its fast pacing. Through Scholastic, he also worked on animated series, and found the painstaking timeframe of it unbearable. Composer Jack Lenz says Siegler would sometimes joke that Deborah Forte was just trying to kill an old Jew by roping him into such a time-consuming medium as animation, so getting through an entire episode of television in a week was exactly what he needed. Siegler also found valued camaraderie with line producer Patrick Doyle. "[Patrick] was a great guy. He and Bill Siegler really hit it off," Steve Levitan says. "They had creative struggles, but I think they had a real mutual respect. I think you can see it on screen, they all really had fun and felt they were in the same boat rowing in the same direction."

Ever the champion of his franchise, R.L. Stine would frequently fly in from New York to make visits to set, not to meddle or consult creatively, but simply to show his support. "R.L. Stine showed up all the time, once every five or six weeks," says Ian Brock. The cast and crew loved having Stine there, and quickly established their own little tradition in his honor. "So, we all dressed in black that day, and he'd sign books for people, to the kids and stuff. So, he'd do his spiel, and then he'd leave, and he'd be gone by noon." Some of the hour-long episodes received the special Stine treatment, with the author filming intros and outros that actor Corey Sevier aptly describes as Hitchcockian. On these days, Stine would be more actively involved in the inner workings of production. He'd learn his lines, give his own performances, pose for photoshoots with the young actors and really get into the thick of it. Actor Judah Katz recalls a copy of the script being passed around the cast and crew to sign, for Stine to take away as a souvenir. For Sevier, the best part of the whole experience was getting to meet R.L. Stine. "We knew there was one day on the schedule where he was coming, so a lot of anticipation is building. 'Oh, R.L.'s coming to set,' and on that day I arrive on set, and everyone on the crew is wearing all black!" Effects master Ron Stefaniuk recalls Stine appearing very happy with how his books were being created in the physical world: "He seemed very pleased by the stuff that had been created, and the scope of the show. I think he was happy to see that." Everybody has nothing but kind things to say about these special days when Stine would be in attendance. It was Stine's wife Jane whose involvement got everybody's backs up. "His wife was hard to make happy, but she was his agent and manager. She was very tough," says Steve Levitan.

Although it would be one of the first ports of call when it came to the show making its initial impact, the credits sequence was among the last things done in Season One's production. "It came together late," explains Steve Levitan. "You don't design the opening sequence until you have a bunch of shows." Steve is very particular about opening sequences. Despite the epic music, he thinks the opening sequence for *Game of Thrones* looks "horrible", and doesn't compliment or live up to the standard of the show itself. *Goosebumps* had a number of episodes in the can before they even thought about the opening credits sequence, which explains the montage of shots from those early episodes that made the final cut. "You don't wanna start cutting stuff together until you've seen what the show actually is, cos it's never exactly the way you conceive of it," explains Levitan. Having had a few months to get the feel of the show and establish its tone, it came up one day that they should probably get going on the title sequence. "I think it just got slapped together, and whoever the director was that had a free few minutes at the end of an ordinary shoot of an ordinary episode, we just put together a shot list and asked him," Levitan says. "I think it was Bill Fruet." Steve Levitan doesn't consider the opening overly ambitious, but fitting to the show and "conceptually obvious". They were so consumed with the many challenges of getting the show itself made that the opening sequence was more of a "tacked on" element than one that had lots of careful planning and storyboarding put into it. "By the time you get around to it, there isn't much left in the budget for anything special," says Levitan. "I guess we had it in enough time so that Jack could write that theme music to those shots."

By this point, Patrick Doyle had established a firm reputation as a jovial and resourceful person. Steve Levitan laughs when asked what exactly line production entails, calling it a fantastic question. It is striking that nobody ever thinks to ask him about what the duties of a particular job title involve, and he is always happy to break it down. Somewhere between producer and production manager, Doyle's job was to handle production quality, budget and all the other bits that lie somewhere between creative and administrative. He'd worked with Steve prior to *Goosebumps*, so they already knew exactly what to expect from each other. "His name was Doyle, so he had a great sense of humor!" Levitan chuckles. "He was a great people person, and he was also a pilot. When we designed that opening sequence with the green letters and the music and everything, we couldn't get R.L. Stine personally to come in. So, Patrick said, 'Well, it's just a shot from behind, I'll put on the overcoat and hat and I'll be R.L. Stine!' And he would make decisions like that because it wouldn't cost us any extra money, which he was very, very proud of." With that, Patrick Doyle became Stine for a day, saving time, money and a plane journey on R.L.'s part.

At first, Steve Levitan threw himself into the production side of things as much as the pre- and post-. "I would show up for production meetings on a Friday, before Monday morning's start of shooting, to make sure all the team was organized and had what they needed. And I would go to the set almost every day. But I would never tell anybody when I was coming, and I would never tell them when I was leaving." He would usually visit during lunch breaks to prevent slowing things down, but the more he did so, the more he realized he was causing unnecessary distraction. This 'Jesus is coming, look busy' sort of effect caused the crew to second-guess themselves and stop what they were doing to ask Steve's opinion on creative choices. Having put together a crew that had his complete faith, he felt this was all unwarranted, and didn't want to pull everybody's attention away from the solid job they were already doing. To this end, Bill Siegler was the one to oversee everything. "I trusted him like a brother with all this stuff. There was no need for me to get that heavily involved at those stages," Levitan explains. "I just let the team do what they needed to do, and got out of the way. They were extremely respectful of the time and the budget and the resources we had to work with. It was never a problem."

No two days on *Goosebumps* looked alike. The variety of Stine's stories and the anthology format ensured that every day offered something new. "It was a great crew," says Craig Pryce. "They knew the machine, but they had challenges, because with anthology, you can't just go back to the standing sets. It's like doing a mini movie. There's no pattern to follow, there's no sets to run into." Monday could be a studio-based day, shooting scenes in a house set, while Tuesday meant shipping everybody off to a corner of Sunnybrook Park that had been decked out to look like a jungle, while large animatronic monsters chased them. Some episodes were totally suburban and required little in terms of stunts and special effects, while others required whole historic buildings to be shut down for production, before being sent away to Brock Jolliffe to work his post-effects magic on. But what every day did have in common was an atmosphere of fun, creativity and passion.

For the crew, half the fun was being presented with a new challenge each week, and a new director through whose lens they would focus it. "I would be working with a series of directors who would come and go," says Brian R. R. Hebb, "and even though they each brought their own sensibilities, it was up to me to set a look, a style and an atmosphere that became the show. I would light the sets and the actors, and be looking through the camera all the time to compose the shots and set the scene." Everybody involved was happy to just get stuck in and enjoy themselves in a way that wasn't always possible in the entertainment industry. "I just took to the show, and got along with everybody," Randy Bradshaw remembers. "I loved the kids. They were fun to work with, and they were also very good about being open to suggestions from directors. It was always a good feeling when you thought you could contribute." Director Stefan Scaini agrees: "It was a great show. The cast was lovely. You just had this kind of family, and everybody was very respectful. And the producers, they were all great."

Director Ron Oliver was always especially adept at making the set a fun place to be. "He was so good with kids," recalls Corey Sevier. "Just the kind of guy where you know, he played music on set, constantly joking, but also wonderful at getting the best out of his actors, because he was so personable." Oliver takes pride in nurturing an atmosphere of enjoyment on his sets: "I always dress nice, and I bring my own music to play on set." His early experience on the *Prom Night* sequels allowed him to gain a lot of wisdom from industry professionals, particularly producer Peter Simpson, who instilled in him some solid directorial values: "He always said to me, 'If the director doesn't bring 50% more to the screenplay, then he's the wrong director,' and I've kept that in my heart always, that it's the energy of the set. Try to make everyone feel like their contributions are welcome. I always tell [actors] the same thing, which is, 'You guys jump as high as you can, because I'll be here to catch you.'" Don McCutcheon concurs: "My recollection is of a very harmonious, very collaborative environment."

Randy Bradshaw would pull what strings he could to make the more grueling aspects of life on set easier, particularly for its young actors. If he could swing it for production to begin at 8am instead of 6am, he would do so, bearing in mind that kids needed their sleep, and the excitement of working on a show like *Goosebumps* might inhibit proper rest. For the kids, it was almost always like a week's paid vacation, full of excitement, intrigue and special treatment. "The kids have their own trailers and they're working a couple of hours a day, and they're treated like little gods!" says Ron Oliver. "There's tables full of snacks, so it's not like it was hard labor or anything."

All this effort on the part of the adults really paid off for the kids. "I've seen some absolutely horrific examples of what not to do on set," says actor Melody Johnson of her decades-long career, but *Goosebumps* proved to be not only a friendly and laid-back experience, but a very enriching one, thanks to her director and co-stars. Of director René Bonnière, she says, "He was just so patient, and he really made you feel like you were in a safe space." She felt the entire crew made the set a great place to be, more so than a number of other productions she had worked on. "There's just some sets that just flow and that they're like a big family, and they take care of the people. That was definitely one of those kinds of sets." For the more experienced people on set, the show was a welcome reprieve from some of the behavior they had previously witnessed in the industry. "The crew that you meet, they're just all happy and it's camaraderie, and you all work together to make this one scene. It's really cool," says stuntman Bryan Renfro. As someone with a bounty of film set experience, Renfro has met his fair share of tyrannical directors and acting divas. "And then you go to something like *Goosebumps*, where everybody's happy and everybody's fun and having a good time, and they're not taking it so seriously. It's like, 'Hey, come on, let's make a movie!'" This particular set was the entertainment industry's equivalent of an oasis in a desert.

Actor Bill Turnbull describes the set as "professional and pretty efficient," but not immune from the industry standard of "hurry up and wait." He says the usual approach was, "They set up roughly, sort of what they want, and then you run through it, and then you have to go away while they set up the lights, and then you come back and you do it again." Amos Crawley also remembers the spurts of tedium between all the excitement: "The thing that you do most of all on any set is you sit around a lot. Sort of an extension of recess. It's like a long, boring recess!" Despite the undeniably dull waiting times that no set is without, Corey Sevier recalls how well the young actors were taken care of. "They're intense days, the kids are in everything, but we're in such good hands," he says. "The team on *Goosebumps* from both my two experiences were incredible. Just so, you know, accommodating to working with young performers. Looking back on it as an adult, and having directed some of my own films, it's a big production to put on in a very short period of time. So I can only imagine how hard they worked to make all this stuff happen. As a kid, you show up on set, and it's all set up, and you know it's kind of your playset." The kids all had such fun being a part of *Goosebumps*, and "everyone, all my friends that were on the show, it's the same thing." The child actor consensus certainly seems to be that there was no greater set than that of *Goosebumps*.

Although Amos Crawley has a very balanced view of life as a child actor, he has incredibly fond memories of working on the show. "Why wouldn't you want to run around in a graveyard at night with fog machines going? I guess that's the defining thing of being a child actor, right? It's kind of like, for all the negative aspects of it, and I believe that there are a lot of negative aspects to it, imagine the games that you played in your backyard as a kid, but with a budget." Among all the play, he recalls the intense but fleeting nature of set friendships that always went with the turf: "One of the interesting things about this industry is you become very, very close with people in a very, very truncated and short amount of time. And they're like your best friends for a week." Although some made lifelong friends on the show, it was common, as it is in more pedestrian working lives, for actors to pretty much go their separate ways once filming wrapped. It was nothing personal, but a symptom of the transient life of an actor.

It wasn't just the kids having a blast in the world of *Goosebumps*. Actor Afrah Gouda describes the set as "very nice, very friendly," and a place where you didn't have to worry about the odd flubbed line, or feel any pressure. "All of them were really very kind. It was a lot of fun to be there, and everybody was very nice. I really enjoyed working with all of them." Veteran actor Judah Katz was well-versed in what made a good set, and *Goosebumps* really fit the bill. "It was an exciting place, and they were so nice. Everybody was very, very, very nice," he says. "We were treated very well. The budget was nothing, right? We all got paid scale. Nobody got rich off of this, but we're doing something that was kind of fun," he fondly recalls. From actor Peter Keleghan's perspective, *Goosebumps* was a great show to work on: fun, laidback, and well-stocked. "I think it was pretty well-paid. Canadian productions tend to pay a little bit less [than American productions] because our broadcast system and our distribution is not what the American system is. *Goosebumps* was a well-heeled production. They had a fairly decent set and they treated actors well." Despite the never-ending workload, the fun of it all is SFX artist Matthew DeWilde's most prominent memory of the show. "We laughed a lot. We used to get so exhausted, we just couldn't stop laughing all the time," he remembers.

Balancing work with schooling made for a really unorthodox arrangement for the kid actors, but it was all part of the fun. "You're doing this scene where your heart is pounding out of your chest, then you'd race down the hall and have this little room where you're working with your tutor. And you know, you do a couple of math questions. 'OK, they're ready for you on set.' And then you race back," Corey Sevier recalls. But the young actors' work wasn't necessarily confined to the set, and in some cases, they'd be brought back in for voice work. "We did ADR because, as always, when you're doing stuff where there's smoke machines and visual effects and animatronics, they make a lot of noise. So you have to redo a lot of the sound," says Sevier. In Amos Crawley's case, he was called in at the last minute to do some dubbing work on an episode that he didn't even act in.

Many cast and crew members recall how well they were provided for on set, with the craft services offering some of the best set food they've ever had. "Twenty years on, I still remember the catering being awesome!" says actor Tod Fennell. Randy Bradshaw agrees: "There was an excellent caterer on the show, too. So, lunch was very good. It was always fun having lunch with the kids. Hot dogs for dinner, lots of ice cream!" For Ian Brock, it was quite luxurious compared to what he was used to on other jobs. "On set, they cook us lunch, and we always have lots of picnics, and if we're going out on the road, we barbecue," he says. "If you're going out the road, they hire the caterers to come out! Because normally, we just run and grab something at a restaurant. So it'd be fun. You don't know how good it got until you don't have it anymore. It was a one-off kind of thing. Not a lot of other shows have been that happy. They were really, really good people, but recently [the industry] has gotten a lot less happy." In many ways, this is something the majority of the cast and crew agree with. Times have changed, the business behind making movies has become more cynical, and the pressure is higher than ever. *Goosebumps* struck the perfect balance of work and play.

Of course, everybody still had a job to do, and there were times when they encountered hiccups, but these never derailed production or made a dent in the positive atmosphere the crew had so lovingly cultivated. It was more an attitude of knowing how to fix things. "It was a great show to work on, because everybody was more than willing to put in the effort," says Randy Bradshaw. Having tackled an early speed-bump with child actors on the set of "The Girl Who Cried Monster," directors (particularly John Bell) quickly developed a sense for which parts of a take were usable, and so powered through shooting with a good idea of when they had got what they needed in the can. There was no Kubrick-style approach to retakes, and directors were always very mindful that they were working with young actors who were largely inexperienced. They rested easy in the knowledge that Bob Sprogis and the editing team, the unsung heroes of the show, would be able to piece together the parts that worked into a cohesive whole. "If there was magic in *Goosebumps*, it was Sprogis," says Steve Levitan. This alleviated much of the pressure on the set, allowing the crew to gently support their young cast and feel confident that it would always come together, one way or another.

As soon as the actors were done for the day, the production crews would be all hands on deck, painting, sawing and otherwise preparing the sets for whatever came next, and it was often an all-night thing. For Canadians, working at such a grueling pace from March to October meant they ended up severely lacking in serotonin. "Young people working on the show, like the twenty-five-year-olds, twenty-somethings that spent like literally seven or eight weeks, all summer, working at night, like the whole summer's gone," says Ian Brock. "And it's so precious here. You know, it's like literally winter for nine months of the year. You lose three of them to the dark, and [end up] just not having a life." It wasn't just Ron Stefaniuk's team that were running on youthful vigor. It was practically the life blood of the show.

With all the puppets, prosthetics, crazy sets and fantastical scenarios the show encompassed, it was a really exciting opportunity for its young actors to hang out with monsters, creep around haunted houses, run, jump and hide. Although the kids were eager to perform their own stunts, it wasn't always possible, and if stunts could be blocked to conceal the character's face and enable a stunt double to take over, they would do so. In the case of the child actors, their stunt doubles were usually short adults, and sometimes diminutive men in wigs stood in for young girls. Not only did this cover safety concerns, but maximized what could be shot once the child actors had clocked out for the day. All the same, it made for a much more exciting job for the kids than the average TV role in a classroom setting or as a secondary player to an adult lead.

"Safety's always first," says Don McCutcheon of stunt work. "There's people that know exactly how to do it and do it safely. You're in the hands of good special effects people and you work with them closely." In the case of "The Ghost Next Door," which required a house fire scene, fire bars were used and fire department professionals were just offscreen to ensure everything was conducted safely. "As a director, you relay what it is you're looking for, what the visual images are. But then you hand it over to the experts, right?" McCutcheon explains. "They're not gonna let you push and step over anything that's going to be harmful to anybody. They've done it before, they know how to do it. They know how to do it properly, and the special effects coordinator and the stunt coordinator work together to make sure that we get the shots."

The fun extended beyond the set, and every year, the season would culminate in a wrap party, in which cast and crew would come together and celebrate their work. Special *Goosebumps* gifts and merchandise were given out, lots of hugs were shared, and "embarrassing drunkenness" would ensue. "We made our own swag for *Goosebumps*, for the crew," Steve Levitan recalls. "We had hockey sweaters with the big *Goosebumps* logo on it, because we had a hockey team at one point. The crew led a hockey team!" Randy Bradshaw proudly displays his *Goosebumps* hockey jersey, remarking that he still wears it sometimes in the winter, and it's a real head-turner. "People say, 'Wow! Is that from *Goosebumps*? Where can I get one?'" he laughs.

The official Goosebumps hockey sweater. Photo courtesy of Bob Sprogis.

The congenial feeling among the group also extended beyond the sets, and crew would often get together for barbecues and other social gatherings. On one occasion, Billy Brown and Dan Angel visited the Levitan family on their farm outside of Toronto, and the pair went out into the fields to play baseball with Steve's collectible ball. It was batted out into the distance and never recovered. "So they owe me a baseball!" Levitan chuckles. The team would even go on vacation together. "We became a family on that show. We took Christmas vacations together," says Ron Oliver. "On one season, we all went to Mexico for two weeks. I mean, it was a real family atmosphere." He recalls being on one such trip, and taking a minute to really embrace the joy of it all. "I remember specifically when we first landed there, and we're having our drinks and talking about the place and thinking, 'This is a really great moment,' and being very proud of the people I work with. That was a big thing."

The *Goosebumps* family wasn't limited to the people on its payroll. Family and friends could frequently be found on set, and were sometimes given bit parts or positions as extras. Ian Brock's niece was in a theater scene in one episode, while Brian R. R. Hebb's wife appeared in "A Night in Terror Tower" and Don McCutcheon's daughter scooped ant food pellets in "Awesome Ants." Bob Sprogis' daughter is seen leaving the magic shop and getting on her bike at the beginning of "Bad Hare Day." When the editor was told the runtime of the episode was over and asked if he could shave a few seconds off the opening scene, he staunchly declined and found another scene that had some to spare. His daughter would never forgive him if he cut her big debut. Even if they didn't get a little job to do, it was very much a family affair, with people bringing their kids to set frequently, allowing them to hang around, explore and just enjoy being part of the movie-making magic.

Steve Levitan's kids "grew up on film sets" and had a whale of a time hanging out on *Goosebumps* turf, causing mischief and getting an array of treats from the craft services table. "They were young enough to have a lot of fun on a set, but too young to realize that's an unusual way of life," he says. Their dad's work had a fleeting impact on them. On one occasion, Levitan's youngest daughter left a note in his briefcase saying, 'Dad, don't you think it's time I got an agent?' As a lesson in the realities of the entertainment industry, he provided his daughter with a list of the best kid agents in town and told her to call them herself. She never did, and to this day works in a completely different industry. He can't say he's not glad.

Kids on the set, getting signatures from Bill Fruet.
Photo courtesy of Steve Levitan.

The phrase 'lightning in a bottle' isn't enough to do *Goosebumps* justice. Through design, and a certain amount of luck, the perfect combination of people was found, not only in terms of their skills but their attitudes towards filmmaking. Every building block came together in just the right way to create a cohesive, and very loving, whole. "The team that worked on the show, everybody from the directors to the writers, were great," says Matthew DeWilde. "Every department really did a great job. We wouldn't know what someone else was working on at all, we didn't know what the set was going to look like. But when we got on the set, it all just came together." For Ron Oliver, he lives every day on set in awe: "I have the best job, I have the world's biggest train set! I don't get people who complain and grumble about being on set. I love it!"

While magic was being made on the sets and in the production offices, Steve Levitan's work was never done. Throughout production, he would be busy going through new properties, handling marketing, talent acquisition and all the various legal stuff, and this required him to travel frequently. "Toronto's nice, but nothing happens in Toronto," he says. But no matter how busy he got, or how often he was called away to handle some other aspect of the show's production, he was never far from the heart of it, where an incredible team of people were doing amazing things. He is very proud of how it all came together, although he says he can only take so much credit. "We were lucky. It doesn't guarantee a good project, but if the spirit on the set is positive and happy, and everybody likes working together… If there's any skill that a producer has, it's in putting the right people together. It's being the best matchmaker. It's always a collaboration. So that's the secret. So just follow that formula, and you'll be successful too."

"One of the Key Under-Acknowledged Magical Elements of That Show"

Post-Production

With all the on-set fun in the can, it was time for the footage to make its way to the cutting room. Bob Sprogis and Peter Light had their editing suites next door to each other in the Molson building, mere feet from the sound stages, so far from being an isolated experience, working on *Goosebumps* was a very social environment, with their doors always open and welcoming to visitors. In fact, they were in such close proximity to the studio that people would periodically ask them to turn their volume down so it wouldn't get in the way of shooting. Sometimes the young actors would swing by and the team would show them the magic that went on in the editing suite, and whenever the guys needed a break from the minutiae of it all, they would wander out to the studio and just hang around and take it all in.

Bob Sprogis' reputation precedes him. "Bob Sprogis is not only a sweetheart as a person, but a completely under-recognised, brilliant, wonderful editor," says Steve Levitan. "He is one of the key under-acknowledged magical elements of that show. Editors don't get a lot of attention. Being on a set doesn't teach you anything, but looking at the dailies and the different shots that you have—and trying to figure out which ten seconds from which shot goes with which twenty seconds from the same scene, shot in a different way—and putting all of that together, it's an amazingly creative activity."

Indeed, the editing team was thrown in at the deep end with *Goosebumps*. The problems encountered on the first episode, "The Girl Who Cried Monster," were a great test of Bob Sprogis' skill and level-headedness. "[Deborah Forte] came into my edit suite after the first day, and she said, 'Bob, we're in trouble.' And I said, 'Just wait,'" Sprogis recalls. He knew that regardless of what was given to him, he could spin straw into gold. "That's what editing's for: take out all the lousy bits, put the good bits together, you know," he explains. It was proof, if ever it was needed, that the show was in very capable hands with Bob Sprogis around. And such a safety net was a necessity for a series that worked primarily with untrained child performers.

"When you're making shows with kids who are not trained actors, you really need an editor who can chop up the scenes that are heavy in dialogue and find ways that even an unprofessional delivery plays really well and doesn't throw you out of the moment when you're watching the film," Levitan explains. "And that's really hard, it's really a skill, and I've used [Sprogis] on almost every other show I've made. He's always my first choice." Indeed, Sprogis' Midas touch with kids' shows would later be the savior of another Protocol production, *Saddle Club*, which filmed in Australia and experienced its own issues working with kids and animals. *Goosebumps* would prove to be the perfect warm-up.

Far from the first-day jitters of "The Girl Who Cried Monster" being an indicator of struggles to come, Sprogis says that working with largely inexperienced child actors was one of the things he enjoyed most about the job. "One of the things I loved about *Goosebumps* was the kids, because a lot of them, it was either their first time or like, second, third," he says. "They were very new, so they were always keener. They knew their lines. They were very good. And you get to see them blossom." He says that the kids' willingness to stick to the script made his job much easier, and that the wider crew were a big help in making sure the material he got was easily workable. "The directors were very good, and the script supervisors were good to make sure we got the lines, and they said them how they were written. So [working with kids] really didn't make that much of a difference, as opposed to like sometimes, actually, adults are worse."

For at least the first two seasons, and probably most of the third, *Goosebumps* was shot on 16mm tape. While the quality of the picture itself got mixed reactions from Ian Brock and Matthew DeWilde due to how well it would, or would not, showcase the intricacies of their work, it presented different issues to the editing team. "16mm is a bit of a challenge, too," Sprogis explains, "because with 16-mil, you can get neg dirt, stuff like that. But we fix all that stuff, so that's just technical things." The final season was moved to a digital format, which Bob Sprogis says had very little impact on how he went about his work. Although he may have received the footage itself at a faster rate, the way he actually edited it remained unchanged. "It's all the same," he says. "We used Avid, which was a nonlinear editing system. And they said, 'Oh, it's nonlinear. Now you're going to be faster.' No, you weren't. It was because the speed of getting it is faster, but your editing process still takes whatever it takes. It doesn't matter if it's digital. 16-mil on tape or digital didn't matter."

Sprogis was working to a target of eight minutes of finished footage per day, and says that this goal was usually met, but where it wasn't, it would be made up for the next day. He worked Monday to Friday, doesn't recall ever working a weekend, and took the twelve-hour days in his stride, considering it just part and parcel of the job and the industry. "*Goosebumps* had a couple episodes where there was a lot of stuff happening. So, did I make it every day? No, but in the end, as long as you made it before the director came in, you were OK," he recalls. The overlapping nature of production extended into the editing suite, and particularly when he was still working with film that needed to be developed, he was just one part of a chain. Sprogis explains what his average working week looked like: "So here's the process: they shoot on the Monday, you get your stuff on the Tuesday because they have to transfer, they have to develop it, they have to do a small basic color correction on it before you get it. So then you edit your stuff, and then you're spilling into next week. And so they're already starting to shoot for the next guy in the other room. So that's how it goes. You sort of piggyback." Randy Bradshaw elaborates: "While you're shooting, the editor is doing what's called an assembly edit. So, it's just all the scenes, scene one, scene two, it's in story order. The work might not be accomplished while you're sitting there, but you talk through it, and there's notes from the producers and the network." Although the editors could largely work their magic in whatever way they saw fit, they would get feedback from various parties that would guide their approach and make sure every mark was being hit.

Directors always got the first cut of the episode, working with the editing team to assemble the edit they envisioned. According to Randy Bradshaw, this was written into the directors' contracts. "The producers were very respectful of the mandated process for directors being part of the contract," he says. Script supervisors were integral to the process, watching dailies and marking the shots that worked, or at least the parts of them that did. Some takes were perfect except for one small thing, necessitating the editing team slicing and dicing it in a way that kept the best and left the worst on the cutting room floor. Just as Ron Oliver is quick to mention the importance of his A.D.s, Bob Sprogis also sings the praises of his editing assistant, Renee Georgacopoulos, who would handle the logging and digitization of the footage and dubbing. Sprogis also liked to pass on as much of his knowledge as possible, and so enjoyed having assistants around to let them have a go at editing scenes for themselves.

Sprogis has a particular method of editing that has, at times, turned off potential clients, but that worked like a charm for *Goosebumps*. "I don't read the scripts, because I expect that when I get the stuff in my edit suite, those dailies should tell me what the story's about," he explains. "I would just do the scenes, and at the end, when I'm done with the scene, I'll read the script." He makes any necessary adjustments after reading the script. It may seem a laborious process, but there's method to the madness. "It makes me do it better, I think, trying to make the story, or what they shot, rather than trying to fit everything into the lines." He says that performance is really at the heart of everything he does, and that as long as a take gives the actor's best, any other minor detail, like camera shake or audio pop, can be dealt with. "Just paying attention to the footage and not worrying about what's in the script," is how he prefers to go about it. Most importantly, as he has shared with young up-and-comers in the industry, "There are no rules." He firmly believes in trusting your gut, and compares editing to music. "Editing is making music with pictures," he muses. "Sometimes it's rap, sometimes it's classical, sometimes it's country, sometimes it's rock. You gotta let your mind go to where it has to go. But gut, gut is one thing that I always do."

By Wednesday, Bob Sprogis and co. would have a rough edit of a few scenes that Steve Levitan would be called to look at, and here they would discuss any issues or suggestions. On Fridays, Steve might be involved in a production meeting for an episode shooting the following Monday, or in the editing suite looking at the current dailies. Once the final picture cut was finished and visuals were locked in, the footage was sent over to the sound department, where Jack Lenz got to work scoring it. The crew would discuss where they thought various musical cues should be inserted, running through ideas, and watching an episode two or three times over while discussing ideas. They would also handle any necessary ADR.

Post-production dubbing was a fairly routine factor in *Goosebumps*, particularly owing to the use of masks and puppets, as well as the high-octane nature of the show. On-set effects like animatronics and smoke machines got pretty noisy, and the amount of running and screaming involved meant that set audio wasn't always usable. So, the actors (sometimes those who'd filmed the episode, and sometimes others brought in just for additional voice work) would be brought into a sound studio nearby in Toronto, where they would watch the existing edits and sync their voices to the action. On one occasion, Amos Crawley got a call one day after school for an emergency voiceover session on an episode he hadn't actually acted in. One scene involved a kid handling a tube of toothpaste, at which point the young actor saw the opportunity to adlib, and throw out the "I hate mints!" line he'd used in both "The Haunted Mask" and its sequel. It went down a treat.

The fun of the set would also extend into the sound booth, and the crew would find creative little ways to screw with each other. "The mixing team would intentionally throw in some R-rated, wild lines in playback, just to see if I was awake or not," Steve Levitan recalls, citing an episode in which a young girl knocks on the door of a cabin, and the voice of a man is supposed to tell her to come in. "The wild line that they gave Patrick Doyle to say over that scene was unprintable. It got past me the first time!" Steve chuckles.

At this point in post-production, aside from trying to sneak cheeky lines of dialogue past Steve, a final mix session was conducted, with dialogue on one track and music on another, courtesy of a great team of mixers which included the likes of Allen Ormerod and Bryan Day. Jack Lenz describes the process as "like producing a record." Once all that was done, the crew could call it a day on this particular episode. "As you can imagine, they had to work fast," says Randy Bradshaw. "They were in first cut, second cut, final cut, getting in the final additions for visual effects. Making sure that they had something ready for the music spotting session, and on it goes, right? Those guys were quite busy." The episode would then be sent on to the broadcaster, who might occasionally send it back with further notes, but was usually happy with what they got.

Although Steve Levitan had set out at the very beginning to avoid post-production special effects wherever possible, there were instances that called for them. "I mean, some of it was just unavoidable," says Don McCutcheon. "We didn't have all the money in the world, and particularly back then in '97, '98, or whatever, the visual effects were far more expensive than they are now. We usually always approached that, 'What can we do? What can we accomplish on the set?' For Levitan, one of his most hated episodes, "Piano Lessons Can Be Murder," holds the title purely because he wasn't happy with how the post effects looked. Sure, they may look hokey now (they may have even looked hokey back in the day), but for the young audience, it was just the right level of believability to be terrifying.

The adults involved could see things a bit more clearly. "You know, by today's standards, when you look at some of the computer graphics, they show their age a little bit, but I think for the demographic at the time, the kids don't care!" says Don McCutcheon. Stefan Scaini agrees that the effects did exactly what they needed them to do. "The visual effects are dreadful, but [the viewers] don't care. For some reason, the innocence of that stuff and the simplicity of it kind of makes it more fun and, weirdly, adds to the creep factor." For those moments that needed help from outside the studio, the expertise of post-production effects wizard Brock Jolliffe was called upon.

Tod Fennell remembers the giant ant in "Deep Trouble" being "half real and half CG. They take a picture of an ant and make it bigger." Continuing the theme of ants, Mpho Koaho recalls the walls of the ice cream shop in "Awesome Ants" being draped with bright green strips, which would later have streams of crawling ants animated on top. For them, it was another fascinating aspect of filmmaking that they were learning on the job, so seeing the finished episode for the first time, having just been staring at a strip of green while on set, was a real thrill. If nothing else came of the effects, the kids who got to witness the magic thought it was a really cool process. It may have been expensive and less than what Levitan hoped for visually, but Jolliffe's contributions always bridged the gap efficiently, and given the time, budget and technological standards the show was working with, he met the brief to the best of his ability.

Talking to other crew members, Bob Sprogis is always brought up as a lovely guy who's great at what he does, and the feeling is mutual. He calls *Goosebumps* "one of the best crews you could ever want. Everybody was good. Everybody was friendly." For him, the feeling of being part of a family was there from the start, and this vibe continued throughout every Protocol project he worked on. "The funny thing was every show I worked on with Steve, it was like that. So, I guess Steve picked good people because that's how it went. Fun! We always had fun. Yeah, there were some serious times and stuff, but most of the time it was fun, you know, and that was half the battle when it's fun."

Let's Get This Show on the Road

Season One

Goosebumps was aiming to debut on Halloween of 1995, and so when it came to selecting the hero episode that would kick the show off, it was decided that an hour-long special would be dedicated to the most prominently Halloween-themed book of the series, "The Haunted Mask". This date and choice of episode was a strategic decision, Steve Levitan explains: "Two reasons, both having to do with Halloween. One: Halloween gives you a lot of production value, you have a lot of extras in scary costumes, which you wouldn't necessarily have in any other show. Two: a Halloween-themed show can be scarier."

While these elements made sure that *Goosebumps* could go off with a bang for its television debut, the thinking behind this decision went further than the short-term. "I guess there's three reasons," Levitan elaborates. "A Halloween show for home video release was the real driving force for the decision of "The Haunted Mask" being the first episode, we would have done it anyway, but we would have done it differently if there wasn't a video release. A video release for people to take home has to be longer than half an hour, that's not good value, so we designed it as a bigger show with more production value. The holiday season is a really good mechanism for having people tune in again. From an audience retention perspective, it gives them another kick at the can, it can get them to rediscover the show or tune in again." The first season of the show would focus quite heavily on the one-hour specials that could be released to VHS, and ten of its nineteen episodes would conform to the format. It was dividing its efforts quite neatly between single and double episodes to see what stuck, and it would later turn out that both were wildly popular, although the double-bills would ultimately go on to fan favorite status in later years.

With all this in mind, the crew were ready to go balls to the wall to make sure this hour-long special made the same impact as the *Goosebumps* books had. Everything was hanging on this first episode giving the now well-established fan base exactly what they wanted. If they screwed this up, it could all go down the pan. Thankfully, despite being the first episode to make it to air, and later to have a home media release, it was not the crew's first rodeo. Production on "The Haunted Mask" took place fairly early on in the grand scheme of things—within the first four episodes filmed, according to Ron Stefaniuk—somewhere in early summer of 1995. By this point, the crew had had time to bond, get to know each other and the show, and establish a rhythm, so they were in a strong position to make sure "The Haunted Mask" lived up to its potential.

The Haunted Masks ready for the blue screen.
Photo courtesy of Matthew DeWilde.

The episode was assigned to Timothy Bond, a well-versed director, particularly in the TV-movie and series sphere, with horror and sci-fi anthology credits to his name including *Alfred Hitchcock Presents*, *War of the Worlds* and *Friday the 13th: The Series*. His strength in this field evidently made him a great fit for introducing the world of *Goosebumps* to TV screens, and he arguably turned out the best of the entire show with its very first episode, getting brilliant performances out of his young actors and showing a real knack for tension-building. For experienced young actor Amos Crawley, Bond was a particularly comfortable choice of director. Bond was an old friend of the Crawley family—a veritable Canadian entertainment dynasty—and had already worked with him the year prior on the TV movie *Night of the Twisters*, which made this exciting new gig all the more appealing.

If the writers, directors and production designers had a weight on their shoulders when it came to setting the tone of the show, the young cast had perhaps the toughest job of all. If they didn't deliver, the show's relatability and scare-factor could be dashed before it even got off the ground. To this end, the casting agents struck gold when they found 13-year-old actor Kathryn Long to play the sympathetic lead, Carly Beth. Although she would have help from a body double whose voice was also mixed into hers in post, she displayed a maturity and emotional sensitivity on screen that few actors of that age can muster. According to Amos Crawley, this precociousness extended off screen. "I recall Kathryn being very serious in a way that I probably wasn't. She was more like the adult actors to be around, like in her approach, in her studiousness." Having to endure heavy prosthetics for a good portion of the shoot made it all the more grueling for Long, but she toughed it out with incredible zeal, much to the astonishment of those around her. It's easy to draw comparisons to a young Linda Blair in *The Exorcist*, in the way that she could transform from a sweet, sensitive, normal child to the central monster of the story, and pull it off convincingly.

The show may have got some good, and even a couple of great, performances out of its young actors for the rest of its run, but nobody would ever top Long for the utter terror that she sold.

But just a few episodes earlier, it was a different story. Production kicked off with the episode "The Girl Who Cried Monster," which, save for one particularly memorable set piece, should have been a good way to ease into what would become an incredibly demanding series. Filming in spring of 1995, it was very much the experimental episode, during which everybody was finding their groove and trying to establish what the *Goosebumps* set would look like. As the first episode, the crew had more time than they would ever have again to prepare, which turned out to be a saving grace, as the actor originally cast as Mr. Mortman the librarian would have to bow out due to illness. Although things would largely run smoothly, the episode ended up presenting the first real problem that production had yet encountered.

Steve Levitan recalls that leading child actor Deborah Scorsone was having issues as soon as she got to set. Despite a great round of auditions, Scorsone was struggling to perform in front of the camera, and with the clock ticking, the crew began to worry. A call was placed to her agent, and then to her mother, who advised that Scorsone was dyslexic, and this was likely the cause of the problem. "We had closed off this one block in downtown Toronto, midtown Toronto, right near the museum, which is in the center. It's kind of like the 5th Avenue of Toronto," Levitan explains. "We couldn't risk having to book an extra day in that location, so we had to make the schedule work. It's your first day, everybody's jittery."

In a bit of a panic, Deborah's elder sister Caterina was sent down to set to act as her cheerleader and chaperone. It ended up being something of an unconventional introduction to a show that Caterina Scorsone herself would later star in four episodes of, but it did the trick. "It's the first speed bump that we had," Levitan recalls. "We got past it, and everything went fine. But if it wasn't for her sister, I don't think we would have successfully completed that episode." In addition to the mentoring from Caterina, the editing team would have to swoop in to save the day. Steve emphasizes that, despite the funny and charismatic performance the finished episode presented from Deborah Scorsone, Bob Sprogis did much of the heavy lifting on this occasion, and the editing was largely responsible for turning out a watchable episode. Sprogis is as humble as ever in his recollection of the event: "There was a bit of a rough thing there, but the girl was very good, just first time doing a TV series."

Pressures associated with location bookings would occasionally crop up elsewhere in the series. In the case of "Phantom of the Auditorium," the school scenes were shot at one of the University of Toronto campuses, only a block or so from where "The Girl Who Cried Monster" had been shot, and so the pressure was on to get the footage shot in the single day they had the location booked for. An issue, which Steve Levitan can't recall the specifics of, did arise, and the crew were sweating for a while at the idea of having to shell out for another day on campus, but with that trademark *Goosebumps* determination and resourcefulness, the problem was soon overcome, and they got out of there on time and with the shots they needed.

Despite the hiccups, much fun was had on set of the very first *Goosebumps* episode, with Steve Levitan's fondest memory being filming the scene of Mr. Mortman, in monster form, eating a tarantula. Actor Eugene Lipinski was a good sport about working with the top half of his face fully covered by an animatronic mask created by the Stefaniuk gang. It had initially been made custom for the actor who'd first been cast, but with no time or money to make any amendments, they had to press ahead with the mask they had. "[It was] an example of how elaborate [Ron's] animatronics were, he built this amazing monster mask," says Levitan. "Because it's in the book this way, the eyes bulge out of its head on stalks and move around independently. The mask literally covers the top half of [Eugene's] head, the only thing we had to keep open was his mouth because the monster eats bugs, and we wanted to actually show him eating bugs. So this animal guy supplied us with tarantulas and showed us how to hold the tarantula so it physically cannot bite you."

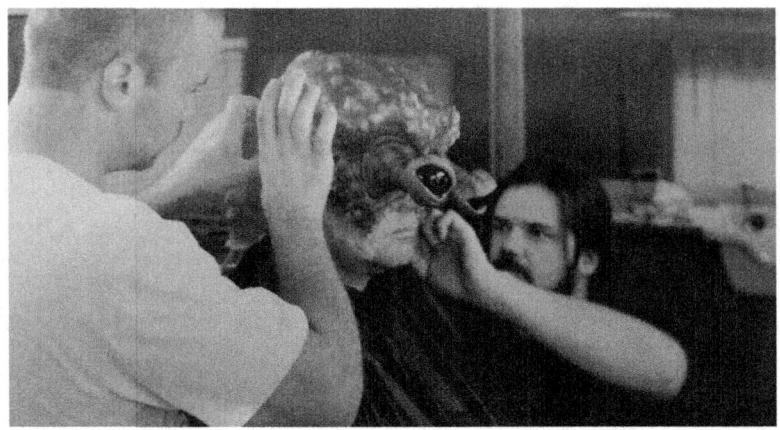

Tony Chappell and Ron Stefaniuk fitting Eugene Lipinski with his monster mask. Photo courtesy of Matthew DeWilde.

Complete with moving antennae, it was an elaborate and impressive piece of costuming that left the actor effectively blind, requiring those off-camera to shout very particular directions to him. This culminated in Lipinski putting a live tarantula almost completely in his mouth. "Eugene pretty much had the entire tarantula inside his mouth before we said, 'OK, cut.' But that's what people did on that show, and it was so fun!" Steve Levitan laughs. The episode turned out to be a very efficient exercise in what was to come: the challenges of dealing with young, inexperienced actors; the pressures of closing off heavily-populated areas of Toronto; bringing in animal handlers. In the space of one episode, *Goosebumps* had already turned its back on the old "children and animals" warning.

Caterina Scorsone's first official role on the show came not too long after, when "Night of the Living Dummy II" started shooting. She went from the real-life big sister role to the fictional one, playing the disbelieving teen sister of Maggie Castle's Amy. This would end up being quite the episode. Ron Oliver didn't know the icon he was unleashing on the world when he was handed "Night of the Living Dummy II." As the TV show's introduction to the now-legendary antagonist Slappy, it didn't strike Oliver as some big debut. It was simply "a fun episode about a possessed ventriloquist's dummy."

When asked whether "Bride of the Living Dummy," or "Night of the Living Dummy II," had taken any direct inspiration from the *Child's Play* series, Ron Oliver cites other sources. Naturally, being the guy who knows every interesting person in the industry, he is good friends with Chucky creator Don Mancini, and insists, "there's only so much you can do with living dolls," but there is one old British movie that certainly did give him ideas. 1964's *Devil Doll* (not to be confused with Tod Browning's 1936 horror *The Devil-Doll*) is the story of an evil stage magician whose dummy, Hugo, may or may not be alive and an accessory to his crimes. "I saw it as a kid and it always stayed in my head," says Oliver, also citing *The Dead of Night* as another key creepy doll feature. "Chucky is a more comical kind of angle on it, and I kind of wanted Slappy to be a little nastier than that." But with Chucky predating the *Goosebumps* series, Oliver says he wouldn't be surprised if Stine's book took a little inspiration from the infamous Good Guy Doll. "These basic plot elements have been done a few times over the years, and always make for an interesting story with a number of possible directions to take it."

In his element as a lifelong lover of the genre, Ron Oliver was firmly in his element with *Goosebumps*, and he was already having a lot of fun with it. Horror fans will notice a certain shot that pays homage to John Carpenter's *Halloween*, one that Oliver is very proud of. Swapping round the dynamics of the shot, with protagonist in the background and antagonist in the foreground, Slappy sits bolt upright, having been presumed dead, just as Michael Myers does behind Laurie Strode's back. Although Oliver and his crew got creative with Slappy, their wild ideas weren't necessarily backed up logistically. Whereas The Muppets work with raised or hollow floors that puppeteers can hide in or under, Slappy was mostly working on a regular old flat surface, necessitating the use of wires and any trickery they could muster. This was where Ron Stefaniuk's creativity would prove crucial, with the puppet-maker lying on the floor and operating Slappy over his head. For Slappy's big death scene, backup was required. As Ron Oliver remembers it, the dummy had two or three backup heads that were good for smashing, allowing second or third takes if required.

When pressed on the mystery surrounding who voiced Slappy and when, Ron Oliver doesn't have all the answers. On the set, he voiced Slappy while Ron Stefaniuk's crew synched his mouth movements. Some say that Stefaniuk did the voice and the puppeteering all in one. The final voice, probably provided by Cal Dodd, was inserted in post, although Stefaniuk and "Return of the Mummy" actor Annick Obonsawin have both been credited with the voice over the years. Oliver doesn't recall directing any voice actors in post-production, which leads him to believe that whoever did the job would simply have followed the cues and cadence of the dialogue he had done on set.

Post-production vocals are a standard practice in the industry, but ADR seems to have been a pretty central issue for the episode "My Hairiest Adventure," a fairly pedestrian episode that didn't require very much pizzazz in terms of production. Neither Steve Levitan nor David Warry-Smith remember much at all about the production of the episode, "which probably means that there was nothing spectacular that happened one way or the other," says Levitan. However, the final product of the episode shows signs of having relied heavily on post-production sound. A lot of the dialogue is slightly out of sync, and there's heavy use of generic background music that *Goosebumps* was certainly not in the habit of using, usually valuing its silences, its abrupt stings, and its thematic motifs. Although it could all be forgiven, particularly as just one episode of an otherwise solid '90s kids' TV show, the sound issues are noticeable, but as ever, the crew did what they could to save the day, and it worked.

But it didn't always work. For Steve Levitan, "Piano Lessons Can Be Murder" is his least favourite episode of the series. "Terrible," is the first thing he says when the episode is brought up, and there's an understandable reason behind his dissatisfaction. "Because of the special effects, you know that ghost thing. Just so hokey," he laments. "It just did not work. And the script really depended on those being effective." Although the effects were certainly passable for a young audience, the way they turned out in the finished episode gave Levitan an early aversion to creating effects in post, and confirmed his existing fears about doing so.

"It's one of those episodes that made me reluctant to ever rely on post effects," he says. "You know, the actress was great, she was scary and old, and she looked like a good, scary old witch. But the effects just didn't work." He is glad to hear that these same scenes gave this writer a damn good scare as a five-year-old, and is quick to credit actor Brenda Devine for making it so. "If it worked, it's because of the actress, because she did a good job of being scary. But I wasn't pleased with that episode." Although it may not have been Levitan's favorite, the episode is notable for having debuted young actor Ben Cook, who would return to the show several times in the episodes "Welcome to Dead House" and "A Shocker on Shock Street." At least some good came of it.

Plenty of good came from Ron Oliver's first foray into the world of R.L. Stine. "Welcome to Camp Nightmare" was the second episode given the hour-special treatment, and with all its homage to the summer camp slashers of the 1980s, Oliver was the perfect choice for director. This was the beginning of a beautiful friendship between *Goosebumps* and Ron Oliver, who would go on to be the show's second most-prolific director after William Fruet. He says that the experience of filming "Welcome to Camp Nightmare" gave the impression that "I was gonna love every second of this series! You had a really big fat budget to play with and we were all staying at some hotel near the camp, so it was like being out at summer camp ourselves. Just fun!"

More than just the prospect of having a fun time away at summer camp, Ron Oliver was excited by the chance to make something that felt like more than an episode of children's television. "Suddenly you're like, 'Oh my God! I can actually make a movie out of this thing, as opposed to a TV episode,'" he says. Indeed, "Welcome to Camp Nightmare" has an undeniably cinematic quality to it, with creative camerawork courtesy of Brian R. R. Hebb and a real sense of slowly-building momentum. The idea of getting to make mini-movies rather than episodes of television was incredibly appealing to Oliver.

Production used Camp Samac, a scout camp based in Oshawa, to double for Camp Nightmoon, and it was the perfect location that needed almost no dressing up from the art department. It had the bunks, the mess hall, even a set of moose antlers hanging from the rafters (which remain in place to this day). Although the cast and crew would stay at a hotel not far from the camp, it proved a fun and very useful location that allowed a lot of logistical legroom. "A tree is a tree, it's all the same," Oliver explains, "so shooting in a forest is actually a lot easier than it sounds. You don't have to move your entire unit from one part of the forest to the other, you just turn a little bit to the left. The audience doesn't know."

Darryl Triebner of Camp Samac posing with the mess hall antlers. Photo courtesy of Darryl Triebner.

Although at first it felt like a shoot that threatened to be laborious, the crew were well-oiled, and with the enthusiastic Oliver at the helm, all were impressed at how quickly they sailed through it. The baseball scene required some forty-five setups, but the cast and crew got it done in a single morning. "Everybody was playing on their A-game, because it was so much fun! And you could feel it was the beginning of something really exciting," Oliver says. In fact, so good a fit was the director, that by halfway through the shoot, he had already been asked to come back. "Whether or not I was any good wasn't so much the question, as it was whether or not I had an affinity for the material, and I really just loved the tone of that show and the feeling of it."

For horror buff Ron Oliver, "Camp Nightmare" was not only an introduction to a show he felt a real connection to, but the chance to make his very own '80s-style summer camp horror. He cites the *Friday the 13th* series, *The Twilight Zone* and the iconic *Sleepaway Camp* (whose star Jonathan Tiersten is another close friend of Oliver's, naturally) as favorites of his that made him enjoy "Camp Nightmare" all the more. In a word, "Camp Nightmare" felt triumphant to Ron Oliver. He fondly remembers sitting out around the campfire on the final night of shooting, with Bill Siegler, sharing drinks and celebratory cigars, and just appreciating how lucky he was to have such a great job. It was most definitely the start of something, and not just for him.

Ryan Gosling, who Ron Oliver affectionately refers to as Goose, was brought on by the director after they had worked together on the *Are You Afraid of the Dark?* episode "The Tale of Station 109.1," his first credited acting role. "We were in the casting room, and this kid comes in, and right away I remember looking over at the producer on that show, D.J. [MacHale] and going, 'This kid's gonna be a star'. You could tell he was gonna be a star," Oliver says of his first meeting with Gosling. The director was so taken with the young actor that he immediately took him under his wing, finding him an agent in Toronto and bringing him over to *Goosebumps*. Although "Say Cheese and Die" would end up being Gosling's only appearance on the show due to a rapid surge in his career, he was invited back for later episodes, including the direct sequel "Say Cheese and Die… Again!"

"Say Cheese and Die" was not unfamiliar ground for Oliver, who had filmed an episode of *Are You Afraid of the Dark?* titled "The Tale of the Curious Camera." It also told the story of a camera that foretold horrific things, and starred future *American Pie* star Eddie Kaye Thomas. He was glad to differentiate the two, at least by the design of the camera itself. He himself mused over possibilities, including turning a polaroid camera sideways inside a space-age looking casing. Although he didn't design the final look of the camera, Oliver adored how the finished product harkened back to the '60s sci-fi era, very much indulging his love for the golden oldies.

There were instances in which other horror classics received tribute, perhaps no more so than in "Return of the Mummy." It required much more elaborate set work, which greatly impressed native Egyptian, Afrah Gouda, and on this occasion, the kids and adults got equally involved in the excitement of the action. Gouda got along well with her co-stars, who she describes as "great, very talented kids." She'd already met Elias Zarou, who played Uncle Ben, at her audition and the two hit it off instantly. So strong was the rapport she developed with her castmates that when the day came to film the confrontation scene between Gabe, Sari and Nila in princess form, she asked the kids to have lunch with her. "I said, 'You know, today in the show, when we are shooting, I'll be yelling at you,'" to which the kids responded nonchalantly, "Yeah, I know. And you're gonna call us peasants!" Daniel DeSanto and Annick Obonsawin were well-versed in their jobs and took it all in their stride, but Gouda had wanted to discuss it prior and make sure they were comfortable with what the scene would require. It all went off without a hitch, and once the cameras stopped rolling, they were all back to being firm friends. The episode would also require some light stunts, making good use of the hollow floors in the Molson building. You'd certainly never look at the sets of this episode and think it was being shot in an old brewery.

Another classic horror setup came in the form of mad science with "Stay Out of the Basement." The episode was filmed over a two-week period in October 1995, mostly at the studio in Toronto. "Exteriors were in a real beautiful home in an area called the Beaches, here in Toronto," says actor Judah Katz. "We shot at one of the really nice ones with that beautiful big veranda in front. But everything else was shot in the studio." The beautiful house in question was at 43 Balsam Ave, Toronto, where external shots of the house, garden and driveway took place over a day or two. Katz recalls the basement set being the only thing to go through much transformation over the course of filming. "The only room that changed was the basement, because it starts off with just my laboratory. And then slowly but surely, they added more plants, and they got to the point where you could hardly move. There must have been like two hundred plants in there!" The plants would eventually go back into the company greenhouse, to be tended to until they were ready for their next closeup.

It was a happy time for those involved, and one that fostered a safe and formative experience for its young stars. "Filming was fun," says Beki Lantos (credited as Rebecca Henderson). "I do remember having tons of fun and laughing a lot." Judah Katz, an experienced and award-winning screen and stage actor, played Dr. Brewer, and despite the surprising menace that he brings to his character, he is remembered as an absolute sweetheart. "I remember loving Judah Katz, my plant dad," says Lantos. "He was so kind and caring, a real support and mentor type. I have nothing but fond memories of Judah." Evidently, his strengths as a nurturer of young acting talent were always there, and he would go on to divide his time between performing and coaching other actors. He has much praise for his young costars, who he watched closely to gauge how they responded to his work. Of Beki Lantos, he says, "She was very good. She was wonderful. Beki was always like a young woman. The kids were very sweet, good kids. I remember [Blake McGrath] was a typical boy. He lost focus at times... I'm sure I do remember [Bill Fruet] having to work with them a lot." Beki Lantos, in true big-sister fashion, found McGrath a little wearing. "At the time of filming, I remember finding Blake frustrating as though he really was my little brother," she says affectionately, "but he was really nice."

Beki Lantos and Judah Katz having fun on set.
Photo courtesy of Beki Lantos.

Although working with children may have required a more involved approach, director Bill Fruet certainly had a knack for getting the best out of his young cast members and adjusted his direction depending on how much support they needed. He gave Judah Katz just enough guidance to have fun with. Between takes of one particular scene, Fruet mused quietly, trying to find the right tidbit to give to the actor. After a long silence, he raised a finger and simply said to Katz, "More plant!" This was all the actor needed: "I know what he's saying. What he's saying was, he wanted more of that cold-hearted, scary character in this scene. It was how hard he was thinking… He was very proud of himself, too. The way he thought for so long, so hard."

The order of the day, as far as Katz was concerned, was intensity, and the episode gave him plenty to work with. "I think the scene that I had the most fun with, yet was the most challenging, was the phone call scene," he says. "It was classic horror, about the hand coming up and grabbing. So that was fun. That was really well shot. And I was the one who came up with the idea of my voice is one character, and my face was in the other character." He adds that Fruet suggested the hand coming out of nowhere to grab the phone.

Although the episode wasn't overly effects-heavy, there was work to be done by Ron Stefaniuk's team, which Judah Katz remembers as presenting some challenges. The pump that was meant to cause the flow of green blood from a cut on his arm wasn't quite working right, and time crunches meant they had little time to get the actor into the appropriate makeup. "They were probably told by the first A.D., 'OK, you got Jude for forty-five minutes, and then we're shooting!' and I'll never forget the panic in their eyes," he says. They also had issues with the bald cap the actor would wear for the final scene, which threatened to snap if he moved too much. The pièce de résistance was the two-dads effects, which at the time of filming, the actor wasn't sure would pan out. "When you're shooting, it never feels right," he says. He just had to play the scene twice, playing one version of the character and then the other, to be spliced together in post. But it was seeing this sequence come together that really impressed him by the time he saw the finished episode. "I went, 'Wow, holy crap! It worked!' I was impressed for what it was. I went, 'Good for you guys.'" It proved that sometimes, the dreaded post-production effects could actually do a serviceable job.

Overall, shooting "Stay Out of the Basement" was great all round: the cast and crew got along famously, inspired each other professionally and creatively, and they turned in a great episode. "It was a very fun, relaxed shoot," says Katz, "I just remember having a good time. They treated us very well." It was a matter of going from one extreme to another for Beki Lantos, who had loved working on the show so much that the prospect of leaving was unbearable. "I was devastated at the idea of having to go back to school and regular life," she recalls.

Another fun, relaxed shoot of the season would end in very memorable fashion. Although *Goosebumps* required a good number of stunt sequences over its run, it wasn't often that vehicles came into the equation, and "Say Cheese and Die" featured a scene of the family's car spinning out of control while on a busy freeway at night. The car interiors were shot in the studio, but the exteriors would be filmed on a cold, dark evening just ahead of a trip to the Caribbean that Oliver and Gosling had planned (something that would become a tradition of theirs in later years). Although Oliver describes the child labor laws in the mid-'90s as more "loosey goosey" than they are now, things were still pretty strict, so the odd loophole could be found, as long as the kid's parents were onboard. "The labor laws are really important for kids because you don't want them in some horrible burger joint working eighteen-hour days, or in the coal mines. But these weren't exactly coal mines!" Oliver chuckles. They piled the other actors into the car after a day of shooting, headed in the direction they were already going along Lake Shore Boulevard, and rolled the camera. Gosling got some cash-in-hand to take on his trip to the Caribbean for his troubles, and they jetted off for sunnier climes the next day.

Oliver would prove a crucial influence in Ryan Gosling's career. He helped him navigate the Canadian television circuit, and later gave him a place to stay in L.A. once he made the big move across the border to really launch his career. Goose later served as best man at Oliver's wedding, with actor Udo Kier officiating. Speaking of Goose's huge success in the industry, Oliver gushes, "It makes me ridiculously proud to have ever been a part of that thing. It's terrific!"

Also among Season One's roster of future stars was a thirteen-year-old Katharine Isabelle, who hailed from a family of entertainment industry professionals, and was an experienced child actor by the time she worked on "It Came from Beneath the Sink." From this early age, she was already proving herself a professional and highly competent actress, particularly suited to the horror genre, which would go on to be her trademark. Director David Winning says it was Isabelle's wide-eyed look of terror that really sold her as a future scream queen. She was in good company on the episode, which was filled out with a number of prolific Toronto-based jobbing actors. Amanda Tapping, who played Mrs. Merton, was a well-known face on Canadian television, modelling and acting in a lot of commercial work, notably for a shampoo brand. The insular and circulatory nature of the Toronto entertainment landscape meant that Winning had crossed paths with Tapping many times before they worked together on *Goosebumps*, and continued to do so afterwards. In the years since, he has routinely quoted *Goosebumps* to her with her line, "OK, everyone—French toast!"

Similarly, character actor Jack Newman was a veteran performer familiar to Winning when they collaborated on "It Came From Beneath the Sink," and given his vast portfolio, the director felt bad about giving him a role as small as that of the school janitor. But Newman, ever the amiable professional, was a welcome addition to the cast, and provided plenty of enthusiasm on set. Still working today, he and Winning have since collaborated on Lifetime productions, and always have a good laugh about his being "the janitor from the sponge show."

Despite airing as the fourteenth episode of season one, "It Came from Beneath the Sink" was the second episode filmed, after "The

Girl Who Cried Monster," just as the whole *Goosebumps* production was finding its feet. It was shot in the summer of 1995, and the weather in Toronto was generally pleasant, something that would cause a thoroughly uncomfortable set when filming in Lawrence Park Collegiate Institution, a high school in central Toronto. Shooting night scenes during the day necessitated blacking out the classrooms, magnifying and trapping the heat, and bringing the internal temperature up to around 120°F. The use of smoke machines to simulate spilled acid made the set even more grueling, but never to the detriment of the cast or crew's performance. "When I think of that episode, I just think of that 120-degree chem lab!" David Winning laughs.

What dampened the experience somewhat for Winning was technical issues. The infancy of the show meant a lot was still being worked out across departments, and the sequence of the sponge expanding on the floor of the chemistry lab was initially intended to be done with practical effects. When no puppet was delivered, however, it was decided that the shot would be achieved in post, so Winning was instructed to shoot the background with a reference point for the sponge to be later inserted on. Once filming had wrapped, the director heard on the grapevine that the special effects department was running into issues. "And of course, who gets splashed with that is the director. But that's the kind of political lesson you learn," he concedes, "but I had a great time on the show."

Also shot at the height of summer 1995 was fan favorite "The Werewolf of Fever Swamp." The episode was shot on location in Pickering, just outside of Toronto, at the house of a strange lady who was in the habit of offering the crew food, only to pull various pieces of roadkill out of her freezer. "She was a real character!" Ian Brock laughs.

Military veteran, actor, stuntman and animal trainer Bryan Renfro was originally brought in to double for the actor cast as the titular werewolf, following a referral from his friend and stunt coordinator Tye Tyukodi. However, his wide range of skills ended up making him a better fit for the role, and he was brought onboard to do all of the costumed werewolf sequences. Ron Stefaniuk's team designed and built the costume specifically to fit Renfro and allow him to be as active as possible, but performing so heavily made-up would inevitably present challenges.

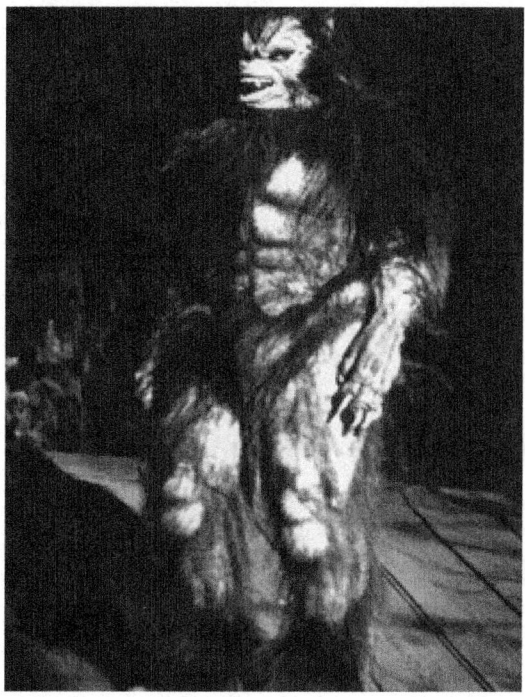

Bryan Renfro in werewolf mode. Photo courtesy of Bryan Renfro.

The role was a physically demanding one for Renfro. Fully-suited in werewolf getup with the mask and headpiece glued to his face, he was virtually unable to eat or drink, and crew had to unzip him at the back between takes to allow for a little air circulation. The costume combined with the stunts made for a fairly punishing shoot, which comprised three consecutive nights. On the first night, an ambitious shot was scheduled, for which Renfro would be required to jump backwards off of a shed roof, so that when played in reverse, it would look like a superhuman leap into the air, while howling at the sky. "Problem was, it was about fifteen feet high, and the only pad that we could use that would be out of shot was a two-inch mat. I didn't know where the ground was, and I hit, straight leg, and it really did a number on my back," Renfro says.

Once this shot was in the can, Renfro next had to dig at the ground of the shed, like the raptors in *Jurassic Park II*, but the plastic fingers of his werewolf gloves weren't exactly well-suited to the task. "So by the end of the night, my back was a mess and the gloves were kind of full of blood!" he recalls. The exhausted stuntman fell into bed around 7am that morning, and by the time he went to get up for the next night's shoot, he couldn't get out of bed. A doctor gave him some pills but, wary of being too zonked out to work, Renfro resisted, and took as little as he could to take the edge off the pain. He ultimately ended up needing surgery on his back, but for the American stunt performer, working in Canada had its perks. "It's socialized medicine, plus if you get hurt on a film set, they take care of you," he reasons.

Playing to his strengths, Renfro would also be tackled by Vandal the dog, while wearing the full costume. Arguably the most nerve-racking job came last, with the werewolf being pushed into the lake. The stunt was full of uncertainties: would the suit float, or absorb the water and drag Renfro down? How would he judge the depth of the water and when to hold his breath when his senses were so restricted? As it happened, the stuntman didn't take a breath at the crucial time, and his costume and mask were flooded with water while his lungs were empty. Ever the professional, he did his best to complete the take without freaking out, and managed to pull it off. "For one second it was a little scary. I don't know if I'm gonna drown! But it's just part of the job, you know. Everybody has an office to go to," says Renfro with remarkable nonchalance.

On the very tail end of a successful first season came another two-parter, "A Night in Terror Tower." Summer and fall had slipped away, and filming continued well into early winter, which was something the crew were not in a hurry to do in later seasons, because in Canada, this meant one thing: cold. Filmed in late 1995, probably in November, over the course of fifteen or sixteen days, "Terror Tower" was different to anything they had done before. For starters, this two-parter was filmed almost exclusively on location at Casa Loma, a Gothic Revival-style castle in Toronto. The cast and crew were given access to private parts of the building, including its tunnels and dungeons, as well as to Toronto's sewer system for a stunt in which Eddie and Sue escape underground and through a manhole. The episodes required a few notable outdoor sequences, and with temperatures consistently fluttering around freezing, everybody was eager to get them out of the way. ""Terror Tower" was a memorable shoot," says cinematographer Brian R. R. Hebb. "I remember it was so cold outside that we rushed through the exteriors to quickly move inside." To top it all off, the episode required a number of night shoots, and with daylight hours already scarce, it proved to be an exciting and unique, practically nocturnal, experience.

The crew freeze on the set of "A Night in Terror Tower."
Photo courtesy of Steve Levitan.

Corey Sevier had started in the modeling world at the tender age of six months, and by the time he was seven had moved his way up through commercials and into speaking roles on television, working alongside Anjelica Huston and Sam Neill on the series *Family Pictures*. The experience gave him the acting bug, and he bagged his first leading role at the age of eleven when he was cast as Eddie in "A Night in Terror Tower." He was not only elated about getting the job as a staunch fan of the books, but excited about the range it demanded of him. "The kids are in every single scene you're doing, you know, dramatic acting, and a lot of horror and fear," recalls Sevier. "It was my first opportunity to play a lead character, let alone in a book that I knew, which was super cool. I had to learn a few lines with an accent and stuff so just I mean, I'm gushing, but it truly was a game-changer for me. It was just the most fun character you could possibly ask for. I was very precocious. I was a pickpocket, and then it turned out that I'm actually this royal prince." This was a big deal. His first lead role, in a super-cool kid-oriented horror show, shot on location and being released as a special on VHS, Sevier felt like a movie star, and enjoyed every second of this incredible experience.

The casting of his co-star Kathryn Short was also a source of excitement for Sevier. She had already played Sabrina in "The Haunted Mask," one of Sevier's favorite books of the series, and she could offer him experience and advice on how the whole *Goosebumps* operation went. The pair were often told how convincing they were as a brother-sister duo, and they quickly formed a close bond.

Although there were almost no sets to build, the production design department were given a lot to play with at Casa Loma, and for the newly-appointed Ian Brock, this episode would be a dream introduction to the show. "Suddenly we were given the keys to this actual castle to shoot for three weeks," he remembers, "so we were given access to places that, you know, the general public couldn't go." Production decked the place out with creepy animatronics, props and set dressing to heighten the historical tourist-trap effect of it all, and enjoyed this thoroughly unique excursion outside the studio. They even got to experience the finer things, with one or two scenes in the hotel requiring a bougie vibe that the show rarely tapped into.

Corey Sevier and Kathryn Short filming a scene for "A Night in Terror Tower." Photo courtesy of Steve Levitan.

Stine came in to film his intro and outro for the episode, and its young stars were thrilled to hang out with him. "He introduced the movie on this spooky little set that they made, and we got to do a photo shoot with him, and he signed my copy of "Night in Terror Tower,"" Sevier fondly recalls. Not only did it get the special introduction courtesy of Stine, "A Night in Terror Tower" stands out as the only episode that released a behind-the-scenes featurette. Appearing before the main feature of "The Haunted Mask" video release, it gave viewers a glimpse at how the show came together, and Sevier was positioned as the presenter. "In between takes, and they'd be like, 'OK, Corey, I want you to just talk about this scene and walk us through this.'" Unfortunately, this was about as close as viewers ever came to getting an inside look at the show, and no more featurettes of its kind ever materialized.

A great time was had by all on "Terror Tower," and it was in this externally frosty, but internally warm and fuzzy fashion, that season one of *Goosebumps* officially wrapped, just as the earlier episodes were starting to air. Although everybody felt pretty confident that they had a success on their hands, none of them dared to dream it would be the overnight sensation that it turned out to be.

Opening Band for The X-Files Hitting the Small Screen

Goosebumps made its grand debut on Friday 27th October 1995 in the 8pm time slot on Fox. It was a big deal for a kids' show to be given such a primetime slot, right before *The X-Files*, no less, and the show was marketed as a big Halloween event, taking advantage of all the seasonal hype that Levitan had anticipated when he began planning the logistics of it all months earlier. Airing in a single night rather than as two separate episodes, the show was a smash success, achieving a rating of 8.2, and got the show off to an incredible start. They'd done it. They'd taken one of the biggest kids' books of the era and successfully translated its magic and horror from the page to the small screen. This really set the ball rolling for fans. Now they'd seen what *Goosebumps* could look like on screen, what would come next? They could work themselves into a frenzy imagining all the books they'd already read and loved, and which might be adapted for this hot new show next.

The first season would largely fall on Fridays, with one or two episodes being repositioned into Saturday or Sunday slots. Either way, *Goosebumps* was commanding the most desirable time slots—only the best, befitting such a major property. As of Season Two, the show would become a Saturday staple on Fox and YTV, and in the era of weekend television being a ritualistic childhood fixture, it quickly became one of the most reliably entertaining shows for young fans. It was made all the more exciting when commercials would tease an upcoming primetime special which, while never achieving the numbers of "The Haunted Mask," would continue to do great business. At this point, says Randy Bradshaw, there was plenty of information from home turf on the success of each episode. "There would always be feedback from the producers about just internally how successful they found the episode," he says. This would not prove to be the case when it came to international markets, so they made do with what data they had and trusted that the decisions they made off the back of it would guide them in the right direction. It usually did.

While kids across the U.S. and Canada, and later around the world, were getting their fill of Goosebumpy goodness, the kids on the screens were handling being at the center of a media sensation with relative calm. While some would receive their own VHS copy of their episode prior to broadcast, this wasn't a routine thing, and for some young actors, they didn't even watch their episode when it aired.

A poster advertising Goosebumps on YTV. Photo courtesy of Bob Sprogis.

What most definitely didn't happen was a big song-and-dance about being the star of this hot new kids' show. While it's easy to imagine the excitement being too much for kid actors not to make a big deal of it, the vast majority of the show's stars did not mark the occasion in any special way. "There was certainly not a screening party, like all my little tween friends came over. Absolutely no way," says Melody Johnson. For Bill Turnbull, he was too old to even host a birthday party without finding the whole affair embarrassing, so there was no way he wanted to put himself at the center of a spectacle. However, his friends found it pretty cool that he was the ghost kid on the latest episode of *Goosebumps*, so he would indulge their curiosity, at the very least.

Beki Lantos had loved her time on the set, and put a surprising amount of seriousness into her work, so she did catch the first broadcast, and was thrilled with what she saw. "I was elated when I saw the final product air," she says. "It was so well-edited, with the cool intro and that awesome theme song. It was especially cool to be able to recognize so many names in the credits. And of course, seeing my own name among them was beyond exciting. I just remember watching it and being so impressed with it. There was a good sense of pride."

For many of the young performers, acting was a way of life that they were firmly accustomed to, and while they may have been proud to be part of it, they saw little reason to make a big deal of their turn on *Goosebumps*. Amos Crawley attended an alternative school that regularly catered to child performers, which took the edge off what might be a remarkable lifestyle to other, regular kids. This firmly ruled out any notion of viewing parties or other celebrations. Additionally, there is a notable sense of humility, even embarrassment, among the actors. "I admit that I have a certain amount of squeamishness at watching myself," confesses Crawley, a sentiment that is far from exclusive to him. Nobody I talk to enjoys watching themselves on screen, and often find themselves picking apart their own performances when they do. Understandably, this problem is only worsened when watching their younger selves who still had room to grow in their craft. While kids all over North America were celebrating this enticing new show, the kids who made it were happy to go back to their lives and pay little attention to the hype.

It was a bit different for the adult actors, who were used to the industry and rarely felt the need to sit down to watch the finished product. They'd shown up, done their thing and been paid, so what more was there to say? If nothing else, they appreciated the artistic elements of the show, like Judah Katz did: "I saw the Canadian broadcast. The music was great, the editing was pretty damn good. They made it dark and scary," he says. Peter Keleghan's first viewing of "Revenge of the Lawn Gnomes" doubled as the first time his young children watched something he had worked on. He sat down expectantly, waiting for his kids to recognize their old man on their very own TV screen, and was somewhat surprised when his first scene failed to rouse any reaction. The episode ran, and Keleghan thoroughly enjoyed it. "I thought it was great. I thought they did a great job," he says, particularly appreciating how carefully the show walked the line of being scary but not too scary for its target audience. As the credits rolled, his daughter turned to him, raised an accusatory finger and said, "Dad, when your daughter said that those lawn gnomes came to life, and they did, how come you didn't believe her?" Keleghan was tickled, not only because the sight of her own father on TV had spurred no real reaction from his daughter, but because at her young age, she was still perfectly willing to accept him as someone else's dad in an alternate universe. Having kids present for the big reveal was something a number of the crew enjoyed about watching the show. Ian Brock recalls his son having friends over and watching an episode on TV. He found one of the kids hiding out in the hallway, eyes covered, asking to be told when it was over. This was more what viewing parties looked like to adults.

Randy Bradshaw was a little more invested in seeing the show in its original run. He recalls receiving a letter from R. L. Stine after the broadcast of "Scarecrow Walks at Midnight," congratulating him on a job well done. He watched the episodes upon first broadcast as often as he could, but says the studio were great at getting a video copy to him well ahead of the broadcast date. "I think they were always, in a way, playing around with release dates for certain episodes, or some episodes may have needed a reshoot or something. So, things get switched around," he says.

It would take a good while for the show to make its way around the globe—unexpected, given that the book series had been a worldwide hit and translated into many languages. Steve Levitan says that what ended up happening with international broadcasts is one of the areas in which the show really failed to meet his expectations, but it wasn't down to quality, or the stories not translating well into other cultures. "That was a big failure in the international marketing of *Goosebumps*," says Levitan of the marketing of the show internationally. "Because Saban was known for the top animated shows in the world at the time and they didn't get live action or what was important about it. They preferred to sell their show than somebody else's, because they were a production company and a distribution company. The one disappointment about *Goosebumps* is that I don't think Saban did a good enough job of selling it internationally."

It's true that outside of North America, and certainly outside of English-speaking regions, the show was not making anywhere near as much of a splash as it could have, and it was given a very staggered start when it did finally make its way over the borders. *Goosebumps* made its UK TV debut on the afternoon of Monday September 1 1997, almost two years after the show had launched in Canada and the U.S. Taking the 4:35pm time slot on BBC One, which on weekday afternoons functioned as Children's BBC (CBBC), the first episode to air was "The Cuckoo Clock of Doom." It is interesting that "The Haunted Mask" seems to have never been broadcast in the UK—speculatively, this is because the episode was just too scary compared to others. After its first four weekly episodes, the time slot was moved to 4:40pm, and continued throughout the remainder of 1997, concluding with "More Monster Blood" on Monday 22 December.

The show picked up again on April 9 1998, with a one-off showing at 4:35pm, before resuming its 4:40pm slot, this time on Thursdays, and now jumping between episodes from the first three seasons. The afternoon schedule was an unusual one, fluctuating between programs for younger children in the four-seven age bracket and those aimed at older children. CBeebies, a slot made especially for toddlers and younger children, would not launch until 2002, so up to this point, CBBC catered to a fairly wide demographic. This might explain why the more extreme episodes never got broadcast.

After a brief break over the summer of 1998, *Goosebumps* had its Monday afternoon slot reinstated, continuing this way until Monday 21 December, with its airing of "Don't Go To Sleep." Season Four was finally broadcast on CBBC between Thursday April 1 and Thursday July 8 1999, with the odd episode from earlier seasons interspersed throughout. The following week, reruns commenced, starting again at the beginning with "The Cuckoo Clock of Doom," both in the regular after-school and weekday morning time slots throughout the week. It would continue airing sporadically throughout 2000 and 2001, and featuring on themed events such as CBBC's Eek! Week and the summer HoT broadcasts. Later, UK-based cable channels would pick the show up and give it periodic reruns throughout the early 2000s. This is just one example of how sporadic the show's international broadcasting ended up being, clearly something of an afterthought for Saban. Given its late start getting international airplay, the show offered the advantage of a considerable bank of one-off episodes that could be plucked out and played in any order, allowing plenty of flexibility for broadcasters. However, it was clear that away from home territory, *Goosebumps* was not given the attention it really deserved.

Because of this, it is difficult to gauge just how big a deal the show was in other countries. There are very few archived TV listings available, with even fewer reporting on viewing figures, an issue that Steve Levitan says they encountered from the off. The analog nature of the industry at the time meant that there was a considerable void between Goosebumps HQ and the various international broadcasters and distributors. "We got very poor reporting on international broadcasts from anybody, so I don't have any good figures for you on that," says Steve Levitan. The programming schedules were handled differently country to country, so while the show was originally created to be played at a rate of one episode a week, some territories were broadcasting it at a faster rate, somewhat muddying the concept of seasons. "Some broadcasters did the same episode twice or even more times each week. So the actual broadcast pattern would differ from place to place, but the production schedule was one season at a time," explains Levitan.

But back home, where it mattered—to Saban, at least—the show was an instant and consistent success, garnering itself the status of the most successful Fox show for three years running. This was enough for the network to greenlight a second season, and keep the ball rolling for the next few years. This show was just getting started.

"Let's Just Make It Fun, Like an Amusement Park Ride!"

Season Two

Season One of *Goosebumps* was a runaway success, and, having tested the waters with a fourteen-episode run (nineteen if you count the second halves of two-parters as individual episodes), Fox was eager to get as much of that Stiney goodness onto their network as possible, and ordered a full, industry-standard twenty-five-episode second season. This meant additional budget, but it also meant a protracted production schedule that would now run for a good six months. If the workload was heavy on the first season, the second would push the crew even harder than before, and to this end, would cause small but noticeable production shakeups. Ian Brock had officially replaced Armando Sgrignuoli as production designer, and Brian R. R. Hebb would willingly start to scale back his involvement throughout the season, citing burnout, and making way for Barry Bergthorson, who would sit firmly in the cinematographer's chair from Season Three onwards. But spirits were still high, with the majority of the crew remaining in place, and now that they had a complete hit season under their belts, they felt more at home than ever, and ventured forward, happy to be back together and eager to see what the future held for the show.

Season Two would have four one-hour specials to its name, with "Attack of the Mutant," "The Haunted Mask II," "Welcome to Dead House" and "Night of the Living Dummy III." It also featured the only immediate sequel that wasn't part of an one-hour special, with "Monster Blood" and "More Monster Blood" airing consecutively, and shooting back-to-back, ensuring the relevant cast members would be present for both. The handful of specials were diluted somewhat by the larger order of twenty-five episodes, and spaced further apart in the broadcast schedule, allowing the single episodes to really have their time to shine, and prove that *Goosebumps* could tell just as good a story in twenty-three minutes as it could in forty-six.

Two such examples are "Be Careful What You Wish For" and "You Can't Scare Me," both the efforts of director René Bonnière and among the first of the season to shoot. It was early 1996, winter just getting around to melting into spring, and the weather was still very cold, as evidenced by scenes in which snow is falling and the actors' breath is visible. "My teeth were chattering!" says actor Melody Johnson. "That's a very Canadian actor's experience. Everybody would have one of those." Despite the weather, "Be Careful What You Wish For" offered an easy start to the season, with minimal effects and sets required. The episode was one of those rare instances in which no studio work took place, instead filming entirely on location at real houses, schools and streets. Mimico Memorial Park, on the corner of Central Street and Hillside Ave., was used for outdoor street sequences, and just up the road at John English Junior Middle School, the school scenes were shot. Johnson recalls the basketball scenes being filmed at a rec center in downtown Toronto, separate from the school. She says that between her lack of traditional school setting and her need to avoid potentially dangerous activities because of her work, "that episode was probably as close to a gym class as I ever got!"

As a seasoned pro and a real actor's actor, her co-star Ellen-Ray Hennessy made a real impression on Johnson, hamming it up as the delightfully sly Clarissa. "That woman is so expressive and she's so funny," Johnson says, recalling cracking up on multiple occasions due to Hennessy's frequent mugging. More than just fun to be around, Hennessy taught Johnson a lot about how to conduct herself as a serious actor. "That's just such a positive experience as a young person, thinking, 'That's the kind of way I want to conduct myself on set.' She's just really professional and was able to hold space." Johnson would take these lessons forward into her own acting career, and *Goosebumps* continued its now firm tradition of making its sets a welcoming, nurturing and friendly place for its young actors to be.

While the early episodes were largely location work in schools and on streets, Season Two would jump outside the suburban box, venturing into a wider range of settings, from farms and swamps to beaches and historic mansions. This meant that Sunnybrook Park got a few more makeovers, and the location scouts had their work cut out for them when searching for places in and around Toronto that could pull off these various environments. It would also prove to be a more monstrous season, with a nifty selection of creatures stalking the young protagonists, and perhaps the most out-there creation was the blob.

"The Blob That Ate Everyone" was shot around April and made good use of local spots. A real video store was dressed up for the episode, with the crew making sure to hide any hint of the adult section that every good video rental place of the time had. Stickers were placed on the covers of all their stock to avoid any legal disputes, and custom video covers were designed by the art department. A short time was spent at 599 Markham Street, just a few steps from the famous Honest Ed's Discount Store, for the opening scene in which the kids sit and listen to Zack's story. All the interiors were shot at the studio, where young actor Scott Pietrangelo was impressed by the pick'n'mix sets, and how whole walls could be removed to accommodate a camera.

On set, it was all happening, thanks to a fun director in Randy Bradshaw, and the wild creations of Stefaniuk and crew. "I'd never done anything like this before," says Pietrangelo of his first time on a professional set. "I didn't feel intimidated. Everyone on the crew, from what I can recall, was just so friendly, and open and happy. Anything we didn't know, they would explain. I just remember it being an entirely positive experience, learning so much in a week."

He recalls the first shot being of him running up the stairs, and moving straight on to the scenes of Zack typing in his bedroom. After this warm-up came the wilder stuff, with blobs, sticky tongues and worm boxes. The blob's tongue was liberally coated with what was referred to in the industry as Ultra Slime, and the box of worms had a layer of real worms over a pile of fake ones. Pietrangelo recalls the effects guy having to stick his hand through a hole in the box, only to receive a faceful of worms. "They're landing on him and they're still rolling, so he just has to keep going. They say 'cut' and they pull him out and he's just covered in worms, real and fake!" he recounts with amusement.

The shot of the blob eating an incredulous Adam was done in a single take, "and he came out the other end covered in slime!" says Pietrangelo, with one of Stefaniuk's crew hiding out inside the blob costume to pull the young actor in. This whole scene was done on location in the video shop, with the exception of the shot from inside the blob's mouth, which was done in the studio. Such was the force of the stunt that the back of the blob was lifting up off the ground, necessitating camerawork that would hide the creature's straining balance. Pietrangelo felt for the creature's operator, and recalls the guy in the blob costume injuring his back while filming the shot in which the creature grabs the typewriter (which was a real, heavy antique) off the desk. Thankfully, they also got that in one take.

The blob required much discussion not just about design, but about how to operate it. Randy Bradshaw recalls that Ron Stefaniuk was eager to be the one inside the blob, but so demanding was his job that he simply couldn't make the time for it. One of his crew ended up taking the role. It was stiflingly hot inside the suit, and the operator needed frequent breaks and a lot of cold water to ensure his wellbeing.

This was something of a stunt-heavy episode, so while the blob operators were left to their own devices, the kids got a crash course in stage-falling from a stunt coordinator, presumably Ty. "He made it all like play for the kids," says Pietrangelo. The stunt coordinator would also take one of the best stunts for himself, according to Pietrangelo, as the businessman falling over a video display in the shop amid the panic, with the other faller meant to be a kid, but really "just a short dude dressed up as one." Toronto's population of diminutive actors got a considerable surge in work thanks to the stunts *Goosebumps* was regularly staging.

While the person inside the blob costume spent their time crawling around on the floor, the actor behind the mud monster in "You Can't Scare Me" was experiencing loftier heights. The episode was filmed early in the season, with frost in the air and sleet falling during filming. For actor Garry Robbins, this was probably preferable. The professional wrestler's incredible stature of 7ft5in made him perfect for the imposing mud monster role, and his full-body costume and mask would have been slightly more tolerable in the more temperate conditions.

The same could not be said for actor Tim Rykert on the set of "How to Kill a Monster." Ron Stefaniuk designed an elaborate full-body costume, complete with animatronic head, for him to wear, and it was about as uncomfortable as it sounds. It was heavy and very hot inside, so it was a relief that the suit itself could be used as a monster body-double when shots required it to be less animated. For the scene in which the monster falls to its supposed death, "that was just us chucking the costume off the balcony!" Ron Oliver laughs. The actor would take the head off the costume as often as possible and drink gallons of water, while production assistants would wrangle him when he was in full costume, to help him get around and make sure he didn't fall over. It was a tough shoot for Rykert, but he evidently made an impression, with Oliver declaring him a "set crush. You know, you get a set crush. It's the best," he grins.

Ron Oliver had been busy both writing and directing for *Are You Afraid of the Dark?* for a while, so it wasn't until Season Two of *Goosebumps* that he got the chance to write his own episode. He was excited to really lean into the swamp setting of "How to Kill a Monster," and took inspiration from Tobe Hooper's *Eaten Alive* and George McCowan's *Frogs*, screening the latter for the crew to get an idea of the bayou atmosphere he was going for. Having directed the scripts of a few other writers on the show to this point, Oliver enjoyed the ease with which he could get into shooting, having already figured out the mechanics of the script and how he would achieve each shot in practice. This was the first episode in which he could be fully in control from start to finish, and write with the practicalities of the set in mind.

Oliver was going for a very tongue-in-cheek tone for this episode, playing with monster-killing tropes and what real-world kids would try if they found themselves in this predicament. "In horror movies, the monster always comes back to life, so we're making fun of that. It was a bit satirical. I liked that episode a lot." This sentiment extended to the portrayal of the grandparents, who he wanted to allow to be equal parts funny and creepy. The episode would rely heavily on the perfect actors to embody this vibe, and when Oliver met Helen Hughes and Peter Boretski in the casting room, he instantly knew he had found his creepy grandparents. "I remember them coming in and just going, 'That's it! They are perfect!' and I love that feeling," Oliver says.

With his actors in place, he couldn't wait to hear them bring his kooky script to life. He wove plenty of quirky dialogue in, and was particularly proud of the "That's just an old storage room full of… old storage things" exchange. He also felt an affinity to Clark, who he saw as the audience-insert character to point out all the problems and logical inconsistencies, while Gretchen tried to keep the peace and ride things out. For the role, he chose young Ricky Mabe, for his ability to be likeable while still a little obnoxious.

The big slimy explosion of the monster's final demise was the episode's simplest trick, with Oliver standing behind the camera with a bucket of yellowy-green slime, and throwing it over the kids. In classic Ron Oliver fashion, this episode was fun, messy and creative. "It was really easy to shoot that show, and really fun!" he says, and the experience was that much brighter for the director, as it was on set here that he received the news that he'd been approved to extend "Perfect School" into a two-parter, and had been allotted additional time and budget for further shooting. "The crew cheered!" he remembers fondly. "Perfect School" wouldn't see the light of day until Season Three, which is indicative of the nonlinear nature that shooting often adopted. With any particular cast only in place for a week or two at a time, getting everybody back, along with location permissions and all the other red tape involved in organizing a shoot, was a hefty task, and such an arrangement was bound to cause delays.

As an interesting aside, according to Oliver, the influence of "How to Kill a Monster" may have reached further than he initially anticipated. He says M. Night Shyamalan has spoken about how *Goosebumps* and *Are You Afraid of the Dark?* inspired his own filmmaking, and posits that *The Visit*—the story of two kids staying with the grandparents they never met on an isolated farm—may have taken nods from "How to Kill a Monster." Others have speculated that Shyamalan's *The Sixth Sense* is based on the episode "The Tale of the Dream Girl," by "It Came from Beneath the Sink" director David Winning. But in the world of sci-fi and horror, it seems inspiration is often taken from previous works. *Goosebumps*, in both the books and the episodes, exhibits hints of predecessors like *The Twilight Zone*, which itself was often based on preexisting short stories. Such is the cyclical nature of the horror fandom, paying loving homage to their generation's old favorites.

Creepy, kooky old relatives were quite the running theme once Season Two kicked off. "Scarecrow Walks at Midnight" could be seen as "How to Kill a Monster" transplanted to a farm, and required equally compelling adult actors to sell the mystery. Director Randy

Bradshaw had worked with actor Michael Copeman on a previous show, and describes him as "a real pro. He took a lot of delight in playing characters that were, you know, kind of a bit edgy or mysterious or darker." Copeman's Stanley is what really makes the episode work, with his shifty eyes and manchild persona, although Bradshaw sings Copeman's praises as an actor, assuring that he is a thoroughly normal and friendly guy when the cameras aren't rolling, and that the kids on set particularly loved him. Just as the haunted scarecrows delighted in throwing creepy curveballs at the characters, production on the episode started with a hitch. First day of filming, there was a pileup on the Don Valley Parkway on the way to the farm location, and Randy Bradshaw worried he would be late to set. The resourceful union driver, however, took him round the backroads, giving him a tour of the countryside that would get him in the mood for the farm-based episode, and deliver him miraculously on time. The rest of the shoot would go on relatively smoothly, punctuated by fun night shoots, and an array of stunts with mechanical threshers, bikes and hay lofts.

The creepy relatives theme continued with "Ghost Beach," director Steve DiMarco's second and final episode. Actor Bill Turnbull found DiMarco "quite outrageous for the time! He was a nice dude, a busy guy on the set. He knew what he wanted, and he knew how to just talk to us as kids, but also as actors." The young actor enjoyed having a handful of contemporaries around him for the episode, and knew co-star Sheldon Smith from the audition circuit. He fondly remembers a schooling session that he and his young co-stars were doing during a day of filming. Sat in an office at Goosebumps HQ, he and Jessica Hogeveen were playfully picking at each other, "not an argument, but it wasn't flirting either," he says, settling for the middle ground of "teasing". When he gave her the finger, Anna Majewski gasped in faux horror and exclaimed, "Sam Sadler!", calling him by his character name. Chuckling, he muses, "It was just like a weird kid thing, learning how to interact with the opposite sex, I guess." On-set tutoring was good for all sorts of lessons, it would seem.

While interiors were shot at the studio, these ghosts needed a beach, which came in the form of Scarborough Bluffs. The production design crew constructed an impressively convincing graveyard set in a field alongside the Bluffs, which would be used throughout the episode. While the gravestones were fake, one particularly spooky addition to the episode was all too real. "We actually got that skeleton of the dog from like a scientific place," says Ian Brock of the picked-clean bones the kids find on the sand, offering further proof of the crew's resourcefulness in making the show.

Bill Turnbull arrives for his interview dressed in a prized possession—a thrifted *Goosebumps* t-shirt with an image of a rat across the front. He turns side-to-side to show how frequently it has been patched up over the years. Although it wasn't a souvenir from his time on the show, it is dear to him, evidenced by the extensive repairs it has been through. His week on the set of *Goosebumps*, under the watchful black-lined eye of Steve DiMarco, is one he thinks of very fondly, and feels gave him valuable experience that he would take with him into his later career.

But while DiMarco was a hit with the kids he directed, there were rumblings going on behind the scenes. The episode "Revenge of the Lawn Gnomes" got caught up in a bit of corporate drama, according to Ian Brock. Steve DiMarco was originally attached to direct, and had got to work, but somewhere along the way, DiMarco's persona apparently became too risqué for Fox. "He was out there," says Brock. Although very well-liked by cast and crew, it would seem that DiMarco's presence ruffled some feathers further up, and Deborah Forte made the call to fire him from the show. "I guess they got into some kind of spat and she fired him," says Brock.

Steve Levitan recalls the incident, and while remorseful, seems resigned to having had little power over the decision. "Steve DiMarco would show up in skinhead boots, big leather lace-up boots up to his knees, fishnet stockings, a black leather mini skirt," he explains. "Sometimes when [executives] show up on the battlefield, they just have to demote somebody or fire somebody just to show who's boss. And [DiMarco] was that guy in the line of fire. He was a sweetheart, he just looked scary." With that, DiMarco was out, and ol' reliable Bill Fruet was swiftly brought in to pick up where his predecessor had left off, two days into prep. Given how tight the production schedule was, and how choice of director was frequently dictated by availability, it seems an unwise choice on Forte's part to disrupt what was a well-oiled machine just because one director dressed a bit too lavishly for her liking. DiMarco's episodes are just as enjoyable as those of other directors, and he was well-liked not just on *Goosebumps*, but on most every other set he worked on until his untimely death in 2020. This incident was a rare sour note for the show.

"Revenge of the Lawn Gnomes" was filmed at the height of summer in 1996, and the weather was hot and humid. "I remember it being hot and muggy," says actor Peter Keleghan, who, as the main parent of the episode, arguably got off lightly when it came to dealing with the heat. The majority of shooting taking place outside made production an at times uncomfortable affair, and, of course, those who bore the brunt of the weather were the actors playing the gnomes. "They were wearing ten pounds of gizmos and hats. They were in a very difficult place," Keleghan recalls, and given that to the actor's recollection, the episode was shot entirely on location at a suburban house, there weren't many of the amenities the studio provided that could offer the actors much respite. The plasticky vinyl outfits worn by the actors, as well as the makeup, were not conducive to comfort, but, by all accounts, the gnome actors were great fun to be around, and relished the opportunity to be part of the fun, relaxing with cigars in between takes.

Keleghan was unfamiliar with the *Goosebumps* world, so while spending a week playing the father of two kids didn't strike him as a particularly impactful job at the time, he was excited to reunite with actor David Hemblen, for whom he had been understudy at a major production for the Stratford Festival in 1983. "He was such a great guy, and he had such a magnificent voice," he recalls of his friend. Hemblen had temporarily lost said magnificent voice back in '83, and Keleghan swiftly stepped into his role with only two hours of rehearsal time before hitting the stage. Keleghan says Hemblen was a great choice for the role of the Major. "He's almost like the character he played," he says. "He was a pretty dour, crusty kind of guy, but his heart was always in the right place. And then always a big smile when he saw you."

Ever the conscientious working actor, Keleghan remembers his fleeting *Goosebumps* experience fondly, not just for the fun of working on the show, but for the impact the series had on his industry. "It was a big sort of institution within Toronto that really helped the industry a lot because of the work, not just for actors and directors, but, you know, caterers and drivers and car companies," he says. For those child actors who continued on in the industry into adulthood, this is a concept they have come to appreciate in their later years. For a major American brand to make the trip over the border and give such steady work to hundreds of industry professionals was a hell of a big deal, and one they still express gratitude for to this day.

There were rare occasions where American creativity was brought on board, and perhaps the most prominent such name to grace the *Goosebumps* screen was that of The Caped Crusader himself, actor Adam West. Past his glory days of *Batman*, West's career was finding a sort of self-aware resurgence in pop culture, often either playing himself or parodic versions of himself or his former characters. He was still far from his stint on *Family Guy*, which would cement his self-deprecating style of meta-comedy, and surprisingly, he was not at all excited when he was approached to star as an aging superhero in *Goosebumps*.

Although Dan Angel and Billy Brown had specifically written the episode with him in mind, "Adam West did not want to make that show," Steve Levitan says. "Adam West, who was a lovely, lovely man, was kind of pigeon-holed. He was stereotyped after the *Batman* series, constantly these high camp characters and types. I gathered from his agent that they were sick and tired of getting approaches from producers to play another person in tights!"

The team fought their corner, and eventually secured West on the condition that he would only be needed for two days' work, and that the costume he wore would never see the light of day. "He went home with that costume!" says Steve. Everybody was awed by the presence of a bona fide legend on set. "Honestly, he was an icon when he showed up on the set. Everybody stopped! Their mouths were wide open. They were just in awe that we actually had Batman on our set!" he recalls. Despite West's reservations about accepting the role, he took it all in his stride and made a very positive impact on not just the show, but those he worked with. "It went swimmingly," says Levitan. "Well, he was totally professional. He was fantastic, did his stuff. It's a great episode. I still remember walking onto the set and seeing him in the middle of all of these pipes, in that costume, and he was just totally a gentleman about it. A great sport. I'm forever grateful to him for agreeing to do it. I can't imagine making that show with anyone else."

While the adults in the industry were happy for the boost in demand for their services, the less experienced child actors were champing at the bit for the weird and wonderful experiences that a gig on *Goosebumps* could throw their way. It wasn't often that the young actors got to play the monsters themselves, so when the opportunity arose for three child performers to be fitted with monster gloves and masks for the episode "Calling All Creeps," they leapt at it eagerly. Matthew Lemche, Travis Kutt and Tonya Johnson were excited for the chance to perform in full creep costume, but the pieces made shooting a rather disorienting experience. They couldn't see or hear very well, and their voices were muffled by the animatronic masks, which led to the crew recording their lines on location, rather than in the booth, to ensure a consistent ambience. The kids performed each shot with the masks off for audio, and then again in costume for the visuals, with their vocals being mixed in post to add an eerie creep factor. It was certainly a memorable early working experience for them.

"Calling All Creeps" was filmed entirely on location in August of 1996, except for the scene inside of the creeps' tent, which was extended at last minute to accommodate more creative camera motion. "So it was probably the cheapest set they built!" laughs director Craig Pryce. This sequence required a half-day at the studio, but everything else was shot on location in houses and Lawrence Park Collegiate Institute. The episode was in the hands of an up-and-comer who was far newer to it all than the other directors on the show. Pryce was young, only 28 or 29 at the time, and had got started in his own feature films, so this pivot towards television was relatively unknown territory for him. "I was still, for TV directors, young," he says, "and they were very supportive, and I also knew exactly what I wanted. At the time, you're just so focused. I get so focused and almost myopic on what my job is as a director. So I felt a little intimidated because, number one, it was a successful show, and you want to make sure you carry on the tradition and the continuity. It was my first or second episode ever, so I wasn't used to a big union crew, I was used to indie horror films and stuff. It was a learning curve. I remember being very young, and everyone sort of treating me that way. Other than the cast, I was the youngest kid on set!"

For Pryce, being given "Calling All Creeps" was a great fit, having completed his second movie, a creature feature titled *The Dark*, not long before he arrived on the set of *Goosebumps*. "It made sense because the creeps were creatures, and *The Dark* was a creature feature. I think there were elements of "Calling All Creeps" that were suited to my last feature," he says. As well as finding the monster premise a great fit for his skills and interests, Pryce had also worked with Ron Stefaniuk on his first two movies, so found himself in good, reliable company with the effects workshop his episode would depend on.

Although Pryce didn't go into the project with any particular inspiration in mind, he is flattered by comparisons of "Calling All Creeps" to the likes of *Carrie* and *Little Shop of Horrors*. "I always let the script tell me the style," he explains. "When I received "Calling All Creeps," I really let the script talk to me about how to shoot it and how to design the shots. The underlying thing on style is that I'm really big on movement. As lyrical as I can, 'motivated' is my big word." He was also intrigued by the direction the story takes, not toward some great triumph over evil, but more a resignation to it. "The ending is really interesting, because for twenty-two minutes, Ricky has a great arc. He's the outcast, he's bullied, and all these things are going wrong. I looked at it as 'power corrupts'. He can be unselfish and save his friends, but now he's becoming the leader and they're the nerds, so to speak. It's kind of a dark ending, it really is, which I love about it. This character, who knows what it's like to be on the other side, and now he has this opportunity. You see good people get power and then they change. Now everything has to have a happy ending it seems, and that's what I liked about the show. Tween shows, they were a lot different back then."

Indeed, tween shows had a rougher, nastier edge to them in the '90s, and Season Two of *Goosebumps* was living proof of it. Having really gained momentum since the Halloween debut of the show almost a year earlier, *Goosebumps* was now the go-to for spooky season entertainment, and Season Two did not disappoint. "Attack of the Jack 'o' Lanterns" was the second Halloween-themed episode, and served as an intro to "The Haunted Mask II", which aired just a few days later to take full advantage of Halloween audiences, and stands out as among the most genuinely horrifying episodes ever made. Production was fully in the swing of things now, and was taking advantage of the opportunities at its disposal, not least of which being the ability to descend on neighborhoods and give them a seasonal makeover.

On the set of "The Haunted Mask II." Photo courtesy of Steve Levitan.

"Whole neighborhoods just go nuts for Halloween!" Ian Brock remembers of mid-'90s suburban Toronto, jokingly musing on whether *Goosebumps* had anything to do with this explosion in all things spooky. "We just take over like whole city blocks, and we just make it like it was Halloween." The addition of some fancy, and very pricy, new helium lights from Italy made shooting exteriors at night a much easier affair, particularly given the night shoots that the episode exclusively consisted of. As ever, the production design team got to work with characteristic thriftiness, with Chinese lanterns painted as pumpkins being a particularly triumphant idea for Ian Brock. When he later spotted the exact same thing in the Martha Stewart catalogue, he didn't know whether to laugh or cry.

"Attack of the Jack 'o' Lanterns" was shot in the Banbury-Don Mills neighborhood of Toronto, with Chatfield Drive featuring heavily. Filmed in the summer, school was out and plenty of local kids were available for recreating Halloween. Extras were gathered from local areas, along with the kids, nephews and nieces of the cast and crew. Erica Luttrell, who had played the minor character of Kim in "Piano Lessons Can Be Murder," was back for her first lead role on the show, while Philip Eddolls of "Phantom of the Auditorium" also returned for his second episode.

"The Halloween shows were always our big-budget shows, because we'd always have to go outside, have a lot of kids in costumes. I'm pretty sure my two daughters were extras in that one," recalls Steve Levitan. "One was dressed as a witch, and one was dressed as a princess or something." Although Levitan was always happy for his kids to experience his thoroughly exciting work life, he was careful not to let being the producers' daughters go to their heads. "They were in the background. Didn't give them lines, that would have been too much nepotism! I remember going there with my two kids, who were super excited about being in a TV show, and my mother-in-law, who was scarier than anybody who was ever in the show, and more dangerous!" he chuckles.

Hot on the heels of "Attack of the Jack 'o' Lanterns" was perhaps the most highly anticipated episode yet. As one of a small handful of episodes to function as direct sequels to previous instalments, and the only one to have received the hour-long special treatment each time, "The Haunted Mask II" is a real standout among the series. Stine's book sequel to "The Haunted Mask" was published the same month that the series' first episode was airing, so at the time of production on "The Haunted Mask," there was no indication that there would soon be a reunion to film part two. But the debut episode had been a ratings hit and got the show off the ground in a big way, and having proven once before that it could be pulled off on-screen—as was the main criterion for books selected for adaptation—it was quickly lined up for another hour-long special episode.

It certainly came as a pleasant surprise for its cast, who were all reassembled, with the sole exception of George Davis as Steve, who was replaced with John White, previous star of "The Cuckoo Clock of Doom." By the time of "The Haunted Mask II", all four main kids had done *Goosebumps* before, with John White and Kathryn Short having worked on episodes outside the "Haunted Mask" universe. Unlike in other such instances, Amos Crawley doesn't recall their swapping experiences much: "I think for a lot of child actors, most of us had done it for a long time, or started when we were really young. It was part of the fabric of our existence in a way that didn't feel notable unless you were around other kids who weren't child actors."

For Crawley, being invited back, sans audition, was "a reward," a sign that he did his job well enough to be given another go. Although he preferred Tim Bond's directorial style, he found working on the sequel an even more rewarding experience because he had more to do this time around. He felt a marked change of pace on set, mostly due to Bill Fruet now being at the helm, and the preexisting relationships he had with his co-stars, but found his second go on the *Goosebumps* carousel more enjoyable than the first, particularly thanks to the sweet gangster getup he was given. He still wishes he could grow a pencil moustache as good as the one they drew on him.

John White has his makeup touched up on the set of "The Haunted Mask II." Photo courtesy of Steve Levitan.

Season Two wasn't just bringing about exciting new opportunities for its cast, though. By this point, cinematographer Brian R.R. Hebb had firmly made his impression on *Goosebumps* and lent it a certain visual style, full of swooping camera movements, Dutch angles and frantic but stylish energy. Although his plate was already full, covering both director of photography and camera operator roles, he fancied trying his hand in the director's chair, so put his hat in the ring and asked if he could direct an episode. Production were more than happy to oblige, and although Hebb didn't get any say in which story would be delegated to him, he was happy with the choice they made. "The Headless Ghost" was officially his, and they went into production.

It proved to be an enjoyable but very demanding job for Hebb. "I did have a lot of freedom but not a lot of time," he says. "Many of the things I wanted to show on screen I didn't have time for. Working as both director and director of photography, especially when I'm operating the camera, is total mental gymnastics." As much as he loved his time directing the show, he was a one-and-done. "I only did the one directing assignment because time didn't permit me doing the three jobs as director, director of photography and camera operator," he says. Producers also shut down any prospect of Hebb directing any further episodes. "I guess they didn't want me distracted from the photography," he posits. More pressingly, he was in the process of moving away from the show altogether, as circumstances in his personal life made him feel that he needed a change of scenery.

The episode brought about a trip to another of the city's notable residences. Exteriors were shot at the historic Cawthra-Elliot Estate, a 1920s house in Mississauga built for one of Toronto's most prominent and wealthy families of the time. Fittingly, local supernatural enthusiasts report that former staffers at the estate claim that the house is haunted. Unfortunately for Hebb, no such manifestations occurred on the *Goosebumps* set, leaving the crew short-changed by the resident specters, and having to create the scares themselves. Typical bougie ghost attitude.

As if no-show ghosts weren't enough for Season Two deal with, the conveyor belt of child and animal stars kept on coming. As before, animal actors were an integral part of the production, and this came with its share of creative scrambles. In some cases, they were easy. Stuntman Bryan Renfro's dog had made quite the impression on *Goosebumps* producers when they met him on the set of "The Werewolf of Fever Swamp." Despite having accidentally locked himself in an office on that occasion, he was well-trained and easy to work with on set. To this end, Renfro was called back in Season Two and asked to bring his dog with him. "He was such a good worker that the producer on the show wanted me to work him again for another episode, so we colored him so he looked like a different dog," says Renfro. "They didn't want to use another dog!"

On the opposite end of the Season Two animal spectrum is "Bad Hare Day." The episode's thirty-five-page script originally contained ten whole pages of dialogue to be spoken by a rabbit. Where scripts were usually delivered on a Wednesday, this one was running late and didn't arrive until Friday morning. With such tight deadlines, this had the potential of a domino effect, something everybody else would have to rush to avoid. Such instances "would drive everybody crazy because there's so much work to prep," says Steve Levitan, but in the case of a rabbit with ten pages of dialogue, there was even more to consider. The three effects department guys were called— animatronics, post and animals—and Ron Stefaniuk, in his ever-ambitious way, assured Levitan he would have an animatronic rabbit ready to go for Monday's shoot. "He said that all the time!" Levitan chuckles. "It was never finished! It was always almost-finished." Ideally, such intricate creations would be ready a couple of days ahead of shooting so that directors and D.P.s could play around with them and get to grips with their functions. "The effects people always said, 'No problem, we'll do it in post, we can do it,' but we can't wait that long. It'll take three or four weeks in post and we can't go back and reshoot," Levitan explains. "It's an anthology, all the people are gone, they're off to other things."

To this end, the animal wrangler was frantically called, who reassured production that he could deliver the goods, and arranged for a camera test on the Saturday before shooting was due to begin—a rare working weekend. The rabbit turned up, and was plonked on top of a barrel, with a camera facing him. Then came the wrangler's magic tool: a water pistol filled with sugar water, which he gently sprayed at the rabbit's mouth from off-camera. Sure enough, the rabbit began twitching his face to sop up the sweet treat, and all that needed to be done now was for editing and voiceover to fill in the gaps. "We hired the late, great Gilbert Gottfried to do the voice of the rabbit," Steve Levitan fondly remembers. "He was terrific at matching the dialogue to the rabbit's movements. And that was the process. Almost every episode had something similar to that because there was always a monster!"

But every now and then, the monster was more man. For Ron Oliver, "Vampire Breath" was a real treat, thanks to the immersive sets and old-timey classic vampire vibe. The self-described horror nerd delighted in doing something that felt like a throwback to the days of Hammer Horror, with plenty of stone, mist and swishing capes. He also loved the staple plot points that vampire stories presented: "Here's a lovely life, and then something terrible comes in, and at the end, your lovely life again — and then a twist! The rules of Vampire World are so strong that you can have fun with it and satirize it a little bit," he explains.

Of course, paying homage to the vampiric greats like Christopher Lee required an actor who could really live up to the charismatic yet intimidating archetype of the classic prince of darkness. Earl Pastko was a Chicago native and experienced theater actor, a quality that Oliver really wanted in his head vampire. "There's this stately quality about him," Oliver says, "and you wanted somebody who had this grandeur about them. He was the linchpin for the episode, and if that guy's not scary, you have no show." Pastko's theatrical presence made him the perfect fit, and he was quickly brought onboard to counter the two innocent child characters, played by Zach Lipovsky and Meredith Henderson.

As one of the most classically horror-oriented episodes of the show, "Vampire Breath" presented plenty of fun to be had with its atmosphere, a job Oliver gleefully handed over to the production crew. "It was spooky, lots of dry ice. That was probably one of my favorite sets in the entire series, and I remember saying to the designers, 'Let's just make it fun, like an amusement park ride, like a thrill ride.'" He liked the idea of combining the metaphorical feeling of *Goosebumps* being a rollercoaster ride with a literal rollercoaster ride down into the bowels of a vampire cave, and wrote in the kids' fast-paced descent to keep the energy of the episode up and maximize the excitement.

The show's use of the Lego set arrangement didn't stop at bedrooms and house interiors: the centerpieces of the cave set had been left over from another show, and were perfect for reappropriating for "Vampire Breath." The pieces were brought into the studio and redressed to give a uniquely *Goosebumps* feel. The final, and arguably most imaginative piece of design that went into the episode was the coffin bunk beds used for the big twist ending, which would add a final splash of fun and light-heartedness to an inherently dark story. A particular favorite among the cast and crew, they all wanted to take them home with them. "That's the kind of bunk beds I'd want my kids to have!" Ron Oliver says.

The season would end once again on a high note, with the return of Slappy in "Night of the Living Dummy III," this time in the hands of Tim Bond, as Ron Oliver was not available to return to his beloved demented doll. Although the two-part episode turned out very well, continuing Slappy's bitchy prankster spell and going on to be another fan favorite, Oliver would have liked to be involved, to take Slappy's antics up a notch before writing him in his final incarnation, "Bride of the Living Dummy." The episode is notable for starring a young Hayden Christensen as Zane, the wimpy cousin of the two sibling protagonists Trina and Daniel, who takes revenge a little too far and ends up tangled in Slappy's web of tricks.

Heading into summer of 1997, *Goosebumps*' first full-length season was a resounding success, and at this point, with Stine continuing to pump out books at a remarkable rate, it seemed the future of the show was unlimited. With these high hopes, the crew would head back into production after a short break for Season Three.

The Era of Kid-Vid

Home Media and Merchandising

It was the '90s, and owning a movie or show on video was the only surefire way to enjoy a piece of media whenever you wanted. Saturday evening trips to Blockbuster or your local mom and pop video store were part of the culture, and kids' videos, or kid-vid, were big business. Disney were raking it in with their relatively new strategy of releasing decades-old classics on video at an incredible $26.99 a pop, and they were dominating the video sales charts on account of this move. The House of Mouse went further still to capitalize on the home media boom, with straight-to-video sequels to their classics, and the *Singalong Songs* series, which at first served as a jukebox of Disney songs, before expanding into short live-action adventures with groups of characters or child actors prancing around Disney parks. Although much shorter in runtime, they still commanded those hefty Disney prices.

Next to these home viewing offerings, $14.98 for a whole hour of rewatchable Goosebumpy goodness was a bargain, and gave kids the freedom to watch their favourite episodes to their heart's content. The first official video release for *Goosebumps* came in March 1996, a while before Season One had wrapped, but a good few months into the show's run, allowing plenty of time for young viewers to get hooked and want to own the videos for themselves.

Video releases were a very specific part of the *Goosebumps* marketing strategy that had been in play from the beginning. Early on in the business dealings of setting the show up, a deal was struck with 20th Century Fox Home Entertainment to release a number of episodes as one-hour features that would be bang for your buck as home viewing experiences, and this established the multiple-parter format. It also played into which stories would be adapted into episodes with a longer runtime. "The video releases had to be longer than the broadcast versions," says Steve Levitan, "with a running time of twenty-four minutes and ten seconds if I remember it correctly, so the structure of the show for home video viewing needed to be a lot smoother, the breaks needed to be smoothed out or eliminated. The videos were sold as one-hour episodes and the broadcast episodes were twenty-four minutes, and we wrote them for that kind of flexibility."

"The Haunted Mask" having served well as the show's opening act, it was a shoo-in for the home media releases, and was unleashed upon the U.S. by 20th Century Fox Home Entertainment on March 12 1996. It boasted a behind-the-scenes featurette of upcoming release "A Night in Terror Tower," as well as a lenticular image bookmark, reminding kids to keep reading. Fox was pushing the release hard, with special point-of-sale signs and graphics to advertise the new release in stores, as well as a website for those advanced or lucky enough to have access to the World Wide Web in 1996. It was a smash hit, selling 2.5 million units by Christmas of that year, and had been on Billboard's top kids video chart for nineteen straight weeks by the time follow-up video releases were announced. Clearly the home video marketing strategy that had been integral to the show's design was working, so further releases were scheduled.

"Stay Out of the Basement" and "A Night in Terror Tower" were released on September 3 1996, with the behind-the-scenes sneak peek having built significant hype for the latter. Next came "The Werewolf of Fever Swamp" on March 25 1997, followed by "The Haunted Mask II" on July 29 and "Welcome to Dead House" on September 23. By November of 1997, over 5 million copies had been sold of the first five titles, making the *Goosebumps* series one of the best-selling kid-vids ever. The curious decision was made to release "Night of the Living Dummy III" in January of 1998, bypassing the lucrative Christmas gift market. Nevertheless, it performed well, debuting at number nineteen on the top kids video charts.

The summer of '98 was where the strategy was shaken up a bit, with the release of two three-episode special videos, combining already-released episodes onto one compilation tape. This approach leaned more in the direction of your average kids' show VHS release, which would compile several episodes onto one release. Fall of 1998 saw *Goosebumps*' final foray into the US video market, with "Werewolf Skin" and "One Day at Horrorland" both releasing on September 15, along with a double feature of "Bride of the Living Dummy" and "An Old Story." This final video release stands out as the only one not featuring a two-parter episode. One would be forgiven up to this point for assuming that the video market angle was to release all two- and three-part episodes, but this was not the case. A number of multipart episodes, such as "Perfect School," "Welcome to Camp Nightmare" and "Chillogy" did not receive a U.S. video release, nor did any of Season Four, which had just debuted on television at this time and comprised entirely two-parters.

Over the pond, the U.K. distributors, 20th Century Fox Video, took a slightly different approach. They also debuted the video series with "The Haunted Mask" in March of 1997, followed almost a year later with "The Werewolf of Fever Swamp," which appeared to ruffle the feathers of governing body BBFC, and received a 12 rating as opposed to a PG. This presented some issues as it meant that kids of the target audience age couldn't buy it themselves, and would have to appeal to their parents to overlook the off-putting certificate and trust that whatever was on this video would not irreparably scar their children. It also apparently meant that this little episode of kids' TV was as upsetting to young viewers as *Titanic*, and scarier than *Jaws*, if certifications are anything to go by. It's a strange choice, given the episode doesn't really stand out as extreme compared to the rest of the show, and that all other U.K. releases skated by with a PG rating.

"Welcome to Camp Nightmare" got its video release here, as did "Return of the Mummy," which as the only single episode of the UK releases was another odd addition to *Goosebumps*' home video catalog. "Stay Out of the Basement," "Night of the Living Dummy III," "A Night in Terror Tower," "One Day at Horrorland" and "The Haunted Mask II" all released in 1999, curiously followed three years later by "Welcome to Dead House." The show saw sporadic VHS releases in other territories as well, including France and Germany.

None of the various distributors opted to release the entire series during the show's heyday. This was admittedly not unusual in itself, with many kids' shows in the '90s releasing compilation videos of three to five episodes with little connective theme or chronology. The industry theorized at this time that TV shows being released to home media was a bad move in the long term, leading to decreased viewership of TV broadcasts, poor sales of videos, or both. *Goosebumps* seemed to disprove this theory, or at least buck the trend thanks to its incredible popularity and young audience.

Amos Crawley remembers the VHS era, and what made home releases so appealing to audiences. "I think the VHS is really what gave [the show] its staying power. I do meet people fairly regularly, even much, much younger people who are like, 'Well, every Halloween, this is what we watch.' That it is a tradition for people. And I think it's because, sometimes it was the only VHS you had. You know, something that our kids will not understand is that there was a time in your life where you watched a movie twenty or thirty times because it rained all summer, and that was the only one that you had!"

The 2000s presented a strange in-between time for *Goosebumps*. The show was officially over, and many of its original audience had supposedly grown out of it, and most pointedly, media consumption habits were on the cusp of a great transformation. The internet was now much more universal than it had been during the show's run, but still had a way to go before the likes of Netflix and YouTube would make viewership more accessible and full of endless choice. Television remained the go-to for the series format, so while the show was still enjoying reruns on various cable networks around the world, it was kind of stuck there. That was until 2008, when 20th Century Fox Home Entertainment released a short, sharp burst of *Goosebumps* onto DVD for the first time.

Marketed as double features despite offering between three and five episodes per disc, these releases showcased some of the multiple-parters that were neglected the first time around on video, such as "Chillogy" and "Perfect School," and marked the first home media release of all the episodes of Season Four. Only twenty-four episodes were included on this DVD release, and it was a good step in the right direction, but there was still a way to go before fans could own the entire show to watch at home.

It wasn't until the 2010s that *Goosebumps* would receive the full, uncut boxset treatment. Revelation Films secured the rights to the show's UK home media distribution, and initially released the show a season at a time. Season One came out on DVD in November 2012, followed by Season Two in March 2013. Seasons Three and Four were condensed into a single release in August of that year, and just in time for Halloween, The Complete Collection emerged on October 28. It had taken almost twenty years, but finally the show was available on home media in its entirety.

The following year, Australia received the same, courtesy of Madman Entertainment, and French and German releases were unleashed around the same time. In France, where the show was known as *Chair de Poule*, Seasons One and Two got individual releases in 2012 and 2013, with Seasons Three and Four being grouped together for a final release in October of 2013. Germany, meanwhile, was lucky enough to get the complete boxset of *Gänsehaut* in 2016.

It was also during this time that Netflix acquired the streaming rights to the show, and this was where the nostalgic boom really took off. Streaming hadn't yet become such a competitive arena, and Netflix largely dominated it, with everybody and their aunt having a subscription. This wide accessibility meant that many now-adult viewers, who hadn't watched the whole series in years, if at all, could finally sit down and binge it if they so desired. The more eagle-eyed viewers might have spotted small but noticeable differences between the finally-uncut version of the show they were now watching and what they saw broadcast on TV in the '90s. Episodes recorded from reruns in the early to mid-2000s evidence a lot of cuts, often during chase scenes or monster sequences. This might strike the viewer as a matter of censorship—the UK boxset DVD release makes explicit reference to BBC broadcasts having been censored—but Steve Levitan says that is mostly not the case. "It was not because of scary content or anything like that. It was mostly because of the nature of the viewing experience for that particular format," he explains. Short answer: the episodes now available on Netflix or DVD releases were the full, uncut versions, which home media could accommodate. But broadcast episodes needed to work around incredibly specific time slots, where every second counted, and it just happened that the more protracted scenes like chases through the woods could be trimmed down to meet these slots without negatively impacting the narrative or overall viewing experience.

As of 2024, all episodes of *Goosebumps* are available to watch for free on YouTube, and each episode has racked up hundreds of thousands of views. While this is nice, it is strange and quite unfortunate that the U.S. and Canada, the nations who gave birth to the show in the first place, have never received a complete series boxset release of their own. With trends leaning back towards owning physical media again after an era of everything being digital, there would surely be an audience wanting to own the show for themselves, where it cannot be retrospectively altered or removed.

It's notable that despite the huge success that the show brought around for the *Goosebumps* brand, it was fairly low on merchandising, especially compared to the book series, which had everything from alarm clocks to toothbrush holders created in its image. According to Steve Levitan, this was an issue they'd struggled with Scholastic over. "Scholastic was not prepared to give up merchandising rights," he says, "so I wasn't able to participate in any of it, and eventually I agreed. Not because I was wise enough to foresee what was going to happen but because there was no other way to do the deal." However, once the show went into production, the company started exploring merchandising options, and brought Levitan into the negotiations.

He attended meetings in New York with various toy companies and other potential licensees, to explore the possibility of licensed t-shirts, school supplies and other such trinkets. However, these talks quickly encountered an issue. "The big problem that became clear, the big obstacle, was that kids merchandising is character-driven," Levitan explains. "Slappy is about as close a character as *Goosebumps* has, so it was really hard. And *Goosebumps* as a word, or as a brand, doesn't lend itself to creating actual toys. You might get a *Goosebumps* t-shirt or a *Goosebumps* logo on a water bottle for kids or a lunch bag, but it's not that exciting to just have the logo. There might be a small market for it but not enough to drive an overall license deal, which is what you need with a big toy company for a line of different products. So, it never really took off."

In addition to its lack of a marketable character who could serve as the figurehead for the show, the wider impact of the anthology format was being felt. For the crew, making a mini movie every week was part of the thrill and creative challenge, but when it came to merchandising, it made everything too inconsistent and lacking in focal point. Levitan says that the anthology is not for the faint-hearted, and that many producers prefer a straight-forward narrative centered around the same characters and locations week after week. "It's not for budget reasons, it's just lazy thinking for producers who didn't want the scary idea of having to recast every episode," he says.

Levitan doesn't necessarily see the show's low marketability as a bad thing, though, and feels that the lack of licensing deals probably freed them up to maintain a level of creative autonomy that they otherwise might have lost. "It didn't need merchandising to be successful," he says. "If we had done a toy deal or a merchandising deal as part of the financing of the show initially, which is the way most kids' shows get done, with Hasbro or Mattel or one of those big companies…if we had had Hasbro as a partner, then we would've been under a lot of pressure, probably, to have continuing characters and create characters or narrators or something that could sell."

The nostalgic boom of the 2020s has brought around a new era of *Goosebumps* merchandise, although most of it is focused on the brand as a whole rather than the television show specifically. Steve Levitan imagines that a lot of these are unofficial, unlicensed products, and wishes their makers luck with handling the lawsuit that will inevitably come their way. Jane Stine remains protective of her husband's work. For the *Goosebumps* show, home media releases were the only other main source of income for the show outside of broadcasting deals, and they certainly did their part to not only rake in more bucks, but to cement the series as a true classic of '90s kids' entertainment. The video tapes are now considered collector's items and fetch considerable sums when put up for sale. Those who kept hold of their childhood VHS tapes are probably glad they never quite outgrew them.

The Beginning of the End

Season Three

Production on Season Three got going in the Spring of 1997, and the show was still flying high on the success it had built through hard work and pop culture prevalence. By this point, home media releases had begun, adding a valuable string to the *Goosebumps* bow and furthering the show's reach. R.L. Stine would continue publishing a new book every month for the rest of the calendar year, at which point the original book series would end and make way for the different-in-name-only *Goosebumps 2000* to capitalize on the slowly building hysteria surrounding the impending millennium. It had now been five years since the world of *Goosebumps* had got going, and it showed no signs of slowing down. As readers and viewers aged out of the target audience, their younger siblings were growing into it, eagerly snatching up the books and video tapes their brothers and sisters now felt they were too old for. There was a continuous conveyor belt of kids ready to get on the *Goosebumps* train, and as long as they were there, Protocol and Scholastic were more than willing to deliver the goods.

Despite the steady stream of books Stine was providing, the writing of the show started to diversify considerably in Season Three, with eight of the stories adapted for episodes not coming from the original sixty-two-book series. These outliers were based on collections of short stories within the *Goosebumps* universe, but were not quite as well known to the audience as the original series. On top of that, Season Three would push the boat out creatively by doing its first, and only, totally original story in the form of "Chillogy."

Penned by Billy Brown and Dan Angel, it was also notable for being the series' sole three-parter, comprising episodes "Squeal of Fortune," "Strike Three… You're Doomed," and "Escape from Karlsville." While the story itself isn't particularly groundbreaking, it is carried on the shoulders of actor Daniel Kash as the deliciously devious villain Karl, and his splendid array of glittery blazers, bringing it a decidedly camp vibe to proceedings. It also marks the return of Caterina Scorsone, and made prominent use of another Toronto landmark. The entire Trinity Street area was cleared out and transformed into the mid-century pastiche of Karlsville, and with the vast space, managed to achieve an authentic feeling of a creepy, otherworldly town. It made use of some miniatures as well, with Ian Brock remembering one of his work friends knocking the mini set together in her living room. As one of the most comically-oriented episodes of the series, it made its mark by doing just about everything differently, and stands out as one of the most fabulously unusual in the show's run.

In fact, Season Three would continue to step out of the box with the more weird and wonderful stories, not least of which being the now-infamous "An Old Story." To this day, the episode is remembered as possibly the strangest—and at worst, most disturbing—to come out of *Goosebumps*. Although told in a relatively innocent way, it is difficult to overlook the implications of this story: essentially, a woman is sex-trafficking her nephews. But the crew never looked at the episode in such a light. To them, it was all light-hearted fun, as *Goosebumps* always was, and most of all, it was a blast to make. "I, of course, was wondering how the episode would be received," says Randy Bradshaw. "But the people at the Fox network loved it. To them, it was just another crazy *Goosebumps* story."

Randy Bradshaw's book signed by the cast of
"An Old Story." Photo courtesy of Randy Bradshaw.

When Bradshaw was first given the script, he loved it, and couldn't wait to get started directing it. Although he acknowledges that the episode is something of a standout for the series, he theorizes that Fox let the show have a little more wiggle room, given what a smash success it had become by this point. "I think they gave everybody a little bit of space," he says. "Not knowing, or thinking, this is, much like you were saying, a bit outside the normal bent of the series." For Bradshaw, it was just another amusing go round on the *Goosebumps* carousel, and one that gave him the perfect opportunity to reunite with an actor he had loved working with previously. He and British actress Kay Tremblay had crossed paths on an episode of *Street Legal* some ten years earlier, and he was determined to bring her on board. "I just loved her, so right away I knew it had to be her," Bradshaw says. She would play one of the elderly women set to gain a mysteriously young-at-heart husband, and the two had a swell time on the set together again.

Kyle Downes and Jordan Allison were just getting started in their acting careers, and were thrilled for the opportunity to be made over into old versions of themselves. They rehearsed their old man choreography with Bradshaw, walking around bent over and suffering from the aches and pains of advanced age. "They just bought into the whole idea, as weird as it was, and the kids loved doing it. It was fun to work with them," the director says. "They were really well-prepared. These kids were spot on the money."

Despite mostly taking place in an ordinary suburban setting, the episode promised to be a fun one to work on, given the heavy makeup that would be involved. "I thought, *How the hell are we gonna do this?! The makeup—how long is it going to take and how were we going to deal with the schedule?*" Randy Bradshaw says. Indeed, the makeup presented a considerable challenge, not just for Ron Stefaniuk's creative team, but in terms of child labor laws. Bradshaw recalls that the kids were able to work for a maximum of eight hours a day, and when the boys were in the makeup chair for several of those hours, it ate into their shooting time at an alarming rate. To help overcome this challenge, additional makeup artists were brought on so that Downes and Allison could have their makeup applied simultaneously and maximize their time with cameras rolling. The effort was worth it, and everybody on set was tickled pink by the results. "When they would see the boys in their makeup, everybody was freaking out! A lot of pictures were being taken!" Bradshaw recalls.

Beyond the physical makeup, a conservative amount of the dreaded post effects would be required for the finale. Aunt Dahlia's big death scene was a simple enough setup, one which required three identical costumes for actress Patricia Gage, so that they could get multiple takes of her character being doused with prune juice, which in reality was just water with food coloring in it. Because of the extensive makeup the young actors required, Bradshaw says they tried to make up the difference by getting through everything else quicker than usual, hence measures like multiple costumes at the ready. Despite these extra considerations, the episode was a blast to work on, and didn't run into any major issues. "It was so much fun!" Randy Bradshaw says, fondly recalling his favourite line of the episode as wisdom to live by: "Good snacks take time."

Similarly out-there episodes were dotted throughout the season. "Strained Peas," about a boy whose new baby sister is some kind of evil, pet-eating monster set on ruining his life, was notable for its casting of young actor Tyrone Savage alongside his real-life parents Booth Savage and Janet-Laine Green. Director Don McCutcheon says that this unconventional casting of a real family was not part of the plan, nor a case of industry nepotism, but "just serendipity, I guess, to a certain degree. I mean, Booth and Janet-Laine are very, very talented. So there was a chemistry there, and they were just right for the roles. It was that simple."

Then, of course, there was the final appearance of series icon Slappy in what was easily his most mischievous, and some may say alarming, outing to date. Randy Bradshaw didn't know that "Bride of the Living Dummy" would be his last time directing the show, and went at it with his usual sense of fun. This episode brought him together with fellow *Goosebumps* director Ron Oliver, who was hired to pen the script, making it the only one of Oliver's scripts that he didn't also direct himself. Given its campy nature, along with being the final instalment in the "Living Dummy" series which Oliver directed the first of, it seems it would have been a good fit for the director. He puts the decision not to direct down to time constraints. "There was a lot going on at that time. I was doing another series. That might have been the same time as *Animorphs*, or it might have been the same time as *PSI Factor*."

Around this time, several shows were being produced in the same studio building, with a floor dedicated to each, making it easy for those straddling more than one show to literally cross over from one to the next. In this way, Oliver says he probably popped by the *Goosebumps* studio to handle the writing of "Bride of the Living Dummy" while working full-time directing a different series.

There was also the matter of new experiences. Having already done the whole "Living Dummy" thing, Oliver was eager to take on new challenges. "It was just that I did that, and I don't really want to do it again," he says. So it was up to Randy Bradshaw to take the reins, and he was going for a film noir feel. As such a puppet-heavy episode, he wanted to go as dark as possible to offset any jokey elements that might have come with the turf. This may have worked a little too well, because by the time filming was in session, some last-minute changes were required. Late actor Michael Vollans once did a Reddit Q&A that revealed there was some back-and-forth about how far was too far for this particular episode, especially with the reveal that his character Harrison had been possessed by Slappy. The final line was originally scripted as "a new body for my new bride," but the implication that Slappy would now be romantically involved with an adolescent boy was a little too far. Randy Bradshaw elaborates: "There was a lot of discussion about the script before we started shooting, too, right? And it was just trying to figure out some of these things and trying to walk this fine line. The line is invisible, but you don't want to cross that line. I think there was a little bit of sensitivity about this whole thing." To this end, the big reveal ended with the line, "Sorry, folks. Harrison doesn't live here anymore," and the addition of *Roger Rabbit*-style cartoon eyes made sure the ending packed a punch either way.

Those in the horror circles may well recognize character actor Wayne Robson as ventriloquist Jimmie O'James. Robson would later make very memorable appearances as the hillbilly father of the mutant clan in *Wrong Turn* and its first sequel. Bradshaw had worked with Wayne Robson previously, and was excited to be directing him again. "He was a very charming guy. Extremely professional, always came fully prepared," the director recalls, comparing Robson to Toby Jones, as a character actor who always made an impact regardless of how limited his role was. In fact, Bradshaw sought Robson out. "Wow! This is a character Wayne could play," he thought, and, "immediately I call up and see if Wayne would come in to chat." As ever, Robson made a lot out of a little, and the location team did the same. The scenes at the theatre were filmed on location at the Factory Theatre at 125 Bathurst Street, just a short walk from *Goosebumps* HQ. While this was an incredibly convenient location to move the action to, this season was not playing it safe, and arguably the most ambitious filming location would be used to kick off Season Three.

For "A Shocker on Shock Street," even Sunnybrook Park couldn't quite measure up to the scale of the story. For this one, they needed a real-life theme park that could be dressed up to fill in for Shock Street Studios. This is where the historic Centreville Amusement Park came into play. The park was closed to the public for a week, and everybody loved the novelty of riding a ferry from the mainland to Centreville's island location for work every morning. Randy Bradshaw and some crew members had a walkthrough of the park during their prep week, throwing out ideas about how they could take its existing components and transform them into a sci-fi dream. They were assisted by ride operators who worked at the park, and sat through a number of safety meetings. Sadly, the limited park staff and demanding schedule meant that the cast and crew didn't get to enjoy all the perks of having a theme park to themselves, but the location alone made for a really unique working week that everybody enjoyed.

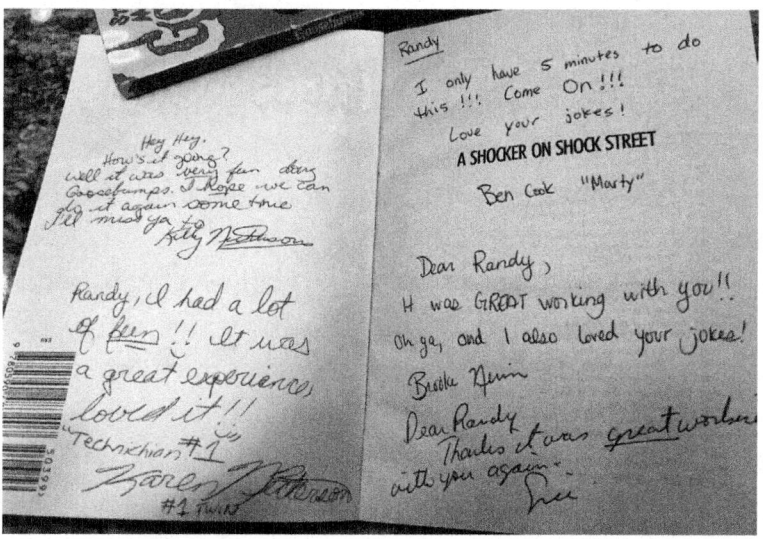

Randy Bradshaw's copy of *A Shocker on Shock Street*, signed by the cast. Photo courtesy of Randy Bradshaw.

Bradshaw estimates that it was a more expensive shoot than most on the show, with higher logistical requirements like security, transport and equipment. The fact that it all had to be transported by ferry made it more demanding. Lori Kirk, Centreville's marketing manager, says that the park's main appeal is that it maintains an old-timey quality, allowing guests to step back in time and enjoy a day out that feels pleasantly nostalgic. Thanks to this approach, the majority of buildings and features seen in the episode are still standing to this day, and the action has a pretty timeless quality to it. An existing dark ride was repurposed into a ghost train, giving Ron Stefaniuk a veritable gallery in which to exhibit all his previous works, with the scarecrows and fish people making appearances, among others.

The episode marks another appearance from actor Ben Cook, and opposite him Brooke Nevin, who would go on to play one of the teen leads in *Animorphs*. It was Bradshaw's suggestion that they hire twins to play Mr. Wright's assistants, with Karen and Kelly Nickerson bringing an eerie, old-school sci-fi feel to proceedings. Meanwhile, Ron Stefaniuk finally got the chance to appear in front of the camera, donning one of his own creations to play the Piranha Person. With the effects master having started out as a performer himself, it seemed like a natural progression to the director. "I think he always had a desire to be an actor," says Bradshaw, "and of course he was familiar with the operation and how to use it, do things without anything getting damaged."

If Season Two was the home of the Halloween episode, Season Three was all about theme parks. Easily one of the most memorable of the hour-long specials, and a firm fan favorite, "One Day at Horrorland" is something of an anomaly for the *Goosebumps* series. With a distinctly tongue-in-cheek tone that borders on the explicitly comical, it still manages to maintain its scares and sense of danger, while delivering some of the most delightfully camp material in the whole four-season run. According to actor Jonathan Whittaker, this wasn't necessarily the idea going in. "I think it just unfolded that way," he says. "I don't think I was approaching it as a comedy." If nothing else, the tone can be traced back to Dan Angel and Billy Brown's script, which is markedly rife with humor, particularly on the part of the various Horror characters, most of which were performed by Neil Crone, with Ron Stefaniuk and a couple of his team wearing their own creations. Out of the entire series, this one seems to have Ron Oliver's name written all over it, and in an ideal world, it would have gone to him, but for those typical scheduling issues. Still, for a director as gruff and straight-edged as Bill Fruet, he pulled off the darkly humorous tone well, delivering one of the most memorable episodes of the show's run.

As ever, it was an enjoyable atmosphere, welcoming to ideas (and, indeed, the families of the cast) at the hands of Fruet, who was "very supportive of all our work," says Whittaker. "Our inspiration and inventiveness was allowed to flourish," which is evidenced by little touches that seem too personal to have been in the original script, such as Heather Brown's pirouette in the House of Mirrors, accompanied by a flutter of balletic piano. When asked about this shot, Jonathan Whittaker imparts, "I believe that Heather did have a dance background. Having come from the music theatre world myself, I have seen enough pirouettes to know good from not so good. Heather's was good, in my opinion."

Another of the defining features of "One Day at Horrorland" is the prevalence of the parent characters, and how well they are played. *Goosebumps* is often memorable for its inept parents, who are largely detached from the spooky action, and spend the runtime not believing their kids' cries for help. In "Horrorland," the parents are squarely in on the action along with the kids, which offers them a fairly unique chance to get into the atmosphere and offer more than annoyance. Kirsten Bishop and Jonathan Whittaker play Peggy and Carl Morris so much like a real couple it hurts: she is the stilted, worried mother who quietly nags at her husband for not getting their station wagon fixed, while he is the laid-back, trusting father figure who thinks his wife simply worries too much. They are both bursting with personality. It's nice to see parent characters in *Goosebumps* get so much development, especially when they don't turn out to be the twist villains, and for their actors to go at the project with the same gusto they would with entertainment not made for kids. "I try to employ the same earnestness in all my work," Whittaker explains. "I don't really believe in talking down to kids. There's more to gain from speaking on a mutual level." And this earnestness comes through on the screen. It's probably easy for actors to approach a kids' show with a certain hesitation, but one of *Goosebumps*' strengths is its earnestness, and adults taking their roles seriously is a major factor in grounding the show in as realistic a world as one can expect from Stine.

The hour-long special was shot in the summer of 1997, aiming for a Halloween broadcast in the last week in October and first week in November. Sunnybrook Park provided the woodland setting for all the Horrorland exteriors, including the parking lot, ticket booths, rides, and the memorable wooden bridge, which shows up in several other episodes, like "Werewolf Skin." With a vast green canvas ready for the taking, it was up to Ian Brock's team to transform it into a creepy and kooky theme park, a job that earned the episode the status of his favorite that he ever worked on.

As the father of a seven-year-old boy, Whittaker was already well-versed with *Goosebumps*. "It's required reading as a parent to an adventurous seven-year-old," he says, and lucky little Taylor really got to enjoy his dad's crazy work assignment. "My son came to set with me when we were filming the game portion of the show," the actor recalls. "He was extremely intrigued by the masks and was given an opportunity to try one on and watch the filming from the production tent and the craft table. Though I think he spent more time at the craft table!"

The show continued to be a family affair for director Don McCutcheon, for whom "Awesome Ants" was a great first gig on the series. McCutcheon had a tradition by this point in his career of finding his three children small roles in his works. This time, it was his middle child's turn, so she became part of the crowd in the final scene, shovelling piles of blue ant food pellets, which were actually beans Ian Brock and his crew had hand-painted with food coloring.

As a writer who had been brought up on the classic sci-fi of the 1960s, Neal Shusterman was excited to get to craft the script for "Awesome Ants." "It was a favorite because I got to go more *Twilight Zone*-y with that one," he explains. It gave him the opportunity to immerse himself in the sort of entertainment he enjoyed as a youngster, and do what Rod Serling was a master of: working towards a killer twist ending. This meant he could focus his creative efforts on building suspense and gathering the momentum for the big reveal. "I wouldn't call it a one-joke premise, but the story played toward that one twist. I would say that "Awesome Ants" was easier because of that," the writer says.

McCutcheon was equally enthused by this *Twilight Zone*-style script, but knew there would be some challenges emerging in terms of special effects. "That's exactly it. It's got a *Twilight Zone* kind of vibe to it," he says, "so it was really cool. I thought, just genius from a story perspective to flip that on its head. But it was a challenge to figure out, *how are we going to do this, and do it properly?* It was challenging," he says. "But I knew deep down that if we got it right it would be a great episode."

To this end, McCutcheon thought very visually about how he was going to attack the episode, and found ways to share his ideas with the crew. At an early pre-production meeting, he freehanded a quick sketch of what he envisioned for the final money shot, of the neighborhood being looked down upon by giant ants. "I'm a terrible artist," he says, "but I wanted to at least try to relay how I saw the final shot of the episode." Sometime later, during a lunch break on set, McCutcheon was called away to oversee where production vehicles would be parked the next day. Thinking this had already been handled but happy to help, he went on this wild goose chase, only to come back to a set full of crew wearing his design on t-shirts. "It was Lena [Cordina] that had the t-shirts made," he says, showing his off proudly. "I was pretty touched. It was kind of fun. We all had a great laugh out of it." The shirt is a prized possession and doesn't get worn very often, but at the suggestion of Mrs. McCutcheon, Don wears it to his interview. He says that of the hundreds of hours of television he has directed over the course of his career, "Awesome Ants" still ranks in his personal Top Five.

Don McCutcheon shows off his "Awesome Ants" t-shirt.
Photo courtesy of Don McCutcheon.

Working with live insects presented its own challenges, and called for the reliable expertise of Jim Bugs. He handled all the exotic creatures, from boa constrictors to cockroaches, and in this case, he brought along hundreds of ants. Jim Bugs proved to be a soothing and rational influence on this strange production. "He was a very calm man, very lovely. He was great. It sounds like it should have been a little more crazy and chaotic," says McCutcheon, explaining that Jim Bugs kept the crew's expectations of insects reasonable. "I mean, they'll only do so much. I want the beetle to go from there to there, well, maybe the beetle is not gonna do that, you know."

The casts of *Goosebumps* usually enjoyed friendly and frictionless working relationships, just savoring their time together and encouraging each other's creativity. "Awesome Ants" was a little different. Its young star Michael Yarmush had a significant credit to his name in the form of the hit children's animated show *Arthur*, in which he voiced the titular aardvark protagonist—a pretty cool job to have to one's name. "Super cool," actor Mpho Koaho agrees, "but he was a prick." Although there's no indication of things coming to blows between the two young actors, Koaho still remembers Yarmush's attitude. "He was so self-absorbed, believed he was a star, and I remember how contentious that relationship was," he says. "As much fun as I had, Mike was a little shithead." Despite this tension, Koaho maintains that it was cool to work with the very first Arthur, and that his love for the show hasn't been spoiled by the ego of its lead actor. It was also a brilliant experience for McCutcheon, who had been made to feel at home very quickly, and was soon to be brought back to work on the show again. Evidently, he had made a good impression.

Having been approved in the previous season, now was the time for "Perfect School" to be expanded. It started out as a standard half-hour single episode, but director Ron Oliver really got the bug for it, and shot much more action than the runtime would require. When asked to cut the runtime by ten minutes, Oliver proposed a different arrangement: "What if we make it into a two-parter?" He got the go-ahead while filming "How to Kill a Monster," necessitating a second shooting period, something practically unheard of on this well-oiled machine of a production.

Because the episode was shot in two separate sessions, different locations were used. Many interiors were shot during the initial five-day schedule, mostly taking place in a nursing school in North York, Toronto, while Sunnybrook Park was used for external scenes. However, the second three-day shoot was such a slap-dash affair that the sets were being built as shooting went on. The scene in which Brian sneaks into Room 21 and goes through computer files was shot to accommodate the lack of set, so the crew started with closeups and gradually drew back to wider shots as the remainder of the office was built. They also needed an interesting way of transitioning from this scene to the next on the stairwell, so the air vent crawling was devised, not only to make sure actor Shawn Roberts got as much action as possible, but to carry from one scene to the next.

While the majority of the episode is planted firmly in the action-thriller category, Oliver had a lot of fun with the misnomer of an opening scene, which operates in the grand tradition of every slasher movie ever. The feet climbing the stairs, the darkened house, and the classic dolly zoom (AKA the *Vertigo*/*Jaws*/*Poltergeist* shot) go all out for a slasher vibe, making it blindingly obvious that the kid brother is about to get slashed. "You're on a zoom lens, and you're zooming out as the camera's moving in," Oliver explains. "It's a really tricky, fussy little shot to get, but when you get it right, it's great. I haven't done one in a while. This may surprise you but there isn't a lot of call for track zoom shots in Hallmark movies!" It took a while to reach the finish line, but Oliver was over the moon with the results, which only proved he was right about it becoming a two-parter. The extra runtime served it very well indeed.

Having previously served as first assistant director on the show, "Teacher's Pet" was one of Andrea "Raff" Raffaghello's first writing credits, and it proved instrumental in launching his career as a producer, as well as the recruitment of Stefan Scaini, who he was friendly with. Scaini was one of the few one-and-done directors to work on the show, which he attributes to a busy work life. "My schedule just didn't permit that I could do more, and then they also had their regulars, which they kind of rotated through," he says. "They kind of brought me in for this one here because it was a little more performance-heavy and I have worked a lot with animals." The living antithesis of that old children-and-animals adage, Scaini was well-versed in everything that is traditionally considered nightmarish on a film set. "It's the grown-ups that scare me," he jokes.

The episode was shot in late October or November of 1997, and the climate lent the episode a lot of mood. "It was kind of a cold, rainy week, which I think added to the look of it. I like that," says Scaini. "Some of the fog that we had was natural, so we managed to get that atmosphere for free!" Interior scenes taking place in Blankenship's cabin were the only ones filmed in the studio, with all other shooting taking place at Studio C, Sunnybrook Park, making it a very outdoorsy shoot. A shell of the cabin was knocked together in the park for the exterior shots, which served as a dressing room for the various snakes and other animals working on the episode. All the animals were accounted for by the end of the shoot, with the exception of a single white mouse, who presumably lived out the rest of his days in the luxurious confines of Sunnybrook. Lucky guy.

A different animal wrangler was brought on this time around, courtesy of the director. Michael Hackenberger was the final owner of Bowmanville Zoo in Ontario, which was home to rescue animals who were trained for movie stardom, including a tiger who had started life as part of a stripper act. Scaini and Hackenberger had worked together before, and the director was determined that the cast and animals would feel comfortable around each other, so made special arrangements. "A week prior to filming the episode we brought in the cast. Within fifteen or twenty minutes, everybody had a snake around them!" recalls Scaini. "I said to the production, 'Guys, we should invest in this. I know it's going to cost money because we have to book the actors for an extra day. We've got to make them comfortable with these creatures.'" Not only did these measures ensure that both animals and actors were happy working together, but it made the shoot much quicker and more efficient than it otherwise may have been. Scaini had been right on the money with this call.

The script was rewritten to accommodate the capabilities of the animals they were working with. Scaini and Raff consulted with Hackenberger on what was achievable, and wrote sequences accordingly. Previous on-set experiences, particularly one with a bear named Misty, had taught Scaini a lot about working with animals. "It was a stark reminder that these are still wild animals. You know, they're not teddy bears. You have to be respectful," he explains. The camera crew wore black and kept as still as possible to avoid startling or distracting the animals, and the cast, having already got to know their scaly co-stars, were able to perform the scenes comfortably and considerately thanks to their extra day of prep.

Despite a newly-introduced embargo on night shoots falling somewhere around this time, "Teacher's Pet" did a couple of them, staggering the working day to start at noon so that day and night sequences could be filmed within a reasonable time frame. "After that they were trying to dial back [on night shoots]," says Scaini, "because it's just expensive, too. It's too taxing on the crew and certainly on the cast."

Scaini was thrilled with his cast, which included Richard McMillan, who had previously played Spider in "Say Cheese and Die." "He's an old theater guy. So, my goodness, he's, like, bomb-proof," says Scaini. "Richard kept saying to me, 'If I'm getting too campy…' I said, 'It's *Goosebumps*. It's OK to be campy!'" The director had previously worked with Asia Vieira, who played mean classmate Sue, on the show *Street Legal*, and the two were thrilled to see each other again. He particularly admired his two lead actors, Michelle Risi and Telmo Miranda, who threw themselves into the episode and really enjoyed the adventure of it all. "Michelle was new, this was one of her first things," Scaini remembers, "and she was fearless, 100% just going for it!"

After almost three full seasons of fun and frolics, it caught everybody off guard when tragedy struck *Goosebumps*. Undoubtedly one of the most notable aspects of "Teacher's Pet" is the closing dedication to its lead actress Michelle Risi, who passed away unexpectedly, shortly after filming wrapped. It was a dreadful shock to everybody she had worked with on the show. "She died of meningitis about a month after," says Scaini. He found out about her death when organizing a screening of the episode for the cast and crew, and the suddenness of it all made the director think that some terrible accident had claimed her life. The revelation of her illness was all the more perplexing. "She was full of beans when we filmed it," says the director, "that was scary." It was decided that the episode would be dedicated to her memory, a touching sentiment that embodied the camaraderie and friendly nature that the set of *Goosebumps* had at its core.

"She was a big part of the show, and the show was like a family," says Steve Levitan. "It was such a shock, how quickly she passed, that we just said, 'We need to acknowledge that.' Nobody knew, I didn't even know that she was sick. It came on really quick and it took her really quick." Regarding the decision to dedicate the episode to Risi's memory, he says, "You can't not do that. It doesn't feel right to not do that. That dedication is literally the very, very last thing that goes on an episode before it's delivered to the broadcasters. It's a big shock, and she's still very much in people's minds." Michelle Risi was only sixteen when she passed away, and it is quite touching that she is immortalized in this fun little outdoorsy episode of a show that meant a lot to many young viewers, and that everybody on set loved working on. If ever *Goosebumps* showed its heart directly to the audience, it was on this solemn occasion.

"Werewolf Skin" was filled with behind-the-scenes drama, and perhaps could be called a turning point for the show. According to Ron Oliver, Dan Angel and Billy Brown were often pushing for more creative control over the scripts. Brown especially also campaigned for "better" actors for the show, something that it didn't need anyhow, and would incur more expense. "Werewolf Skin" was at first deemed unproducible, which for some reason didn't stop it from being added to the production schedule as would usually be the case. Angel and Brown's script was on the extreme end of the scale, with elements like a deer having its head torn off by a werewolf, and the duo stood by their work. As Oliver tells it, they threatened to quit the show if the episode weren't done their way, and when they got word that this wouldn't happen, they stuck to their guns and hightailed it out of there.

"Deborah Forte came to me and said, 'We need you to step up to the plate and take this over,'" says Oliver, to which end he became a producer on the show, and hurriedly rewrote the script while on the flight to Toronto. That's not to say the trouble was over though. The episode marked a certain change in the way that *Goosebumps* would be shot from now on: no more night shoots, by order of Lena Cordina. Not only did it mean less of the cost and effort required to shoot overtime night scenes with young actors, but given that a shooting season tended to run from early summer into fall, they could get more done during the day with the longer daylight hours. But this move meant that all night scenes from here on in would be shot day-for-night, an old-timey technique that involves putting a blue filter over the lens to darken the image. Of course, it is not simply the brightness of the image that conveys nighttime, and shadows and light reflection are often the tell-tale signs of the technique. "It always looks bad!" Ron Oliver says.

To top it all off, a key scene was getting the show into hot water with the network, which given everything they had got away with so far was quite the novelty. Oliver had lovingly crafted a *Rear Window*-esque scene in which Alex spies on his aunt and uncle removing their werewolf skins in the neighboring house. Logically, the pair would be naked underneath the skins, and the dailies showed their bare backs and shoulders. In Oliver's mind, the scene would have a fairly sexual subtext, playing on the horrifying experience many kids can relate to of walking in on their parents getting it on. "I was sort of mortified that anybody figured it out, because I was just doing it for my own amusement," Oliver chuckles. "The network freaked! They made me recut it maybe three times."

This is one episode that a specific date can be put on. Ron Oliver remembers shooting at night (evidently just before the ban was enforced) for the scene in which Alex buries the werewolf skins. It was raining lightly, and Oliver was busy trying to shoot the fairly demanding scene, which required Ron Stefaniuk and his crew to be buried under the dirt wearing werewolf gloves, thrusting their hands up through the ground to grab at the kid as he whacks at them with a shovel. Meanwhile, some of the crew were gathered round a television watching the live broadcast of Princess Diana's funeral, placing it on September 6 1997. Reflecting on what Diana's death meant to the people of Canada, and particularly to the gay community, Ron Oliver posits that everyday life doesn't allow for much emotional catharsis, leading people to latch on to opportunities to grieve, not only for whatever tragedy is currently befalling them, but for all the tragedy in their own lives that has gone unprocessed. He says the same is true of horror. "People have horrors all the time in their lives, but they don't always have the chance to scream. But in a horror movie, you can express that fear."

By Season Three, things were changing for *Goosebumps*. The set was still a bright and lively place to be, the crew were still getting along famously, and it was still proving a massive hit for Fox, and by this point, Saban, who had acquired international broadcast rights to the show. But in a number of ways, its success would prove to be its downfall, a decline first indicated by the departure of writers and showrunners Billy Brown and Dan Angel.

Ron Oliver describes Brown and Angel quitting the show towards the end of Season Three over lack of creative control. Steve Levitan recalls it differently. "By the time Season Three ended, they were very much in demand," Levitan says. "They had been the showrunners of, at that point, probably the most successful scripted television series for kids ever, and they had tons of opportunities, and they were not happy." As is often the case, the duo's breakthrough opened them up to a world of possibilities, and having made their mark on the show, they were eager to see what else they could lend their talents to, both as a team and individually. Angel and Brown decided to quit while they were ahead and embrace the many opportunities that *Goosebumps* had brought their way. "I hated to see them go. Everybody did. But it was the right decision at the time," Levitan muses. "I think they got tired of working together as a team as well. It's a marriage where you have a new child every week. Every single time from the beginning, and every child is different. You get tired of that process."

As Levitan remembers it, Angel and Brown continued to write for the show, but Bill Siegler took over as showrunner. Ron Oliver says his position on the show also became more senior, and that he picked up some of the slack left by Angel and Brown. With the show's creative driving force now gone, things were feeling different. Of course, they had been with the series long enough to have guided it into a very firm pattern, so it's not as if nobody knew what to do without them, but they were sorely missed, and their absence marked the beginning of the end.

Steve Levitan says that the Canadian television marketplace has its own unique set of issues that often make it less fun, and less rewarding, to produce shows there, despite the many incentives. "It's not really an industry that is looking for hits," he says. "It stands on the 49th parallel," he explains, referencing the Canadian border with the U.S.—the world's largest undefended border— "and looks north, not seeming to care that that horizon has nothing on it. It's just wasteland!" So quite fortuitously, Protocol had managed to secure the right property at the right time, and find the perfect team of creative professionals to bring it to life. It was lightning in a bottle, a hit of such magnitude that it was very much outside the norm of Canadian television. This rampant success would ultimately be the key to the show's undoing.

The conventional wisdom of the industry at the time dictated that animated children's shows had much more rewatchability, making networks resistant to live action entertainment. By the third season of *Goosebumps* however, Fox determined that these live-action anthology episodes were holding their own against animated competitors, and finding great repeat business with young viewers. While this was a victory for the medium of live-action children's entertainment, it proved to be a double-edged sword, one that would come down on the show's lifespan. So popular were the existing episodes in their reruns, that Fox saw little value in continuing to produce the show, and soon the ax fell.

Steve Levitan explains what was going on at a corporate level: "Fox had had a change of command, and Fox Kids disappeared shortly after Saban, which had the international distribution rights for *Goosebumps*, took it over. I think [Rupert] Murdoch was taking it over around that time. Margaret Loesch, who was the head of Fox Kids, was an unbelievably fantastic children's television executive. I think she went to join Nickelodeon, and there was no reason for them to spend the large amounts of money that they were spending on a kids' show when the repeats held up so well. In kids', unlike for adult television, if your target demographic, which for *Goosebumps* I would say was for ten- to twelve-year-olds—there was always a younger character than the main characters—by Season Three, the young siblings of the kids who were watching *Goosebumps* were old enough to be the core audience and watch them from the beginning. It's just as large an audience. You're defeated by your own success."

When presented with such a situation, it would be easy for producers and showrunners to beg, haggle or negotiate. But over the decades, the TV landscape has been littered with shows that overstayed their welcome, ran out of steam, or simply couldn't translate their success to later times. Having put so much into making sure that *Goosebumps* lived up to what the fans really wanted, the crew was not about to go cutting corners or compromising their vision for the sake of longevity. They knew they'd had a really good thing going for several years, and rather than fizzle out, it was decided the show would go out with a bang. "We could have, I suppose, fought harder and tried to drop the budget and make it more financially attractive," Steve Levitan says, "but that would be dangerous because it would be a different show, and we really did want to keep the quality of the show."

This would definitely be the point to leave on a high. Not long before, the crew had attended the annual MIPCOM industry trade show in Cannes, and found that swag bags embroidered with the *Goosebumps* logo were being handed out to attendees. "I guess Saban paid for that," Levitan says. "That meant all ten thousand of the international television people are walking around Cannes with bags that say *Goosebumps*, and that's an unbelievable source of pride!" The show really was at the height of its success, which is why Fox's reluctance to keep investing in it was so perplexing.

In addition to Fox seeing no need to continue pouring money into production, the Canadian government was also reassessing. By the third year, they refused to find the show eligible for subsidies, due to a perceived wealth of financing from outside of Canada. "They thought, 'You're successful, why should we help you?'" Steve Levitan says. "By then, I think Fox was facing some financial difficulties." In a very short space of time, both of the show's main financial backers had found the show too successful to sustain their interest, and the rug was beginning to be pulled out from under *Goosebumps*.

Fox was willing to order one final season, but this in itself indicated that the end was nigh. With twenty-six weeks in a typical television season, the average order was for weekly episodes to run throughout the season, which the show had secured for its last two seasons. The final order that came through was for just eight episodes. The most striking characteristic of *Goosebumps*' fourth and final season is that it comprises four two-part episodes, and there was a reason for this arrangement. "Cheaper," says Levitan. "The typical order was twenty-two or twenty-six episodes for a season, but Fox knew they were winding down, and said, 'OK, we'll give you one more season,' and make it what we call a short order—less than a full season. And the reason for the two-parters is that the video market for these episodes was strong enough that we thought we could release more special versions in a one-hour format for that market. Mostly, they were two-parters for financial reasons."

It was somewhere during Season Three that Protocol began to expand its catalog, which now included the rights to K.A. Applegate's children's sci-fi book series *Animorphs*, another Scholastic title. The show went into production in late 1997 or early 1998, with many of the crew dipping back and forth between *Animorphs* and *Goosebumps*, and one of the floors of the Molson building being allocated as studio and HQ for the new show. While it would be the end of an era for *Goosebumps* to come to a close, it wasn't as somber a farewell as it could have been, because the majority of the team made the transition from one show to the other.

"[By the end of *Goosebumps*] We were really busy as a production company," Levitan recalls, "but I was really sad because I loved working with Bill Siegler, I loved working with Dan and Billy. We got very attached to that show and it was sad to see it go. I didn't want to see it go, I wanted to keep doing it, but I didn't want to keep doing it in a way that made it feel like its best days were behind it. It's better that it leaves them wanting more." It was with their heads held high that the gang headed back once more for their final adventure in the world of *Goosebumps*.

"What Have We Got to Lose?"

Season Four

It was spring 1998, and the home stretch had arrived. Billy Brown and Dan Angel were gone, and Ron Oliver was, by his own admission, "the showrunner, if you will." *Goosebumps* was officially on its way out, and although everybody involved was sad that this once-in-a-lifetime job was coming to an end, they were determined to make it as big, bold and exciting as ever. With only eight episodes ordered, it was decided that four stories would get the hour-long treatment, giving everybody the opportunity they loved so much to dig deep, expand the action and give the characters decent arcs. The stories selected for adaptation would be some of the most adventurous ever.

Season Four would kick off with "How I Got My Shrunken Head," and the crew set off one last time for Sunnybrook Park. The art department dressed the woodier parts of the park up with moss and vines to simulate the feel of the deep jungle, and everybody enjoyed the tropical feel of the set they would call home for the next ten days. "We were all living in that campsite!" Ron Oliver recalls. "We were all there all the time and it became an actual subculture. And that's something you can't get these days because you would shoot a lot of stuff now against a green screen, which I hate." It was this environment that Oliver was so keen to capture on screen, again in another throwback to classic movies he'd enjoyed since childhood. "I wanted to make an homage to those 1940s jungle movies," he explains, so plenty of attention was given to khaki outfits and explorer hats, tents, maps and Jeeps. An animal wrangler was brought back once again to help acquaint the cast with snakes and other jungle creatures, and would end up curing at least one phobia. "It was the first time I got to really 'get to know' a snake," Beki Lantos recalls. "Before this, I'd always kind of feared them, but the wrangler was so nice and shared their passion for the creatures so deeply, I was moved and my fear of snakes went away. I reflect on that from time to time as I find so often sharing a passion makes for such a wonderful connection."

Lantos returned to the show, having first starred in "Stay Out of the Basement." She and Ron Oliver had worked together on the *Are You Afraid of the Dark?* episode "The Tale of Laughing in the Dark," which had been her very first TV gig. Although she knows she auditioned for the role in "How I Got My Shrunken Head," she doesn't remember doing so, and posits that having previously worked with Oliver helped her secure the job. "Directors often like to work with the same people once they know they're reliable," she says. Although she was glad to be back, and enjoyed being back with the wonderful crew for a second time, it was very different on this occasion, because of her experiences since her last stint on the show.

"I was also a very different person," she explains. "I was fifteen or sixteen and had endured a lot more bullying and abuse. I was not a happy person and had absolutely no self-worth or self-esteem." Viewers might not have recognized the actor at first, given she was now several years older and had swapped her long, dark, wavy hair for a sandy-blond bob. It had been an attempt at reinvention after getting out of a very traumatic relationship. "I'd convinced myself that dyeing my hair would let me move on and leave all of it behind, as though the transformation would make all that had happened unhappen. Of course, it didn't. I was simply left with terrible hair. But hey, what can you do? I got two acting gigs with it so who knows if it was such a bad idea after all," she says.

Although she doesn't like to look back on the episode, given how it effectively serves as a time capsule of a very difficult period in her life, she says that the experience of shooting the episode was an important one. "I think being in the show saved me a little bit, as it helped me to remember what I loved and was good at, but it was so fleeting as it was just a two-week project," Lantos explains. The atmosphere on set, with co-stars she became very fond of, and a director she describes as "fun and outgoing, maybe even a little crazy," was exactly what she needed at that point in her life, and although she would take a considerable hiatus from acting not long after, one last hurrah with *Goosebumps* was an experience she is glad she had.

It was an adventurous shoot, full of action, animals and stunts. Daniel Clark was hung upside down by his ankles, and although it was fun to watch, Beki Lantos was pretty bummed about not being allowed to perform the stunt of falling into a pool of shrinking potion. The greatest story to come from behind the scenes of "How I Got My Shrunken Head," or perhaps the entire show, is of one of Ron Oliver's frequent cheeky attempts to have fun on set. To this day, Oliver likes to have souvenirs made up for his cast and crew to commemorate their time together, and on this occasion, he rocked up to set with a box full of t-shirts with the caption, 'I spent the night in the jungle with Ron Oliver, and all I got was a little head.' They were top-quality shirts, because, as Oliver puts it, "If you're gonna do something that vulgar, it better be high quality! That was in 1998—I couldn't do it and get away with it now! To me, that was screechingly funny." It was a pitch-perfect example of the utterly unique character that is Ron Oliver.

While the majority of the cast and crew found the stunt just as hilarious as he did—young actor Daniel Clark desperately wanted a t-shirt, but was denied—word reached higher-ups about this vulgar little gift, and there was a scramble to recall the offending shirts. However, a number of rogue t-shirts remained in the hands of the team. Oliver recalls running into Clark years later, "and he says, 'The greatest regret of my life was not getting one of those t-shirts!' You couldn't get away with that anymore, because everybody's lost their sense of humor." In classic Ron Oliver fashion, he gets a kick out of the t-shirt story still floating around. "I love that that story still exists," he laughs.

Ever the showman, Oliver was determined to have his final time directing *Goosebumps* be the most spectacular of all his episodes, and with this in mind, he wrote "Cry of the Cat" as a loving homage to the horror genre and, in fact, to the show itself. When Ron Oliver submitted the script for the episode for the Stines' approval, he received a phone call from Jane Stine. "OK, so this is either the worst idea we've ever read, and you're crazy, or this is going to be the best episode of *Goosebumps* ever," she told the director. Regardless of any doubt, it seems the couple were willing to take a crazy chance, and they signed off on it, sending the two-part episode into production. It was a very different flavor for the show: it ran in the vein of *Scream*, or *Seed of Chucky*, taking a meta approach to its own existence, and inviting the audience to see horror from a different angle. Centering on two young actors starring in a horror movie, it took viewers deep into the core of moviemaking.

It will come as no surprise to anyone who knows Oliver that there are a number of self-insert characters in "Cry of the Cat." The director, played by Arthur Eng, dressed in tie and baseball cap, is based on Ron himself, and the assistant director is based on an A.D. he had previously worked with on the show, complete with her favorite cowboy boots (presumably Samantha Snidal). It was a particularly fun experience for Oliver and his crew, in that they could really exploit the meta format and put a lot of themselves into the episode. "There were a lot of inside jokes for my crew on that show, because we'd all been together for so long," he says. They had time and money uncharacteristic of the show since pre-production of Season One, and so found they could really let loose this time and just enjoy themselves.

In the spirit of meta celebration, it felt only fitting that the episode would bring back two of its previous young stars. Hamille Rustia returned following "Calling All Creeps," to play the leading lady on this horror film project, while Corey Sevier was delighted with the chance to play a stuck-up child actor, a role far removed from his previous work on "A Night in Terror Tower." At the time, Sevier was unfamiliar with the classic horror movies that the opening sequence of this episode was paying homage to, but it was an element he came to appreciate later in life, and the kids had a blast getting to essentially play at doing their jobs. Sevier and Rustia quickly bonded over their respective histories on the show, and found a lot of fun in sharing stories of their previous episodes. "I remember her just being so kind," he says.

It was one thing getting one last go at *Goosebumps*, but for Sevier, the real thrill was getting to play a character quite unlike any that had featured on the show before. "I remember reading it and going, 'This is so cool, because I get to play this pretentious actor,'" he recalls. More than that, it called for him to do some stunt work. He loved the wind effects and being grabbed by a monster through a door, but the pièce de résistance was getting to run away from an explosion. "I had to do a scene where I was running away, and this explosion goes off behind me, and I dive through the air and land on these mats. I'll never forget the feeling, the adrenaline of running down that hill. As you jump you can feel the heat on your back. Such a cool experience!" He also loved that he got to close the show with a big twist ending that involved him eating a mouse, which was substituted with liquorice. It was the wildest time anybody could have at work.

While the script was pretty radical by *Goosebumps* standards with its meta approach, the production of the episode itself ended up blurring the lines of reality even further. Oliver's pride and joy of this particular story is the one-take shot near the beginning that reveals the action to be a movie within a movie, before the assistant director calls cut and a break for lunch. Indeed, after a few rehearsals, the shot was achieved in one take at the tail-end of a half-day Friday, at which point lunch really was called on the set of *Goosebumps*, and Oliver took the crew out for drinks at a local pub. "That was one of the best days we ever had," the director remembers fondly, "and doing stuff like that made it really special to me."

Not only was the episode a joy to work on, and a great swan song for the show's favorite director, but it would bring Ron Oliver one of the highlights of his time on the show—his second Director's Guild of America Award nomination for Children's Programs. Although the award would ultimately go to Mitchell Kriegman for the *Bear in the Big Blue House* episode "Love is All You Need," it was a profound moment for Oliver. "That made me very proud, because I am a kid from this nowhere-land with no contacts and no chance whatsoever of getting into the business. Suddenly you're going from that world to the Director's Guild of America Awards twice! That was a very proud moment," he beams.

While Oliver was going all out on the show, knowing that the end was nigh, the same couldn't be said for Don McCutcheon, who doesn't actually recall knowing that "The Ghost Next Door" would be his last time directing an episode of *Goosebumps*. Because of this, it doesn't stand out in his memory as a particularly significant experience. He went at it with his usual zeal, and had a great time with the challenges it threw his way, namely playing with fire, which required extra health and safety precautions, including a local fire department team waiting in the wings. Like "Cry of the Cat," the episode also brought back previous players, including Cody Jones, who had played Carly Beth's obnoxious little brother Noah in "The Haunted Mask" and its sequel, Dov Tiefenbach from "Bad Hare Day," and Diego Matamoros of "A Night in Terror Tower," as the voice of the shadow figure. As McCutcheon's first and only two-parter, he was thrilled at the chance to put more time and character growth into an episode of *Goosebumps*, an effort that evidently paid off, as the episode remains a favorite among fans, particularly for the twist that comes at the end of part one.

After a long spell as the show's most frequently-used director, it only made sense to have Bill Fruet return for one last episode—*the* last episode. The time had finally come. *Goosebumps* was officially coming to an end, and "Deep Trouble" was to be the two-parter that would provide the show's swan song, so it was a big deal to get cast as the leads in *Goosebumps*' final episode. Tod Fennell was already a huge *Goosebumps* fan, having read all the books and watched the show, and cites "It Came from Beneath the Sink" as his favorite. He was thrilled to get to audition for the show, and when it became evident that he had bagged the lead in the last ever episode, it was more than he could have imagined. To top it all off, he and co-star Laura Vandervoort became firm friends right away, bonding over their mutual love of martial arts and Magic: the Gathering. It was all shaping up to be a fun and memorable job.

Unlike the previous episodes, which were produced on a rolling basis, everybody on set knew that this was the end, and they were determined to enjoy it. Shooting on Lake Ontario towards the end of summer 1998, Tod Fennell remembers it being a fun and laid-back experience. "Deep Trouble" was a special occasion, and in some respects, this made things much easier, with a more relaxed approach to deadlines. "It meant more shooting days, so more time with the cast and crew. It was the end of a massive show," says Fennell. There was one big disappointment though: "The day we got to set, everybody was talking about how R.L. Stine visited the set for the episode previous to ours! And we were like, 'But this is the two-part series finale!'" Fennell recalls. "We had to hear about it, which made it even worse."

The episode was filmed on the shores of Lake Ontario, and the beach was dressed up to lend a more tropical feel to the episode. Marring the faux-Caribbean vibe of the location was a looming nuclear power plant—most likely the Pickering Nuclear Generating Station—which was plainly visible in the distance. "They kept framing that out," says Tod Fennell, "like, 'OK, well, we can only shoot from this angle.'" This emphasis on the power plant got somewhat under the skin of the two teen actors, who were required to wade around in the water. They sought reassurance from the crew that the water was safe for them to be in, and approached it with more than a little side-eye. It was around August, so the water wasn't quite at the peak of its Canadian frigidity yet, but it was still uncomfortably cold, if not radioactive!

The house scenes were filmed in a real residence a little further up from the waterfront, located on Enola Avenue in Mississauga. The Derry House is located right on the waterfront with a little forestry separating the house from the lake. Unlike many other houses used for exteriors on the show, The Derry House served as the interior location as well. "I felt bad for the owners because we were slinging that green slime everywhere, and it was hard to get off!" Fennell says. It wasn't until the cave scenes that anything was done in the studio. "They had built this huge cave, and everything was real that you could interact with. They built the entire thing and you could go up into the caverns," says Tod Fennell. "I would eat my lunch super-fast and then I'd wanna go explore those caves!"

The sets and creature effects were as top-notch as ever, and promised the show would go out with a bang. The giant fish that shoots poisoned spines was built with a blow dart mechanism that packed a punch. The shot of the kids hiding from it in the cupboard required the actors to keep their distance for safety's sake. "We were told to stay far away from the door, because it's going to come right through the door," Fennell remembers. The elaborate makeup effects Ron Stefaniuk and his crew designed and implemented for the fish mutants in the finale were also among the most ambitious they'd done yet, and the blow-dart fish remains one of Stefaniuk's favorite creations for the show.

Steve Levitan says there was "no particular reason" that "Deep Trouble" was positioned as *Goosebumps*' finale. "We avoided water shots as much as possible, as they're extremely difficult on our schedule. I do remember saying, 'Let's try this one, cos we've avoided that kind of episode for a long, long time. Let's just finally give that one a shot, cos what have we got to lose?'" This was the time to throw everything at the wall, so they went with a water-heavy episode with tons of special effects, makeup, location work and action. Although some say they didn't prep and write it with a finale in mind, it ended up serving that purpose very well indeed. It was firing on all cylinders.

So, with that, filming wrapped on Season Four, and on *Goosebumps* entirely, and it was an emotional time for all involved. The crew were determined to go out with a bang, so soaked up every moment of their time on set and in the offices. The final yearly wrap party would take on a particularly poignant air. "This one is a bit sentimental," Levitan recalls. "It was such a happy production experience, and such a good result. It was, you know, kind of like a university graduation party instead of like most shoots." Everybody gathered to celebrate their many accomplishments over the show's impressive four-year span, and shared laughs, drinks, cigars and memories. Steve recalls the impact of the cancellation on the production team, saying everybody felt "wistful," and that given the immense success of the show, they had perhaps been lulled into a sense of security. Theoretically, as long as Stine kept on writing, they could keep on shooting. But any entertainment professional knows that all good things come to an end, and at the very least, the core crew wouldn't be parting ways, with most of them continuing on with *Animorphs*, so it wasn't a case of packing up their desks and wandering off into the sunset. "The relationship stayed, although the particular task wasn't the same, and everybody was really proud to have worked on *Goosebumps*," says Steve Levitan. It had been a wild ride, with much fun, laughter, adventure and spirit, but *Goosebumps* was officially over.

"Splendors Situated Beyond the Tomb"

Living With Goosebumps

Talking at length with the many wonderful people who helped to bring *Goosebumps* to life, there is one particular common thread that runs throughout the discourse: the show was simply a joy to be involved with. From its inception, through the production of each episode, and into the continuing legacy of *Goosebumps*, everybody loved it. The set was always a place full of fun, laughter and imagination; watching each episode as it aired was a triumphant, memorable and at times surreal moment; mentioning having worked on the show, even decades later, elicits excitement and limitless intrigue. Now, with the incredible legacy that it has amassed thirty years on, it gives its crew and performers an immense sense of pride.

During production, the school run became a routine mobbing for Steve Levitan. His daughters' classmates would trail him from the car and back, begging him to make an episode of their favourite *Goosebumps* book and asking how they could be on the show themselves. Little did he realize at the time that this same enthusiasm for the show would follow him the rest of his career. He still gets mail to this day, with fans asking him questions about the show and telling him how much it meant to them.

For Randy Bradshaw, it has been a wonderfully nostalgic experience getting to talk about *Goosebumps*, one that has brought up some long-dormant memories. For him, the real treat was getting to work with such a talented and widely diverse group of people. His involvement in *Goosebumps* has always been a talking point when people meet him, and he boils it down to the old saying, "Whatever it is, it's nice to be remembered."

Bob Sprogis echoes the sentiment shared by many, that when asked about their happiest or most enduring memory from their time on *Goosebumps*, there isn't one particular incident they recall, but more of an aura of happiness. "Working with all those people, that's the biggest thing. The general feeling of the whole show was one of the great things about it," he says.

"*Goosebumps* was really more of an overall special moment," says Don McCutcheon, "and it's interesting. My recollection and my fondness is more about the people that we worked with and that's what you don't realize at the time. Do you realize that there's gonna be a legacy to the show? I think later about the relationships, how special that group of people were. It's a mix of the show itself, what you're doing, and then the people and the creativity involved. It takes a little while for that to finally go, 'Oh, you know, that was a good time, that was a great thing.' So I think that that's really my special moment is just sort of realizing how much fun it was."

The kids involved in making *Goosebumps* probably had the most intense of all the experiences. They were of the generation that the show was entertaining. While most of the young actors' peers were used to them being on TV or in movies, this was an entirely different beast. It was *Goosebumps*, and it was cool! Tod Fennell felt the brunt of this distinction, having got his big break on *Lassie*, a show his contemporaries considered babyish and well, kinda lame. They soon changed their tune, however, when Lassie boy got to play the lead in the last ever episode of *Goosebumps*. The majority of the kids agree that acting was one thing, but acting in *Goosebumps* was about as big as it got for a kid growing up in the '90s. It made them special. "This is as good as it gets. It had some serious cred when you're in the 6th grade!" says Melody Johnson.

Unfortunately, this was not a universal sentiment, and if there's any population that can be little dicks about almost anything, it's kids. Beki Lantos didn't have such a great time at school in the first place, with her acting career making her something of an outcast.

She moved to a new school shortly before getting the *Goosebumps* gig, and largely kept her other life as an actor a secret. But she was so excited by her work on this incredibly popular show, and finally wanted to share what she did. "I was so excited and I wanted to share it all with my friends," she says. "I was proud of what I'd done. I told my mom I was going to tell everyone and even though she tried to persuade me otherwise, I did it. Perhaps my way of doing so wasn't the greatest, but I was a kid! One day I showed up to school wearing the *Goosebumps* hat the director had given me. I don't know if it sparked conversation or not, but eventually everyone in my grade knew I was going to be on the show and I was the talk of my grade." This brought a new wave of negative attention her way, with kids at first feigning friendship, then getting jealous and even becoming violent.

Kids who had already antagonized her were suddenly calling her Margaret and asking snide questions about her plant dad. Having spent such a joyous fortnight on the set of *Goosebumps*, the aftermath really soured the whole experience, and when the dynamic quickly turned physical, she was removed from school by her mother and taught at home. "It was one of the worst times in my life," she explains. Although this terrible period didn't put her off returning to the show in Season Four, it was not what she had hoped it would be. However, she looks back on her time on *Goosebumps*, particularly "Stay Out of the Basement," as a wonderful and formative thing, and remains immensely grateful for how everybody on set nurtured her as an artist, and protected her as a child.

It was easy for the adults involved to underestimate, or not even consider, the cultural impact that their work would have on the kids who watched it. For many, it was just another job, albeit a wacky and very enjoyable one. Indeed, for Ian Brock, as much as he had loved working on the show and the wider Scholastic catalog, he found his professional name somewhat marred by the words "kids' show," a label he did his best to shed. He didn't want to be tied down by his previous work. Mostly, people seem to have escaped the confines of children's entertainment since their involvement in the show. Even still, all it took was one episode of a legendary kids' show to sear them into the minds of a generation. So when they started getting recognized as having worked on the titan that was *Goosebumps*, it took them by very pleasant surprise.

While shooting *Merlin* with Jason Connery on location in Scotland in 1997, "It Came from Beneath the Sink" director David Winning was approached by a little girl, an extra of no more than five years old, who asked him, "Did you do *Goosebumps*?" When he replied in the affirmative and asked what she thought of it, the precocious youngster replied, "I thought the sponge was very effective." He was profoundly touched by this experience, not only by its sweetness, but because it demonstrated just how far-reaching the impact of *Goosebumps* was. Here he was, over three thousand miles from Toronto, and young viewers had not only seen his work, but loved it, and wanted to talk to him about it. "You never know, when you're making shows, if anybody's gonna watch it. I mean, that seems weird now. But it means something to somebody, somewhere," he says with fondness.

The enduring legacy of *Goosebumps* seems to have seeped into pretty much every aspect of the show's production. "It's always nice to be working on something that people have actually heard about. It was also nice to have a reasonably high-profile, recognizable credit on my resumé when looking for work back then," says orchestrator Jim McGrath. Not only did the *Goosebumps* seal of approval aid in finding him other work, but it went a long way in landing street cred with the younger generations. "I was teaching film scoring to a class of twenty-somethings in the 2010s, and they were somewhat underwhelmed with all the work I had done. Until they found out I'd worked on *Goosebumps*, and they all freaked out and said, 'You should have led with that!', so that was pretty funny!"

More than name recognition, some of the actors have found their faces strike a chord with strangers who can't quite figure out why they know them. They get sideways glances and double-takes, and sometimes the stranger manages to place them. Amos Crawley has had people say to him, "It's been driving me nuts why you seem so familiar to me, and now I figured it out!" It has only become more prominent in recent years as the generation who grew up with the show have started rediscovering it, and harvesting the power of the internet to find out what the *Goosebumps* gang are up to these days. "I guess it is a nostalgia thing," says Crawley, who totally gets it, and spent much of lockdown digging out the CDs he listened to on repeat as a teen. "There was this weird desire to, like, relive something." The funny thing to him is that, as is almost always the case, he had no idea what a big deal he was in the middle of until he was way out the other side. "Thirty years later, you're like, 'Oh, wow! I was part of a thing!' Maybe I should have paid more attention at the time. But you rarely know, when you're working on something, whether it's even gonna be good or not. You're in this unique position of, like, you did this thing when you were a kid, and as a result, you are part of somebody's memories. Which is fortuitous, I don't know what else to call it. It's just lucky, and it's kind of cool."

Melody Johnson also encounters people who recognize her from the show. Around 2019, she met a guy on the set of a TV show who exclaimed, "I remember you from *Goosebumps*! You were a little girl!" She finds these periodic reminders of *Goosebumps*' cultural relevance pretty neat. "It's cool, right? Like, that's the fun bit!" she says of being remembered from her childhood work. Of the legacy *Goosebumps* now holds, she says, "I think it's well-deserved. I think that it was such a big part of the cultural zeitgeist in the '90s. I was happy to be a part of that whole thing early in my career. It probably helped me kind of propel into what I was to do later."

Tod Fennell, similarly, can't help but awe at the impact this one television gig has had on his life and career. "I went to an anime convention for some of my work in video games, and there were more fans that came up with mint condition *Goosebumps* books! I was like, 'Whoa! That was twenty years ago!'" In the longer term, *Goosebumps* would be a talking point for everybody involved. Many working actors find themselves faced with the awkward question, "What would I know you from?" It's a query that vastly underestimates the life of an actor, who dashes between TV guest spots, walk-on roles and character parts in movies. Everyone on the screen, from the leading man to the waitress in the background, is making their living as an actor, but that doesn't mean the average person will recognize them. So having to list off highlights from one's resumé, only to be met with a look of bewilderment, is embarrassing for all involved. However, if there is one title these actors can boast of, and get an immediate reaction from, it's *Goosebumps*.

While all the adoration is quite novel, and most certainly touching, Amos Crawley says that the reverence of actors, or of the entertainment industry in general, is a largely North American phenomenon that does everybody an injustice. He recalls working on a West End show in London, and being amazed that known actors could just step out onto the street for a cigarette and not be bothered by anyone. "Whereas in North America there's very much an attitude that acting is magic. We've sort of created a mystique around it here that I really try to dispel. It really is just a job. So, while it is fun when people go, 'Oh, my God, I saw you in a thing,' you also kinda go like, 'Yeah, but like, you drive a truck and you're a delivery guy and you're a car salesman. That's also your job. My attitude toward it is I would like to sort of dispel some of the mystique about it, because I think that it results, frankly, in actors not being as good at it as they could be."

While the young actors who worked on the show seem to most appreciate that they were a part of something culturally relevant, many of the adults attach a sense of pride to what they achieved in their careers as a result of the show. "I have always felt proud of the work that I accomplished," says Brian R. R. Hebb. "With *Goosebumps*, the work was so intense and satisfying that I am left with a good sense of achievement. It was always about storytelling. Were the stories told well? I hope so. They were definitely special." Indeed, the stories were special. So much so that when Hebb retired, he approached the library at the University of Victoria with his collection of scripts from his work. They most happily accepted them, and they can be viewed there to this day. The cinematographer poignantly recalls a memory from his youth: "As a young boy, I was once asked by a teacher what I wanted to be when I grew up. I said, 'I want to be a clown in a circus.' Well, with *Goosebumps* and all the other shows, I feel that I made it to the circus. However, I still haven't made it to clown status!"

For some, the real circus was the friends they made along the way. For Tod Fennell, all the excitement and wonder of acting on *Goosebumps* was one thing, but it was the relationships he forged during those two weeks in 1998 that made the experience so special for him. He met his onscreen sister Laura Vandervoort while shooting "Deep Trouble," and they have been best friends ever since, frequently collaborating on projects well into adulthood. "That relationship is the best thing to come out of *Goosebumps*, for sure. We still have that brother-sister dynamic," he says adoringly. Although they never worked on the show together, Corey Sevier and Tod Fennell have been close friends for decades since working on *Lassie*, and their shared *Goosebumps* history is just another element that brought them together. Meanwhile, Ron Oliver maintains a staggeringly wide friendship group, nurtured by his many years on film sets, and Ryan "Goose" Gosling is still an important figure in his life, no matter how much of a big deal he becomes. Many friendships were forged on the set or behind the scenes of *Goosebumps*, but even those who didn't stay in touch remember each other with great fondness, and have been more than happy to reminisce about the wonderful people they once worked with, and the impact they made on their lives and careers.

And the show made a hell of an impact. Many of the kids who carried on acting would find that *Goosebumps* had been the perfect professional springboard, both in terms of exposure and the experience it had to offer. Corey Sevier's career went from strength to strength after the show, and he feels that being given a lead role at such a young age set him up well for his future. "I don't know if I would have been as confident playing a lead in a series, had I not done that *Goosebumps* episode," he says, "so that was really pivotal for me." He says that the show gave him "a very prolific opportunity to grow as an artist, as an actor, so it will always have a special place in my heart. And to this day, you know, it's one of the things that I will get recognized for."

Bill Turnbull says that his work on *Goosebumps*, and his wider career as a child actor, set him up well for the industry in adulthood. "I got the experience that's so crucial when you're in your early twenties to book stuff." He says that whereas adults get to take classes on acting on camera, kid actors were usually just thrown into things and guided through it—learning on the job, so to speak. Through his work on *Goosebumps* and other gigs, he learned how to hit his marks, how to prepare adequately and, most importantly, how to bring the best out of himself. Describing himself as "a bit of a nervous guy", he learned from an early age that the best way to work through the nerves was to get through the first take, after which everything feels a bit easier. As a nervous guy who hates getting up early and hates doing the same thing over and over again, Turnbull jokes, "It's almost like I'm in the wrong business," but he has always found the merits of his work. "It's exciting, and it's awesome when you do a good job, like if you make the crew laugh, or you feel like you're connecting with the other actors. If I hadn't done that as a kid, I never would have gotten the opportunities as an adult."

It's not just the impact of the show that contributes to its legacy, but the ways in which it was made and the opportunities for creativity that it provided. Speaking of using inventive camera work, such as the dolly zoom, in his episodes, Ron Oliver says, "It's one of the few things that when you do it, you really feel like part of a filmmaking legacy. We've all got the same equipment, we've all got the same camera, dolly and pan and tracking shots and so forth. But when you do something like that it feels very special." Meanwhile, Matthew DeWilde reveled in working on a show that brought anthological horror to younger audiences. "I love the concept of the show because I love anthology TV series like *The Twilight Zone*," he says. "I love that this was the same kind of thing, like a monster show for kids. I thought this was fantastic!"

Actor Peter Keleghan views things more broadly, and is thankful for the opportunity that such a major American IP brought to Canada and its many talented industry professionals. "I think they did it justice and so they deserve all the success they had. Thank you for coming to our country and giving us uniforms and baseball bats and money to do what we want to do," he says. When asked how he felt about being part of the *Goosebumps* legacy, he had one word to offer: "Terrific." Fellow actor Tod Fennell also recognizes what a big deal it was for the show to snub the entertainment capital of the U.S. in favor of Toronto. "I'm grateful that it wasn't something that was shot in L.A. They came to Canada and gave the opportunity for a lot of local actors to be a part of this thing. So that means a lot to me," he says.

As those who worked on the show grew up, became parents or grandparents, they could more fully appreciate just how impactful the show they worked on back in the '90s had been, and continued to be. For Melody Johnson, *Goosebumps* has proven useful when it comes to sharing her work with the younger generations of her family. "It's one of the only things that I can show my nieces and nephews that I've done!" she says. Tod Fennell has also had the experience of sharing his childhood acting with his young family. One time, his wife and son were visiting friends in her hometown, and the family's children were gathered round watching *Goosebumps*. "My son was there and he's like, 'That's my dad when he was little!' Kids are still watching the show." Brian R. R. Hebb has also shared the show with the family. "When I first met my present wife in California, her son had bought the VHS tape of "A Night in Terror Tower." We sat and watched it together," he recalls fondly.

Amos Crawley doesn't remember watching his episodes of the show back when they first aired, but has made it a family affair in the years since. "My memory of watching it is much more recent. We watched it one Halloween with my kids. So the excitement for me was getting to watch their reaction to it. But I got a little taste of the sentimentality of it. Because, frankly, if you're one of the kids on the show, you're probably too old to watch it." In Stefan Scaini's experience, this couldn't be further from the truth. "I've got four kids, ages currently eighteen to twenty-five, and they still get a kick out of it! I know a lot of their friends go back to the old episodes, and love those," he says. Afrah Gouda remembers catching "Return of the Mummy" back when it first aired, and sometimes rewatches it when a nostalgic mood takes her.

Living not far from Vancouver, where the rebooted *Goosebumps* show filmed, Randy Bradshaw put some feelers out among industry contacts to see how it was shaping up. "Basically, the message I got back was, they were going in a different direction and weren't really too interested in the directors that had worked on the original show." It's certainly true that the 2020s take on *Goosebumps* adopted a more mature and serious tone, centering its action around high schoolers in the twenty-first century. It's their loss that they didn't choose to bring back any of the creatives from the original show's run, but its very existence is testament to the nostalgic power of *Goosebumps*. Thirty years later, it still resonates with audiences.

When asked how he feels about being part of the legacy of not only this iconic show, but its wider impact on the cultural landscape of the '90s, Ron Oliver says, "How do I feel about it? Love it! That was an era that will not happen again, for lots of reasons. But that was fun. We had a great time making the stuff that we wanted to see. I used to make those shows for the twelve- or thirteen-year-old version of me sitting in front of the TV set. We carry those shows with us into adulthood. These shows will last. So, we have to be extra careful to make them as good as we possibly can, because they're gonna have a legacy themselves. They're gonna live on long past us." Not only is he grateful to have been such a key player in the show, but he is touched to learn just how wide an impact it has had on people. "I've had people say to me specifically, 'I got into the movie business because of *Are You Afraid of the Dark?* or *Goosebumps*. They got into this because they looked at it and thought, 'I want to do that,' and that to me is, that's a proud moment. To have encouraged creative imagination in an entire generation. The older I get, the more I love it, the more I appreciate what we did and how it has impacted culture. The Disney sitcom world that took over from kids' entertainment in the '90s is, in my opinion, exactly why we are where we are right now, culturally. Because suddenly everything devolved into just absolute junk."

The current cultural landscape may be a rough one, but it has brought about a wave of rediscovery, of reappraisal and reminiscence. Judah Katz gets a real kick out of seeing *Goosebumps* receive this treatment. "Watching these, what do they call them? These reaction videos. A lot of these people who watched these shows when they were kids, and now they're in their twenties or thirties, and they're rewatching it again, and they're commenting on it. That's kind of fascinating for me. Because I get to hear what's going through their head.

And they talk about when they were a kid. How this scene scared them. Some people said that [my character] gave them nightmares. From a psychological point of view, this is kind of interesting. There's a whole culture in *Goosebumps*. This is still the most popular thing I've ever done, and I still get fan mail. It won't go away. It's a phenomenon. I get letters and emails from all over the world. The only time I would get recognized on the street was after I did *Goosebumps*. When you're an entertainer, you like the idea that somebody was entertained by it," he beams.

Bryan Renfro also appreciates that people are going back to *Goosebumps* all these years later. "It's a cool thing that people are starting to look at this again," he says. "I really like it and I'm really happy that I did it. It was a great experience, and it's nice to do something like [this book] where people appreciate that kind of work." It's a sentiment that many of the cast and crew express to me, much to my joy and gratitude. "I'm really excited about what you're doing, writing a book about *Goosebumps*!" Tod Fennell tells me. "Because it's such a phenomenon! And it's such a cool part of pop culture history to be a part of. There are so many fans and everybody remembers it."

As a music man, Jack Lenz understands perhaps better than most the power of emotion, and its relationship to cultural endurance. "There's very little that endures," he explains. "You know Mozart endures and Beethoven endures. I think that's a very difficult thing to achieve. Pop culture is pretty elusive, and things don't last very long. It is kind of strange and remarkable for something like this to endure. And I think it is definitely because kids grew up with it. And so they continue to remember what they felt like when they watched the show, meaning it is more likely to endure. Baudelaire said a very interesting thing. He said that art in its highest form will often reveal the splendors situated beyond the tomb. Now, if the tomb's scary, maybe *Goosebumps* could qualify," he says with a smile. "I gotta tell you I get emails from fanboys several times a week. I've never had a girl that grew up with the show. It's all guys, which is also an interesting phenomenon when you think about it. It was quite refreshing to hear that it was a woman writing this book."

"Beyond surprised and really, really grateful," is how Amos Crawley feels about the legacy of the show, and his part in it. "It's really cool. It's cool that people associate you with a happy memory. It is dumb luck, just chance. But I'm super grateful for it." So full circle have things gone that in his capacity as an acting coach, he has worked with young actors on scripts for the reboot *Goosebumps* show, and another Stine property is also on his radar. "Funnily enough, where I live, just down the street from me, they are filming the latest instalment of the *Fear Street* movies." Clearly, the world of R.L. Stine is best viewed through a Canadian lens.

Many of the adults who worked on the show have been pleasantly surprised by its resurgence, and the many happy memories attached to it. "It's funny because originally, I didn't think about it," says Craig Pryce, "and then when the movie came out, I saw it and went, 'Oh wow, this is still around! And I was part of the infancy of that. I wasn't a big part of it, but I was part of that journey. So I just felt really proud. It was a great feeling!" Don McCutcheon is equally surprised and touched that *Goosebumps* has shown such staying power. "You don't know that it's gonna resonate for decades," he says. "Yet, here I am, how many years later? Decades later, and we're still talking about *Goosebumps*! It's very gratifying, but you never work alone. It's all a team effort. And everybody, you know, everybody should take credit. But you know, at the end of the day, we do make them for audiences, and you want people to enjoy it and recognize it. You want the show to be popular."

One of the souvenir statuettes made up for the cast and crew.
This Haunted Mask one is captioned 'Goosebumps 1995.
Thanks for Scaring.' Photo courtesy of Bob Sprogis.

Given the frantic pace at which he worked on the show, Matthew DeWilde "never thought *Goosebumps* would ever be a popular, long-lasting thing. I just thought everything was not my best work. It was such a rush all the time. So it's surprising me that it's impacted so many people. Artists and people have talked to me on Instagram. It's been incredible. I'm happy for that." David Winning feels that they all must have done something right to be here now, talking about it still. "Anything that people still talk about thirty years later is amazing to me. I'm really proud of it. I think it turned out well," he says.

Many of the people who worked on the show are still based in and around Toronto, so although the industry may have changed around them, the place where this special, once-in-a-lifetime career experience took place is still near. Corey Sevier crosses paths with Terror Tower itself, Casa Loma, fairly frequently. "Anytime I drive by, it gives me that little bit of a flutter," he says, remembering the amazing time he had filming there as a kid. He plans on taking his own children along someday soon, and previously visited with his grandmother. He is always happy to take a trip down memory lane.

In fact, everybody I spoke to for this book has been, and it has been my very great pleasure to be the conduit of this mass reminiscence of such a special piece of media. Of being a part of this legacy, Tod Fennell says, "I'm honored. It really means a lot to have been part of pop culture history." He is also happy to have been a small part of a franchise that encouraged kids to read. Having, quite by coincidence, found a bundle of *Goosebumps* books at his local phonebooth-turned-mini-library just days before we spoke, Mpho Koaho felt it must've been written in the stars that now was the time to look back at that special, highly-coveted role he secured as a fourteen-year-old. "I'm very humbled," he says of his involvement in the show, and my approaching him to be a part of this book. Corey Sevier understands that in a frantic world, everybody needs the chance to slow down and remember who they used to be, and beloved media is a great way of doing it. "I think a lot of people go, 'Oh, my God, I forgot how much that meant to me,' because life gets busy. I feel very fortunate to be a small part of the legacy."

For Steve Levitan, the guy who bridged the gap between one of the '90s most prolific children's authors and the TV screens of a generation, the show remains a source of great pride, and one that he has been incredibly obliging in telling the story of. "It's nice talking about this show. I love this show, I loved making it," he says. For him, too, the real magic of *Goosebumps* was the people who went to work every day to create it. "It was a very happy team," he concludes.

Ultimately, *Goosebumps* spoke to kids. It gave them that sense of thrill, danger and excitement from the comfort and safety of their living rooms. It opened their imaginations, it sparked ideas, and it encouraged them to pick up books. Randy Bradshaw sums up its legacy perfectly: "The kids, wherever they be, whatever circumstance that they happened to be in, while they were watching an episode, they were being entertained and transported to a world where kids could just have fun. What's better than getting *Goosebumps*?"

Afterword

Compiling the history of *Goosebumps* has been the most surreal, thrilling and rewarding experience, and it all started with an email. The day I got a message from Steve Levitan, saying he was happy to talk to me about the show, my life changed. Something that I'd dreamed up over a year before, but had sat on month after month, certain that this was my definitive project, but never quite feeling confident enough to just go out there and make it happen, had now come to be. Probably without realizing it, by clicking send on that email, Steve had offered me the next step in my life and career.

Over the sixteen months that I worked on this book, I reached out to every single person involved in the show that I could find. I wanted to hear it all, directly from them. Some I never heard back from, one or two very respectfully declined, but an awful lot jumped right on board, thrilled to look back on a kids' TV show they made decades prior, and talk about what it was like to bring to life. Through it all, everyone was so kind, so gracious, so encouraging. I have had hours and hours of great conversations with interesting and talented people, made new friends, and had the privilege of seeing *Goosebumps* from the inside, from a completely unique perspective that I could never have imagined.

This '90s kid was only four or five years old when introduced to *Goosebumps*. In the local library of a tiny fenland village called Haddenham, one small shelf was dedicated to VHS tapes. Two dark spines stared out from the top left-hand side: "The Haunted Mask" and "A Night in Terror Tower." I took home "The Haunted Mask" and was scared shitless, but the funny thing was, I couldn't leave it alone. I kept renting that tape, and when the UK finally started broadcasting the show on TV, I caught every episode I could. As the 2000s came around, I found every VHS I could on eBay, at bargain prices because parents were clearing out their attics. I even found a seller who (quite illegally, I'm sure) was selling homemade compilation videos of *Goosebumps* episodes, having recorded them off the TV. This was my first real means to watching episodes that I never caught showings of.

Over the years, I never shook my love of the show, and as my career started to follow the film journalism trajectory, I always knew I would write books. I just didn't know when, or what. As the pandemic came around, I hit on the idea of *Goosebumps*. I loved it, and I knew lots of other people did. This could be my first big project. It took a while for me to muster the courage to take the leap into what would become a massive, overwhelming and at times incredibly stressful project. But once I did, in February 2024, it set the ball rolling and, I am sure, changed my life forever.

It would be lovely for this book to be a hit, and for the fans to like it. Admittedly, it changed shape constantly over the course of writing it, depending on what information I could find, who I could talk to, and what seemed right. The final product is not exactly what I anticipated it to be, but I am very pleased with what it became thanks to the input of so many amazing people. You may not find every single piece of trivia within its pages, but I hope that I have captured the essence of *Goosebumps*, and told its life story warmly and accurately. This book is really about the show as a whole, about what it was, and when and why, and the many amazing people who made it that way. It is a record of how a sensation came to be, and a reflection of its impact, and I hope that the love and appreciation that I, and fans all over the world, have for it is captured in every page.

Printed in Dunstable, United Kingdom